WORLD
POPULATION

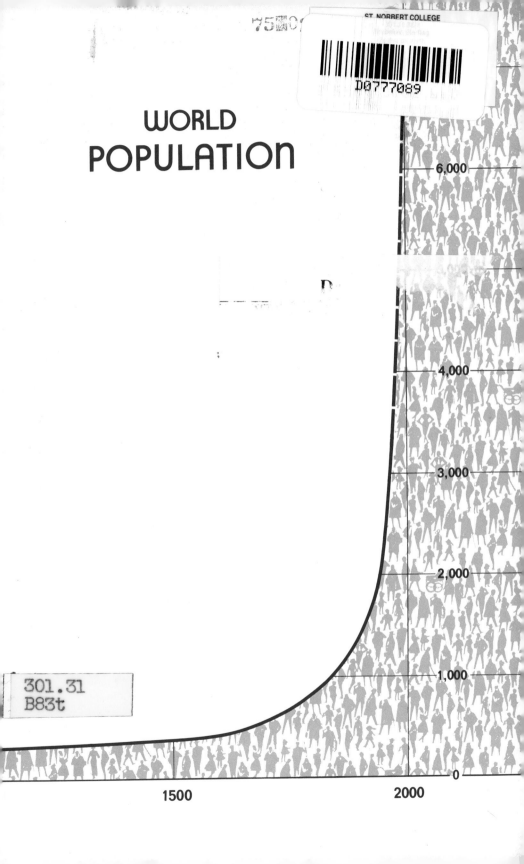

6,000

4,000

3,000

2,000

1,000

0

1500

2000

TO LIVE ON EARTH

Man and His Environment in Perspective

STERLING BRUBAKER

TO LIVE ON EARTH

Man and His Environment in Perspective

A Resources for the Future Study

Published for **RESOURCES for the FUTURE, Inc.**
by The JOHNS HOPKINS PRESS, Baltimore and London

FOREWORD

After dozens of books and hundreds of articles during the past few years, why still another publication on man and his physical environment? The reason, as people in Resources for the Future see it, is that the basic problems have not yet been put in perspective in quite the way that will best help the concerned citizen to form opinions on the short- and long-range choices that will have to be made.

In the long run there is no answer to the argument that control of population is the key to man's survival on his planet. Even the lowest rate of increase, if projected far enough into the future, points to discomfort and finally disaster. But there may be shorter cuts to extinction; for the first time in human history advances in technology have enabled man to make rapid and far-reaching changes in his environment. Some seem good, or at least harmless. But alterations in climate, extreme degradation of water or air quality, nuclear contamination, or general impairment of intricate life-supporting systems could bring the gravest consequences.

Thoughtful and eloquent writers have pointed out these dangers. Their contribution to the chances of human survival has been great; without it the current widespread concern with environmental problems might have been longer delayed. On the other hand, some may have overshot the mark with too gloomy a picture for the public to accept. Prophets seldom pause to weigh all the pros and cons. Moreover the more extreme warnings have called forth a counterbarrage. Persuasive, often cogent, cases have been made, some generally affirming the promise of economic growth and technological advance, and some uncritically defending the status quo, or more specifically, the use of this or that pesticide or industrial process or product.

What can one believe, or, more to the point, how can he participate intelligently in the public decisions that will have to be made in the immediate future and in the next two or three decades? This book is an attempt to offer some answers. Its greatest contribution, I believe, lies in classifying the many kinds of problems and the degrees of ignorance that attend them. By ignorance I mean not only great gaps in scientific knowledge of situations and their consequences but also lack of consensus on goals and institutions for achieving them.

Sterling Brubaker has made a perceptive and objective study of the data that are currently available. "Objective" is, of course, a relative term. Even the most dispassionate analysis must rest upon certain assumptions and viewpoints. This is particularly true of man's relation to his environment now that he has so much power to modify that environment instead of merely adjusting to it. Anyone who thinks and writes on man's future on earth has his own ideas about goals and possibilities in the back of his mind. Mine and, if I read him right, Mr. Brubaker's, lie in a middle ground rather than at the extreme margins.

At one extreme is the idea of cutting back world population to the dimensions of some earlier time, or even of holding it where it is. This is a dream—a most attractive dream, I must confess—and when coupled, as it often is, with a wish to cut back industrial production, it resolves many of the intellectual dilemmas that bother most of us. (No weighing of needs for new power plants against dangers of pollution at the sites that might be selected: just don't build new plants.) This idyllic picture is often imbued with the concept of nature as something apart from man, or at least apart from modern man with his powerful instruments for change and domination.

At the other extreme is an uncritical acceptance of the blessings of economic growth with the comforting corollaries that technology will find a way around any difficulties that may arise and that adaptable humankind will come to accept—even to like—conditions of crowding, regimentation, and artificial environment that now are distasteful to most of us. According to this view, although no one contends that population can keep on growing forever, the time to start worrying is far off, or perhaps will never come at all because whatever population checks are required may take place automatically and be benign and pleasant. This outlook, too, is a dream.

Under the middle-ground assumptions on which this study rests, modern man is part of nature. He need not turn his back on improved methods of agriculture or on the extraction and use of fabricating and energy materials, but he must count the environmental costs of his activities. There are some ecological principles that must not be breached and many of them are still understood imperfectly, if at all. Population *is* a problem. Although it is most unlikely that anything short of colossal disaster can keep present numbers of people in the world from more than trebling, conscious steps need to be taken now toward reducing the rate of increase and stabilizing the total number as soon as possible. Economic growth must continue, if for no other reason than to give a chance to the poor and disadvantaged, both individuals and nations. In this effort, however, it will be wise in the future to put less emphasis on material goods, at least in more affluent countries, and more emphasis on cultural and recreational services. And much more effort must be made in cleaning up the pollution and litter that already have accumulated. Our economic system—and from all appearances that of socialist countries as well—has concentrated on production of goods with little heed to the wastes engendered in the process. In this view of today's world there are many grave problems, but reasonable grounds for hope.

The present study deals principally with the United States, although in some cases it looks beyond our borders. Accumulation of carbon dioxide in the atmosphere, for instance, is a global problem in the broadest sense. So are the possible effects of discharging wastes into the oceans. Rivers and air currents do not stop at national boundaries. Population pressures can spill over from country to country, and international trade can introduce problems when some nations emphasize pollution control measures and some do not. Even with its primarily domestic focus the study will, I hope, be of interest and value to other countries, because many of the problems and responses of the heavily industrialized United States have already arisen in other economically advanced nations and similar situations can be expected later in the less-developed.

Perhaps the most disturbing impression one gathers from Mr. Brubaker's survey is how much we still do not know, despite the widespread public concern of the past two or three years and the considerably longer period of attention to some specific threats to the environment, notably soil erosion and water pollution. It is impossible to say with any authority that, for the nation as a whole or for any sizable area, *this* is the present level of, say, air or water quality, that *this* was the level twenty years ago, and that *this* level is the threshold of danger. Often it seems that we know the least about the largest questions—those that many people think offer the most serious threats to human well-being or survival. For example, will continued burning of vast amounts of fossil fuels have dangerous effects on world climate? Among the reputable scientists who think it will, some believe that average temperatures will drop, others that they will rise. Pesticides are known to increase agricultural productivity and to control diseases like malaria. Could the long-range effects of some of them be so harmful in other ways that use of certain products should be stopped until we are sure? Or is it still prudent to move ahead cautiously, in each case weighing benefits against possible ill effects?

The present study points clearly to the need for large-scale research aimed directly at the situations that appear to have the greatest long-range potential for danger. But a book that did only this, perhaps along with balanced comments "on-the-one-hand-and-on-the-other," would be disappointing indeed and would add little to public understanding of the current situation and what can be done about it.

This study sorts things out. It analyzes the underlying factors—demographic, economic, and technological. It surveys their effects to date and their possible direction and force in the future. It explores the alternatives likely to be open in the next few years and those of the longer future when changes in viewpoints and institutions as well as in technology could open a wider range of possibilities.

Though sobering, the analysis invites neither panic nor resignation. Along with the large long-range problems that still are dimly seen are a host of immediate or short-range ones about which we know quite a lot already. There is a mass of data (far from complete, of course) on the causes and effects of air and water pollution and as the generation of solid wastes and other offscourings of GNP. We know a great deal about techniques for dealing with these evils, and even a little about institutional changes that might help. And we have some idea of what remedial actions would cost. It happens that most of the ills that can be tackled now are more in the nature of nuisances and ugliness than of threats to the human race. But some do have long-range implications, so that in dealing with them today we may alleviate the larger problems of the future.

By analyzing the underlying causes of environmental threats, classifying them according to their nature and seriousness, and differentiating short-range from longer-range problems, the new study will, I believe, help to promote clearer thinking and more effective action to bring man more nearly into harmony with his natural environment.

Although this is Sterling Brubaker's book, it is much more of a corporate enterprise than most of RFF's publications. Many staff members, some RFF grantees, and a few others brought forward ideas and raw materials from their special fields of interest. More specific mention of major contributors will be found in the author's Acknowledgments.

Joseph L. Fisher

ACKNOWLEDGMENTS

As Joseph Fisher mentioned in his foreword, this book is something of a corporate effort. I am more aware of this than anyone, for I have benefited from my colleagues' assistance at every stage. The idea of having Resources for the Future prepare a nontechnical book on the environment was first advanced by Professor Edward S. Mason of the RFF Board of Directors, who hoped that it could be done quickly under group authorship. But soon after work started, it became apparent that some one person would have to worry it through. I undertook the task, imposing my own structure and style on the material at hand.

During the planning stage, I profited especially from the advice of Joseph L. Fisher and Hans H. Landsberg. Once an approach had been decided upon, a number of RFF staff members contributed background material from their own areas of expertise for integration in the volume. I drew most heavily on Allen V. Kneese, Marion Clawson, and Hans Landsberg. Kneese, whose writings in this field are original and extensive, was especially helpful in dealing with air and water pollution, and his material was incorporated at other points as well. Clawson provided most of the information on the agricultural economy, soil erosion, and recreational land use, drawing on his many years of broad-ranging work in these areas. Landsberg's versatility was helpful across the board, but he made his most direct contributions to the section on the economic and demographic factors and on the consequences of fertilizer use in agriculture. Other RFF staff contributed as well. John Krutilla prepared a concise background piece on ecology and Michael Brewer assembled information on pesticide use. William Frisken of York University, while a visiting scholar at RFF, prepared background material concerning man's impact on the global climate. Joel Darmstadter became an unwitting contributor when I was able to draw on his work on energy consumption which became available while I was at work on this study. Also, my colleagues Orris Herfindahl, Ronald Ridker, and Pierre Crosson, in addition to all of those mentioned previously, offered useful comments on an earlier draft of the manuscript. My debt to them all is so great that I am tempted to forgo the usual author's disclaimer that I alone am responsible for errors; however, in deference to protocol I shall not—let the ashes be heaped on my head.

My gratitude and absolution also go to the numerous other persons who commented on all or parts of an earlier draft. Hugh Keenleyside, Lauren Soth, and Luther Foster, all of the RFF Board of Directors, offered useful comments. William Seltzer and Frank Notestein of the Population Council were helpful on population matters, as well as more generally. Valuable comments also were received from John H. Gibbons and Joanne S. Gailar of the Oak Ridge National Laboratory, Helmut K. Buechner of the Smithsonian Institution, and Robert M. White of the National Oceanic and Atmospheric Administration. Specialized comments on parts of the manuscript came from Karl Z. Morgan of Oak Ridge, Edward Burger and John Buckley of the Office of Science and Technology, Professor Martin Alexander of Cornell, Professor Merril Eisenbud of New York University, Paul Gerhart of the Environmental Protection Agency, George Stanford of the U.S. Department of Agriculture, Lyle Alexander, formerly of USDA, Martin O. Stern of International Research and Technology Corporation, and Ralph Lapp, currently with Quadri-Science, Inc. My debt to all of them is great, as it is to others, not listed here, who have helped me in various ways.

Henry Jarrett, of RFF's publications staff, has given more than the usual editor's attention to this book. He made very useful suggestions on organizations at all stages, and his questions on substance have compelled greater clarity at many points. Both he and Nora Roots, also an RFF editor, deserve whatever credit is due if a sometimes complex manuscript has emerged as a readable book.

Finally, I am especially grateful to the diligent Sally Nishiyama for help in ferreting out materials and bringing them to my attention and to Helen-Marie Streich, who typed so merrily and corrected my grammar so unobtrusively.

Sterling Brubaker

CONTENTS

LIST OF TABLES

TO LIVE ON EARTH

Man and His Environment in Perspective

NOTE ON SOURCES

Since this book is aimed at the general reader rather than the specialist, no effort has been made to document the argument extensively. Only sparing use has been made of reference citations, and the bibliography does not attempt to be comprehensive. However, for each chapter where it is appropriate a selected bibliography has been included listing the general references found to be of most value as well as more specialized sources for some of the information found in the chapter. Some works of general interest also are mentioned in a brief bibliography at the end of the book.

ONE

ENVIRONMENTAL CRISIS:
An Introduction

In an age of explosive technical advance, rapidly increasing income, and continued population growth, there is ample reason for concern over man's relationship to his physical environment. But the suddenness with which a long-standing concern has become a source of mass alarm in the United States and the intensity of the public discussion that has arisen are both perplexing.

In focusing attention upon important and neglected issues, the current ferment is all to the good. As a basis for action it leaves much to be desired. The discussion has not had time to mature. It has left us disposed to act in circumstances in which our understanding of the nature and causes of environmental problems and of their possible cures is seriously deficient. Above all, perspective is missing. We need a much better sense of dimension, relative gravity, and priority if we are to respond constructively to the threat of environmental degradation.

The sense of crisis burst upon us in the fall of 1969. In an age of participatory democracy, private firms as well as governments have become the targets of diversified pressures and protests. Each siting of an industrial establishment, especially an electric power plant, a refinery, or a chemical works, is guaranteed to touch off a battle. The once-sacred argument that an industrial plant brings jobs and economic betterment often is brushed aside. Major new public works—dams, roads, canals, airports—are more commonly viewed as threats than as progress. While the silent spring has not yet arrived, the once-somnolent corporate board room is enlivened, as agitated citizens and even stockholders demand ecological responsibility from managements that heretofore have listened to the public only via sales charts. Our impatient youth have celebrated Earth Day, performing as shock troops of the new crusade. The United Nations, moving more ponderously, has scheduled a world conference on environmental problems for 1972.

Legislators have been quick to recognize the bite in the issue and have sought to stake out positions, sometimes abandoning long-defended interests in the process. The flow of legislation has been quickened (air and water pollution acts already on the books are being strengthened); administrative agencies have moved with considerable alacrity to limit the use of DDT and certain other chemicals, to doom the burning of leaded fuels, and to arrest some public works that threaten special environments. The system bends. Who says it is unresponsive?

The environmental movement comes as an abrupt awakening after years of prosperity and of reassurance that economic growth is the key to most social problems. That comforting panacea is now challenged, and the medicine—growth—is blamed for the environmental illness. A sense of disillusionment has become pervasive. The more cynical discern a plot to divert attention from other problems that they find more pressing (Vietnam, race, poverty, urban ills), but plots rarely explain anything in the United States. Corporate and governmental responses to the movement have been skittish, mindful of image, uncertain of what will be required of them. Industry and government have proved willing to act or make commitments without their usual insistence on factual proof or study of costs. They are impressed by the breadth of the movement, uncertain that they can influence or predict its course effectively, or seem unsure or confused about the substance and validity of the case.

This uncertainty is not too surprising, for the environmental movement consists of a number of diverse strains. It is a blend of the holders of traditional antimaterialist, conservationist, and naturalist views together with neo-Malthusians, ecological pessimists, elements of the consumer protectionist movement, action-oriented youth, and air-breathing citizens. With some, the uncertainty extends to questioning of the social system, the value of economic growth, and the man-centered ethics of western civilization. The movement has plenty of vitality but no unifying doctrine. However, the major strands, interwoven as they always are, can be discerned.

One major theme is the fear that man-made insults to the environment will bring ecological disaster. Pesticides, fertilizers, and the energy industries are viewed as the chief offenders. Pesticides are seen as threatening the survival of other species, especially at the end of the food chain, by inhibiting reproduction. It is also pointed out that as more pesticides are used, resistant pest strains develop while their predators may be decimated, leaving man and his crops defenseless against future insect depredations. Fertilizers, it is alleged, may impair the action of soil bacteria and damage soil structure, compelling still further dependence on the chemicals. Migrating into streams and lakes, the chemicals foster luxuriant aquatic plant growth, which in turn creates an excessive demand on dissolved oxygen and thus impairs life in the water. It is observed that nitrates in the water in sufficient concentrations are harmful to man. Energy offends in several ways. At the simplest level, the heat in water discharged into lakes and streams after it has been used for cooling in industrial plants alters the conditions for aquatic life. The burning of fuels, whether in the production of electricity or in autos, adds to the air a heavy burden of carbon monoxide, carbon dioxide, nitrogen oxides, sulfur dioxide, hydrocarbons, and other contaminants that are directly harmful to plant and animal life. An irreducible product of combustion is carbon dioxide, whose mounting concentration in the atmosphere will, it is feared, have a significant effect on climate. A switch from fossil fuels to nuclear energy presents the problem of containing and disposing of radioactive wastes whose presence in the environment can bring genetic and physiological damage. Dangers of this kind are related directly to aspects of technology as practiced in advanced countries.

One important group within the environmentalist movement would accept most of the foregoing but sees it primarily as the inevitable consequence of unbounded population growth. In this view the exponential growth of population is the sure road to disaster, which not only ensures the ecological consequences that others fear, but will bring catastrophe even earlier through inability of most of the world to feed itself. It is thought that the new technology of miracle seeds, fertilizers, and pesticide use cannot be adopted quickly enough to avert starvation in much of the world, and that even if it could, it would provide only temporary relief. Reserve productive capacity in the United States and elsewhere is considered neither adequate nor easy enough to mobilize to come anywhere near meeting the problem. Some see doomsday in the sense of mass starvation as less than a decade away. While they concede that the United States will escape that immediate fate, they feel that it will be part of an increasingly dangerous and tension-ridden world, and that meanwhile, our own crowding detracts from the quality of life in the United States.

Crowding, inconvenience, the loss of contact with nature, and the degradation of that which remains—these are the aspects of the environmental problem that impress themselves on most people who have not paused to quiver about doomsday. The sheer noise, dirt, and physiological and psychological stresses of urban living appear to grow more intense. The trip to work is ever longer and more exasperating. The city becomes less inviting as a setting for enjoyable human activities, yet it keeps encroaching on the countryside. Lakes, streams, air, and landscape share the sickness. It is clear that the environmental movement gets much of its force from these conditions.

One major thrust is toward cleaning up the polluted aspects of the environment familiar to city dwellers—streams, air, streets, beaches, vacant lots. Another is preservationist, aimed at saving the attractiveness of a countryside esteemed for its qualities for healing the ills of an urban civilization. Some conflict occurs between those who are anxious to share the valued out-of-doors with others and the purists who find greater value in the more pristine wilderness—by definition an area lightly used. The conservationist-naturalist view typically is suspicious of materialism and of the advance of technology; sees population growth as an evil; and sees values in nature that are important to man but also transcend him.

To some extent attention to quality has led to revival of concern about resource adequacy. As people become aware of the limits to the earth's capacity to assimilate objectionable residuals, they once again become impressed with its limits as a source of materials and sustenance. This fear of running short is inherent in the population problem where the first question concerns the adequacy of land resources to support food production. However, it is asked anew not only with respect to food production but also to energy, minerals, and forest resources. Heretofore technical advance has staved off the day of shortages in resources, but to many environmentalists technology itself is suspect as the source of many environmental ills, especially in agriculture. The alternative is often seen as a return to less sophisticated technology, which may be more extensive in land use and more costly. Any reversion to earlier technologies in the face of increased population and continued insistence upon high living standards would soon confront us with a problem of resource adequacy.

Environment is an emotion-laden cause. In part this may arise from an atavistic human attachment to the natural world in which the race was formed. In part it seems to reflect a cultural sense of having been unjustly deprived of something previously enjoyed—this generation feels cheated of its inheritance and guilty about having even less to transmit to its heirs. Many seeking a banner to rally under have found this one convenient. The consumer movement sees shoddy, short-lived merchandise as adding to the pollution burden, and views industrial pollution as further evidence of the irresponsibility of industry. Those who are alienated from the society may see its materialism as the principal source of the problem and urge a simpler Thoreauvian style of life as the solution. Others, equally alienated, are convinced that the property and profit system is the problem and seek a solution through political action for social change.

If yet another book on the environment is warranted, it should contribute something toward better perspective on the problem. That is the aim of this book—to define a range of concerns, to discuss causes or sources of the problem, to sort out those aspects most deserving of attention and get some estimate of their characteristics, magnitude, and immediacy, and to discuss technical and economic trade-offs and the range of choices that are open to society.

Environmental quality could be construed to include social as well as physical aspects of the environment—in effect, all that with which the individual interacts. With riches beyond the dreams of most peoples, we have learned that chrome-plated affluence is no substitute for such elemental social prerequisites as decent personal security, a healthy social environment for children to grow in, or institutions to ensure free discussion and orderly public decisions. In full recognition of such problems, and of the constant interaction between the social and physical environment, it seems best to restrict attention in this study to the physical environment and the way in which we manage it. Man is still a major actor on this scene, but his role ranges from that of principal creative agent in urban environments or in engineering works to substantial modifier in the case of agriculture all the way to occasional interloper in the wilderness. In every case, man's values, aspirations, technology, and social organization condition the result.

Urbanized areas, which are almost exclusively the work of man, fail to achieve either functional efficiency or aesthetic appeal, and these defects may be among the most exasperating in their effect on the quality of life for city dwellers. In terms of cost and of attention required, they probably dwarf other aspects of the environmental problem. Moreover, the way in which they are attacked can have major implications for the remaining environmental concerns. However, we tend to see ugliness and inconvenience in urban environments as something tolerable that can be dealt with over time and that does not carry the threat of disaster. By contrast, most of the alarm has centered on the natural aspects of the environment—air, water, soil, sea, ecological systems—and on the effect of man's activities on these interrelated ambiences and the consequent threat to his own and other life. Since this is where the argument is focused, it will get the most attention, but with full recognition that many of the problems are made acute by our cities and by the way we organize our activities in space.

Dramatic warnings of impending disaster have done their work. While it is undeniably moving to soar in prose alongside the imperiled peregrine falcon, if we are to grapple successfully with our problems we had best get down to earth and try to size them up. It is not sufficient to blame advanced technology, high income, increased population, or "the system" in blanket fashion. Instead we must try to determine which of these factors relate to which kinds of environmental insult. We must see how they have interacted and try to establish some prognosis for them. Many of our concerns are with dire warnings of calamities that have not yet occurred—climatic change, the death of the ocean, the end of photosynthesis. It is worthwhile to assess the extent of scientific evidence on these matters before proposing policies to deal with them; often the first conclusion is that much more research is required before even this can be done. Other problems—and some of them may be the source of the most immediate daily annoyances—are ones that can be managed if we wish to pay the cost and devise the organization to do so. It is important to distinguish these kinds of problems from the first because they merit a somewhat different management approach. There are many things that can be done bit by bit along technical, economic, or administrative lines within the present system. This is the normal way in which society copes, and it is much less painful and usually quicker than fundamental changes in values or social system. However, it is equally important to discern where the more drastic kinds of action may be required, in response to which sorts of problems, at what pace, and to discuss ways of moving in the needed direction.

The structure of this book reflects the belief that there are various degrees of environmental threat that require different approaches. First, however, we shall look at the economic and demographic trends which underlie all of the many threats to environmental quality (Chapter 2). Here, as elsewhere, the United States is examined in most detail, although the problems of other countries are borne in mind, sometimes explicitly, more often by implication. Certain categories of economic activity that are identified with environmental pressures have been singled out for more detailed attention—food, energy, waste disposal, and use of space for outdoor recreation, urbanization, etc.

From a policy standpoint, it is useful to think of environmental problems in terms of their gravity. It is foolish to belabor the offensiveness of discarded beer cans in the same terms as potential threats to life on earth. The urgency of the response, or the tolerance of damage, should be related to the potential seriousness of the consequences. Therefore Chapter 3 offers a rough classification of various types of environmental threat according to the scale of gravity.

On the basis of such a taxonomy, Chapter 4 examines some of the principal sources of danger which are potential threats to man and to other life. The emphasis here is on recounting the evidence on how such hazards can threaten the environment and on the state of current knowledge about the existence of significant thresholds at which insult is converted into serious damage. This review deals with possible effects of energy use upon global climate, radioactivity from use of nuclear energy, the use of pesticides and fertilizers, and soil erosion.

Chapter 5 considers the many other kinds and degrees of environmental hazards in terms of their present or potential effects upon the receiving media, principally water and air.

Unaltered trends are not assumed, for much of the point of this study is to identify problems to see how they can be coped with. Chapter 6 considers appropriate basic objectives and then examines the possible contributions of technology, along with the economics of dealing with environmental problems in the world as it is today. The methods of management that are considered include redesign of the present system of incentives and a broadening of the scope of economic analysis, as well as alternative administrative measures.

But not all environmental problems can be confidently approached in such a familiar framework. Some will require a reexamination of social values and institutions, although here, too, technical and economic information also must be taken into account. Although no attempt is made to propose solutions to such grand questions, in Chapter 7 they are discussed in the context of their proper relation to other aspects of the environmental problem that can be appraised by more familiar standards.

The principal conclusions of this study are summarized in Chapter 8.

Selected References

Cole, Lamont C. "Can the World Be Saved?" Paper presented at the 134th meeting of the American Association for the Advancement of Science, December 27, 1967.
_____. "Ecological Soundings Awareness." *Environmental Science and Technology*, vol. 2, no. 2 (December 1968), pp. 1069–71.
Commoner, Barry. "Can We Survive?" *Washington Monthly*, December 1969, pp. 12–21.
_____. *Science and Survival.* New York: Viking Press, 1963.
De Bell, Garrett, ed. *The Environmental Handbook*, prepared for the First National Environmental Teach-In, April 22, 1970. New York: Ballantine Books, 1970.
Ehrlich, Paul R. "Ecocatastrophe." *Ramparts*, September 1969, pp. 1–5.
_____. *The Population Bomb.* New York: Ballantine Books, 1968.
Mitchell, John G., with Constance L. Stallings, ed. *Ecotactics: The Sierra Club Handbook for Environmental Activists.* New York: Pocket Books, 1970.
National Academy of Sciences–National Research Council, Committee on Resources and Man. *Resources and Man: A Study and Recommendations.* San Francisco: W. H. Freeman, 1969.
Rienow, Robert, and Leona Train Rienow. *Moment in the Sun: A Report on the Deteriorating Quality of the American Environment.* New York: Ballantine Books, 1967.

TWO

MAN'S ACCELERATING USE
OF THE ENVIRONMENT

The human race has survived adversity for millions of years. Why, in the last half of the twentieth century, should we become agitated about the viability of our planet? The answer, of course, lies in the power and momentum of man's effect on his environment and the comparative recency with which this has arisen. Heretofore human progress was slow. Although the antecedents of science and medicine can be traced back for thousands of years, their mass impact in most parts of the world is quite new. They have given us the means to break the natural checks on population and to support vast populations independently of nature's usual rhythms. It is the combination of numbers and per capita consumption that creates the problem. Because there are earlier precedents of environmental ills, it is easy to underestimate the extreme recency of our current problem. It has come on with a rush and is proceeding at a pace that is difficult to comprehend. We are right to be concerned.

What is our time scale? Ten thousand years ago the world had about 10 million inhabitants. By 1850 there were 1 billion; by 1950, 2.5 billion; and by the end of this century a population of 7 billion seems likely. From population growth rates that once were about 2 percent each thousand years we come to a rate of 2 percent every single year on a world basis.[1]

If 7 billion people three decades hence seek nothing more than to eat at improved dietary standards, they must about triple the 1950 world output of farms and fisheries—a feat likely to be accomplished only at considerable environmental cost. In fact they will aspire to more. If people throughout the world should emulate the affluence and consumption levels of the developed countries and especially of the United States, the prospective use of energy and materials becomes overwhelming. Moreover, we provide a constantly moving target, for our own rate of growth does not diminish.

The logic of compound growth rates, which is so frightening at the 1 percent or 2 percent rates applicable to population growth, becomes even more compelling when employed at the higher rates appropriate for economic growth. The approximate doubling time, which is 70 years for 1 percent annual growth, drops to 35 years for 2 percent, 14 years for 5 percent, and 7 years for 10 percent. Although income does not bear a direct and necessary relationship to environmental burden, most income is translated into demands for agricultural products, energy, or chemical and mineral products; therefore high income has meant a large throughput of materials and consequently a heavier draft upon natural resources and a greater volume of wastes to be disposed of.

Wholly plausible economic and demographic growth rates soon can pose intractable problems in their meaning for the environment. It is useful—indeed essential—to understand the dynamics that are at work, even though the results of such an inquiry are quite limited. Attempts at quantification do not yield confident predictions very far into the future—at most a generation or so for population, less for economic variables. Moreover, the possibilities for technical change mean that even less can be said with certainty about environmental effects. Finally, even in cases where we appear to have a generation or more of grace, this prospect does not give us long-term reassurance. The measured tread of that 1 to 2 percent population growth rate compounded by even more rapid per capita economic gains allows us no respite from attention to environmental consequences.

Before examining some of the implications of growth, let us first review briefly how the ecological system works and how man's economic system has aggravated economic problems.

[1] Philip M. Hauser, "World Population Growth," in The American Assembly, *The Population Dilemma*, ed. Hauser, p. 13.

Nature's Ecological System and Man's Economic System

Natural systems are credited with order and a degree of stability. The economic activities of man disturb these systems, sometimes needlessly. We must understand the principles of both systems in order to minimize the conflict between them. To ecologists there are two global processes that define the conditions for all life. One is the energy system—an open-end flow from sun to earth where, after doing much work, energy is radiated back to space. The other is the closed nonenergy portion of the nutrient cycle which circulates the minerals required for living organisms.

The Ecological System. Until our recent success in tapping nuclear and geothermal sources, all energy was derived from the sun. Solar energy drives the atmospheric and the hydrologic systems, and it provides the energy for photosynthesis. About 1 percent of the solar energy reaching green plants on land is fixed as carbon in the form of carbohydrates. Such plants are known as primary producers and provide forage for primary consumers, who in turn are preyed upon by predators. Analogous processes occur in water. The energy transferred from plants is largely dissipated, with only about 10 percent being used at each succeeding level in the chain. Eventually, decomposition converts organic remains into waste heat and releases the basic nutrients they contain. The only exception has been the slow accumulation of fossil fuels. All life relies upon the continuous receipt of solar energy.

Life also needs additional ingredients, especially nitrogen, phosphorus, and trace minerals. These are circulated in two large systems, with the atmosphere the principal reservoir for gaseous forms of nitrogen and carbon, and the lithosphere the reservoir for other elements such as phosphorus or sulfur, which are released through the weathering of rock. Nitrogen is recycled from plants to the atmosphere and back in a complicated process whereby organic material is converted into ammonia, nitrites, and nitrate by successive armies of microorganisms. The nitrate, if not looped back through plants or lost to deep percolation, is then denitrified, and the nitrogen is returned to the atmosphere as gas where it again is available to nitrogen-fixing plants. Phosphorus undergoes a simple transformation, having no gaseous phase and simply moving into and out of organic form. Under natural conditions nutrient cycles are more or less in balance. Man's use of the land for agriculture removes nutrients in the form of crops, thereby disturbing the natural balance. The principal nutrients are replaced with a commercial fertilizer.

These global energy and nutrient systems provide the setting for smaller ecosystems. Ecosystems, which are composed of a biotic community and its physical habitat, are of both terrestrial and aquatic types. These vary greatly in scope and overlap in complex ways, making classification difficult. As the diversity in plant species increases, the stability of the system is enhanced. A tropical forest is complex and stable—a one-crop agriculture is a very simple and a very unstable system.

Industrial man must disturb the natural system if he is to maintain his standard. Yet society also has an interest in preserving the fund of genetic information that the natural system contains, for this often has proved to be of value to us. And we derive pleasure from observation of biotic communities in their natural state.

Human economic progress would have been impossible at the rate we have known had we not had access to the reserve of energy stored as fossil fuel. Though we are still dependent on this, we have the prospect of escape by way of other energy sources. But we have faint prospect of escaping our dependency on the photosynthetic portion of the energy cycle, and we must make sure that it continues along with the other life associated with it.

The natural system tends to preserve its equilibrium. The most familiar example is in species populations where the natural checks on numbers apply. But the natural system also reprocesses and reuses organic material by way of the work done by decomposers and dilutes and alters wastes in the air and water through washout and precipitation of inorganic matter. Man always has relied on the natural system to receive his wastes and perform these assimilative functions. Locally we often overburden its capacity to do so. On a global basis the most ominous effects on the natural system would come from seriously disturbing the energy flow (on which the atmospheric and hydrologic system depend as well) or from damaging photosynthesis directly through the use of exotic and powerful chemicals. Lesser but still important effects of man involve the destruction of genetic information or the setting in motion of changes that impair the capacity of the natural system to reconstitute its original balance.

Primitive man was directly dependent on an unmodified natural system for food. His tools were limited and his own muscles supplied his energy. By the same token his needs were biological rather than economic, and his numbers were held in check by the same forces that limit other species. Technological man alters the natural system most extensively in agriculture where the process of photosynthesis is channeled so as to greatly increase the capacity of the land to produce food. In step with his mastery of techniques for acquiring and processing the earth's minerals and for drawing upon its stored

energy, he develops and can satisfy needs that are culturally and not biologically determined. These are the needs that are reflected in the growth
rates cited below. Economic growth is the aspiration of modern man irrespective of his economic system. Nowhere except perhaps in the jungles of New
Guinea are men unaware of its potential or immune to its lure.

One recurring issue confronting man since he departed the natural system
has been the adequacy of resources. The yield of the environment can be
increased through technical advance and that is what we have relied on
mainly, although in the past Western man has combined this with territorial
expansion as well. We increased the yield of agriculture, and improved our
skill in finding energy and in finding and processing mineral ores of descend-
ing quality. The potential yield of photosynthesis is enormous if properly
organized. Likewise, since matter cannot be destroyed, the basic elements of
the earth remain to be reconstituted in such combinations as we choose.
However, the energy requirements of acquiring and processing inorganic
materials would be far different if we had to produce them from crustal rock
or seawater rather than from the concentrated sources we call ores. Energy
thus is a key to the availability of other resources, and, since we mine energy
from finite deposits, in the long run the continuation of man's economic
activity hinges upon finding alternative sources of energy. Fortunately we
have that prospect. While we cannot say that resources are not a problem, we
can see ways of coping with that problem.

The Economic System. The economic system required to order the productive activities of technological man is extremely complex, and in order to
understand it at all we must resort to highly simplified and often inadequate
mental constructs. Theoretically the system could be operated in a variety of
ways. In practice in most of the Western world, and especially during the
period of rapid economic growth which the West has led, it has been found
that giving wide play to individual initiative, including the right to retain the
resulting gains, has helped to make the system highly productive. Even its
severest critics do not fault it on that score. Moreover, the system is dynamic
rather than static, actively seeking and incorporating new technology. Again,
although critics can cite instances in which private interests have arrested
progress, a far more valid concern of environmentalists is that progress has
come too fast, so that we are inundated with goods. Despite the seeming
chaos of having millions of persons making private uncoordinated decisions,
we achieve a fair degree of order through the functioning of markets.

This system is not only productive and progressive but (subject to varying
degrees of dissent) has been considered socially desirable as well. Its under-

lying assumption is that the private desires of individuals expressed in the market—in choice of work or choice of goods—should govern the disposition of economic resources. This criterion of the responsiveness of economic resources to individual desires requires that they be deployed where demand is greatest. Private property and the profit motive occupy a key role, since private holders seeking gain are motivated to provide what the public wants. The private holder can also be expected to manage his property as well as possible in order to conserve its value. The concept of private property has been extended to include land and minerals—neither traceable to man's labors—with the result that their products have been made available on a timely basis in conformance with consumer demand. Moreover, within a system of law, property owners are expected to be responsible for damage that the use of their property inflicts on others.

It has always been recognized that the system has faults. The sort of income distribution it generates, its premium on the manipulation of consumer tastes, the oscillating nature of its activity, and the lack of competition in some sectors have been obvious failings. In addition, private time horizons expressed in markets may not coincide with social preferences in the rate of resource use. Also among the failings has been the existence of externalities— the fact that in the course of using his property an owner creates side effects that are burdens for others. The classical example has been factory smoke that increases neighbors' cleaning bills. While in theory the damaged persons have a claim against the offender, in practice the diffused nature of the effect or the inequality of the parties makes it almost impossible to effect the claim.

At one time externalities were not thought very important. Most of them were transmitted by way of air or water which diffused or diluted the effects. Moreover, these media have some capacity to absorb or neutralize the burdens placed on them. Now, however, we can see how rapidly the environmental burden rises, for all of the materials generated by continuing economic and population growth must be returned to the environment. Far from being the exception, externalities have become the rule, and the assimilative capacity of the environment is overburdened.

Part of the problem is caused by a system of incentives which is biased in the direction of the production of goods and away from protection of the environment. While goods-producing resources are in private hands, giving owners an incentive to maximize output, the environment that receives the physical residuals from materials employed in the process has not benefited from the same economic incentives. Many resources of value to man such as the air, most watercourses, the sea, and aesthetic qualities of the landscape, cannot be captured by anyone for his exclusive use. Yet these common property or open-access resources are used as free dumps for the mass of residuals generated by private activity. Since access is unrestricted and cost-less to the private operator, no individual is motivated to limit his use of these resources or to enhance their quality. Indeed, quite the reverse—it is futile for him to show private restraint. As a society, however, we cannot escape the cost of this abuse, whether reflected in lost amenity, health, or higher eco-nomic charges.

Free use of open-access resources ensures their misuse. Those who use them—and that includes consumers and public agencies as well as industry—have no incentive to desist. Much can be done to limit the amount and modify the form of residuals so as to render them less harmful. At present the market does not provide an incentive to do this, but with modifications it could. If we realize these opportunities, we may be able to obtain the same level of services from our use of materials and energy with less return of objectionable discharges to the environment. In that case environmental dam-age need not rise in proportion to our income. We need all the help we can get in bringing this about, for as we approach the limits of natural assimilative capacity, and in more and more cases pass the point at which natural systems break down, damage threatens to rise more than proportionally.

Demographic and Economic Factors in the United States

The United States, as the world's most economically advanced country, can serve as an indicator of what other countries may yet experience. We shall briefly examine the record and prospects with regard to the main economic and demographic factors and then see how, in the kind of legal and institu-tional setting we have, these are translated into environmental burdens.

The record of demographic growth is easily enough grasped—a population of under 4 million (excluding Indians) at the nation's birth, 31 million at the onset of the Civil War, a diminished growth rate thereafter coinciding none-theless with our largest absolute increases (almost 28 million in the 1950s), and the expectation of 300 million by the end of this century—this in a mere 200 years. Although net migration has been important, the largest factor at work has been the excess of births over deaths. The death rate, which was about 17 per thousand at the start of the century (when the population had a much larger proportion of young people) has held steady in the neighborhood of 9.5 since 1950. At that level it reflects not only our advances in public health and medicine but also the fact that our population is still relatively youthful. Meanwhile birth rates have behaved more erratically, dropping from over 30 at the outset of the century to under 20 during the depression, undulating since to a peak of 26.5 during the postwar baby boom and dropping to a figure of 17.6 in 1968. The postwar baby boom is now expected to have its echo as young women of that vintage enter their reproductive years. In 1968 there were 41 million females aged 15-44. By 1980 the figure will rise to 52 million, with the greatest increase in the high-fertility younger ages.

Given this age structure, we could obtain zero population growth immediately only if we were to cut the birth rate in half, allowing about one child per family over the next 15 to 20 years. Such an abrupt fall in fertility rates is just not in the cards. If we set a less exacting standard by which each generation would reproduce itself (a net reproduction rate of one), the average number of children per family would have to be about 2.25 instead of the 3.0 that has prevailed in recent years. This would not be easy to achieve. Even if it were attained, the population would not become stationary for several decades into the next century and would still rise to about 270 million. This is a considerably lower number than the Census Bureau expects by the end of the current century. One consequence of achieving a stationary population, whenever it occurs, is a sharply different age structure in which the number of children under 15 would be about equal to the number of persons over 60, instead of about twice as many, as at present. An abrupt switch to zero population growth now would yield a wildly distorted age structure.

Although judgments differ about the appropriate size of our population, for the next few decades demographic growth is not likely to be the critical contributor to our environmental problems. Currently population growth in the United States is not in an explosive phase, being about 1 percent per year. This rate, which may be tolerable for a generation, becomes quite intolerable when extended for centuries. But there is little doubt that we can afford to proceed toward a net reproduction rate of one rather than hastening to the more drastic immediate zero population growth.

Economic growth rates in the United States are universally higher than demographic rates. We are accustomed to per capita increases in output and income. In fact, Gross National Product (GNP) has grown at over 3 percent yearly in real terms since the early years of the century and has speeded up in recent decades; the GNP figure doubled between 1950 and 1970. On the common assumption that growth will continue at 4 percent annually (1 percent labor force growth and 3 percent productivity improvement), we will have three times the 1970 figure by the year 2000. The fact that these rates will apply to a rising dollar base heightens their significance. During the years of rapid expansion of 1922-29, annual growth was $4 billion, while in 1958-65, another period of growth, it was $25 billion, all measured in constant dollars. The annual increase in U.S. per capita income usually amounts to more than the total per capita income of such countries as India, Indonesia, or Nigeria.

Industrial production has grown somewhat faster than income. The Federal Reserve Board index (1957-59 = 100) rose from 25 in 1919 to 173 in 1969, almost a sixfold increase over 50 years. Growth in the past two decades was faster than for the whole 50-year period. Even on the modest assumption of a 4 percent rate, industrial output, like GNP, will triple by the end of the century. By that time a single year's increase will almost equal the total output of 1919.

Industrial activity has a more direct bearing on environmental quality than does the more inclusive measure of GNP, and the closeness of the tie becomes clearer when we remember the law of the conservation of matter: when materials are used they are not really consumed but only changed into other forms. If no allowance is made for imports or exports or for accumulation of useful stocks, such as buildings and equipment, the weight of residuals cast out upon the water, air, or land must equal that of the raw materials that enter the system—in fact it is somewhat larger because of oxygen taken from the atmosphere during production or processing operations.

In the United States the weight of basic materials production plus net imports was about 4¼ billion tons in 1965. Deducting 10 or 15 percent for accumulation of stocks would leave a total of well over 3½ billion tons.

If we then exclude stone, sand, gravel, and other minerals used for structural purposes, more than half of the total can be considered as "active" inputs. Most of this remaining weight—perhaps three-quarters—is currently discharged to the atmosphere as carbon—either carbon monoxide (CO) or carbon dioxide (CO_2)—and hydrogen (in the form of water, H_2O). Discharge of CO_2 can be considered harmless in the short run. We shall discuss possible long-term effects later.

Residual gases such as CO, nitrogen dioxide (NO_2), and sulfur dioxide (SO_2) are potentially harmful even in the short run. Dry solids like rubbish and scrap and wet solids like garbage, sewage, and industrial wastes suspended or dissolved in water comprise the remaining residuals. Most of them are troublesome in one way or another.

Technology, of course, affects the scale and pattern of industrial production in many ways. Some observers regard technology as a third major factor, along with population and income, affecting environmental quality. They point out that the substitution of synthetic for natural products is counterecological because the natural system has no means of recycling the synthetics. Implicit in this argument is the view that materials that are not recycled result in a shock to the natural system (overload or deprivation) that must be harmful. This is an important consideration. But *a priori* there is no reason why it must hold in all cases. Some materials may simply be inert and not affect the life process. If so (depending on their volume) they are not counterecological in any serious way over a time span of interest to man. Moreover, total reliance on natural cycling would either compel greatly reduced levels of activity or invite the risk of substituting one hazard for another. For example, if fertilizer use should be curtailed, yet more people with higher incomes still had to be fed, an alternative would be to use more land in agriculture. But as poorer lands are brought into use, increased erosion might set ultimate limits on food supply as land becomes exhausted. While it is true that technology has yielded a number of troublesome residuals of great potential harm, the entire blame cannot be laid at its door.

The Principal Trouble Spots

Overall indexes of population, economic activity, or amounts of residuals are only rough measures of environmental danger. Although sheer size is impressive, some of the more destructive environmental insults are measured not in millions of tons but in parts per million. Also, most of the serious environmental problems are associated with a few categories of human activity. It is in those areas where the pressures of population, income levels, and industrial production bear the hardest upon environmental quality. That is the reason why we shall look with some care at the present situation and the future possibilities in four lines of activity. First among them are the many and varied consequences of energy use. A second important cluster concerns the environmental impact of food production, given modern methods of agriculture. Third are the diverse categories of industrial and consumer activities that generate most of the other residuals that burden the environment. Fourth—and apart from the effects of unwanted residuals that result from the flow of materials—are the ways in which we use space; these also strongly affect the quality of the environment. Here, major sources of pressure are the rising demand for outdoor recreation, the growing interest in preserving natural areas, and the continuing spread of urbanization. Again, the underlying forces are population and income and, as with physical wastes, their effects are unevenly distributed. Most of us perceive our surroundings in terms of the convenience and pleasure (or their opposites) that we derive from city and country, and hence we are greatly affected by the physical form that they take.

All of these problem clusters interact with one another. For example, the energy required for urban transportation is affected by the structure of the city, and farm and forest practices can greatly affect the recreational possibilities and aesthetic appeal of the countryside.

The Energy Economy

In the United States the energy sector contributes the largest volume of active and troublesome residuals to the environment.[2] Many factors influence a nation's total consumption of energy, among them its industrial structure, efficiency in use, and climate. Changes in energy consumption over time tend to be roughly related to income. Energy use per dollar of GNP in this country is now about the same as in 1945. The longer-term decline in this ratio may have been arrested.

Most forecasts of future growth in energy consumption for the United States still shade this relationship slightly, projecting a growth rate of 3.5 percent in energy until the year 2000, accompanied by a 4 percent growth in GNP. The stability of this relationship cannot be taken entirely for granted, however, for the overall projection of energy consumption is composed of many quite different components. It seems reasonable to expect some categories, such as space heating, to approach limits not closely related to income growth; and an economy more oriented to services could require less energy in relation to gross output than a goods-oriented one. On the other hand, our hunger for mobility seems insatiable; we haven't yet tamed the summer heat as thoroughly as the winter cold; and any major shift toward recycling materials is likely to require large inputs of energy.

Sources of primary energy in the United States over recent decades are shown in Table 1. The most notable continuing trends have been the declining position of coal and the rising share of gas. Petroleum, which by 1950 had replaced coal as the largest energy source, has maintained its share since. Hydroelectricity occupies a minor role, and the controversial nuclear source is

---

[2]Energy data on which this section is based were adapted from Joel Darmstadter, "Trends and Patterns in U.S. and Worldwide Energy Consumption: A Background Review."

Table 1. Total U.S. Consumption of Energy by Source and Use in Electric
          Generation, Selected Years, 1910-1969   *(trillion Btu)*

	By source					By use	
Year	Coal	Natural gas	Petroleum	Hydro and nuclear[a]	Total	In electricity	In other uses
1910	12,714	540	1,007	539	14,800		
1920	15,504	827	2,676	775	19,782	1,663	18,119
1930	13,639	1,969	5,898	785	22,288	1,965	20,323
1940	12,535	2,726	7,781	917	23,908	2,458	21,450
1950	12,913	6,150	13,489	1,601	34,153	5,142	29,011
1960	10,414	12,736	20,035	1,631	44,816	8,444	36,372
1969	13,458	21,037	28,374	2,776	65,645	15,748	49,897

Source: Joel Darmstadter, "Trends and Patterns in U.S. and Worldwide Energy Consumption: A Background Review." A revised version of this paper will appear in *Energy, Economic Growth, and the Environment* (Baltimore: Johns Hopkins Press for Resources for the Future, forthcoming).

[a]Nuclear energy amounted to 141 trillion Btu (or 0.2 percent of total energy consumption) in 1969.

still very small. Since total consumption has risen, even coal consumption was higher in 1969 than for any year since 1948.

The role of these energy sources in coming decades is constrained by supply availabilities and environmental concerns. Coal is in ample supply, but it tends to be the dirtiest fuel to burn and it also has adverse and sometimes devastating environmental consequences at the site of production. Petroleum shares some of these disadvantages, creating environmental burdens in production, transportation, and use, although it is somewhat more manageable in burning. Domestic supplies are more restricted for petroleum than for coal, and resort to imports raises questions about the security of supply. Natural gas burns with fewer residuals in most cases than other fuels but known domestic supplies are limited. While the shortage of gas reserves is partially the result of regulatory policies, we face earlier exhaustion of this source than of other fuels. Imports are increasingly feasible but again at some peril in security of supply. Nuclear energy availability depends very much on technical developments. If these progress as anticipated, the atom will be our most ample source of energy. (The environmental effects of nuclear energy are discussed in Chapter 4.) Hydroelectricity is a very clean source of power, but low-cost sites in developed countries are virtually exhausted, and exploitation of those which remain often is opposed because it would inundate valued landscape features.

Although substitution among energy sources is possible over a wide range of uses, to some extent the demand for a given source is related to the sector in which it is used. For the United States in 1968, electric utilities consumed 22.5 percent of primary energy, 24.5 percent went to transportation, 31.5 percent was used in industry, and 21.1 percent in households and commercial establishments. At present coal dominates the electric power generating field and is important to industry, especially for the smelting of ferrous metals. Petroleum even more heavily dominates in transportation. Easiest possibilities for substitution among sources occur in electricity generation and space heating. While other energy sources could be employed in metal smelting and transportation, to do so would entail major changes in technology and massive new investments.

Electricity is an extremely flexible form of energy with respect to both primary sources and existing and potential uses. Its convenience and cleanliness at the point of use favor its growth. In the past 30 years electricity generation has grown about twice as fast as total energy consumption, at a rate of 7.7 percent per year. At this rate output more than doubles each decade, and even allowing for some slowdown in this rate of growth, we can expect by the end of the century to use 7 to 8 times as much electricity as at present. Improvements in efficiency could hold gross energy inputs for generation to about 6 times the current figure, but, even so, electricity generation will use nearly one-half of all primary energy inputs instead of the one-fourth it uses at present.

Where the electricity will come from depends on both economic and environmental considerations. Coal was the primary source of over one-half of the nation's electric power in 1969, and generators used about 55 percent of all coal burned. Most of the remaining electrical energy was produced in the West and Southwest from hydro and natural gas. Residual fuel oil burned by power plants produced nearly 12 percent of the total, mostly in the East. Despite some shift to oil and gas from coal, the total consumption of coal in power generation rose from about 50 million tons in 1940 to over 300 million by 1970.

Coal and oil burned in thermal electric plants and in other stationary sources contributed major fractions of all sulfur oxides (~74 percent), nitrogen oxides (~49 percent), and particulates (~31 percent) emitted in the United States in 1968. (See Table 2.) Recent limitations on allowable sulfur content of fuels and increased use of devices for removing it from stacks will alter these figures. In the case of particulates, however, the figure prevails despite long-standing efforts at control.

Table 2. Estimated Nationwide Emissions, United States, 1968

(million short tons)

Source	Carbon monoxide	Particulates	Sulfur oxides	Hydro- carbons	Nitrogen oxides
Transportation	63.8	1.2	0.8	16.6	8.1
Fuel combustion (stationary)	1.9	8.9	24.4	0.7	10.0
Industrial processes	9.7	7.5	7.3	4.6	0.2
Solid-waste disposal	7.8	1.1	0.1	1.6	0.6
Miscellaneous	16.9	9.6	0.6	8.5	1.7
Total	100.1	28.3	33.2	32.0	20.6

Source: Environmental Quality, The First Annual Report of the Council on Environmental Quality. Transmitted to the Congress August 1970 (Washington, D.C.: Government Printing Office, 1970), p. 63.

Projections of gross energy inputs in generation by the year 2000 cluster at about 6 times the current figure. Some expect two-thirds of the increase in energy inputs into electricity will come from nuclear generators. Even if the relative share of coal declines, about three times as much coal could be required then as now. The type of fuel used depends largely on cost and security of supply. Oil has the potential to compete strongly with coal provided it is available on a secure basis at an appropriate price. The other unknown is the future competitiveness of nuclear energy. Recent sharp rises in the cost of nuclear reactors have blunted their penetration of the market. Renewed competitiveness of nuclear plants or the successful development of breeder reactors in coming decades could give the edge to reactors. Rising fuel prices reflecting the cost of pollution control for plants using fossil fuels may speed the day.

In any case environmental considerations may intervene. Both coal and oil are relatively dirty fuel sources. Unmodified reliance on them would mean that in a matter of decades we would be multiplying present emission levels on a geometric scale—surely an insupportable prospect. Either we must make great progress in reducing noxious emissions per unit of fuel burned or we must turn increasingly to reactors. Some expect nuclear generators to account for over one-half of our electric power by the end of the century with coal providing 30 percent and the shares of oil and gas much reduced.

Transportation accounted for 24 percent of all energy use in the United States for 1969. All but a tiny portion was petroleum products. This sector consumed well over 300 million tons of fuel plus additives, 180,000 tons of which were lead. As Table 2 shows, transportation (principally automobiles) is the chief source of three principal types of air pollution—nearly two-thirds of the CO, over half of the hydrocarbons, and two-fifths of the nitrogen oxides (NO_x).

Passenger transportation in the United States is overwhelmingly automotive.[3] In 1965, 82 percent of all workers went to work by car, and most of the rest by bus. Cars and buses accounted for more than 90 percent of intercity passenger miles and airlines for 6 percent. Although most freight still moves by rail and barge, trucks carried about one-quarter of the ton-mile total and monopolized local distribution of goods.

In terms of fuel consumption the predominance of cars, trucks, and buses is again apparent. In 1966, 224 million tons of petroleum fuels and lubricants went into internal-combustion engines used in transportation. While a small part of this amount was diesel fuel, which causes few air pollution problems, over 200 million tons were gasoline. Aviation (a rapidly increasing sector) used 39 million tons and marine and rail transport 28 million tons. However, most fuel used in aviation is consumed above 3,500 feet, and fuel used in ships is away from harbors—in neither does the emission of their residuals into the air plague us much.

Between 1950 and 1965 the number of vehicles on the road about doubled, attaining a figure of 90 million. Somewhere between those two dates we appear to have passed the point of public tolerance of automotive air pollution. By the end of the century there may be 200 to 250 million vehicles. If present trends continue, even without allowance for the likelihood of higher compression ratios, increased idling time caused by congestion, and greater annual mileage put on cars by a restless population (all of which increase pollution per vehicle), we still may face emissions of 4 to 5 times the level once thought tolerable.

It seems likely, however, that a combination of measures can be employed that will reduce emissions from new cars by about 90 percent. However, the add-on devices that would do most of the job degrade with age and wear; control cannot be sustained in the face of poor maintenance. Over the life of the car the net reduction in emissions may be more nearly 50 percent. It is clear that the anticipated increase in number of vehicles will soon swamp the gain from pollution control devices. More radical approaches will have to be considered. Some of these are suggested in Chapter 6.

---

[3] This discussion on pollution from autos is adapted from Allen V. Kneese, Robert U. Ayres, and Ralph C. d'Arge, *Economics and the Environment: A Materials Balance Approach*, pp. 24–28.

The remaining categories of energy use—industry and households—present diverse problems. Industry is an important user of coal, especially in the metallurgical field, and thereby a major contributor to SO_2 and particulate emissions. Industry used almost 41 percent of all coal burned in 1969 and derived 27 percent of its primary energy from that source. Data for 1965 show that about one-half of this was coking coal. The best quality low-sulfur coals (containing ~1 percent) are used for coke; therefore the average sulfur content of industrial coal is somewhat below that used by utilities. Industry is a heavy contributor of particulates, however.

Both industry and households rely heavily upon natural gas and fuel oil for space heating and industry also uses them for process heat. Natural gas supplied about 48 percent of primary energy to industry in 1969 and petroleum another 25 percent. For households and commercial establishments the figures were 50 percent and 46 percent. The latter two users are the principal markets for natural gas. The fuels used for space heating are comparatively clean. Fuel oil has a low ash content (0.5 percent) and a small amount of sulfur (0.25 percent), while gas is virtually free of both.

The share of total primary energy taken directly by industry and households will shrink considerably by the end of the century, chiefly because a growing share of their energy needs will be met by electricity. If the primary energy used to generate electricity is allocated to ultimate consumers, households will increase their share of total energy consumption from 33.6 percent to 37.8 percent, while industry's is expected to drop slightly from 41.9 percent to 39.6 percent. In both instances absolute magnitudes would increase sharply. But direct increases in primary fuel consumption of industry and households would amount to little more than 50 percent for each of the two uses. Much of this increase is likely to be greater use of natural gas and will present few environmental problems. As coal is phased out of its remaining use in space heating, and improved collection devices cut particulate emissions from coal burned in industry, there may very well be no additional environmental burden from these sectors. We must recognize, however, that much of the problem simply will be transferred to the electric-power sector where it will create difficulties.

Energy use trends, especially in electric generation and transportation, pose severe problems for environmental management even under favorable assumptions about controlling emissions and about the progress of nuclear energy. Moreover, nuclear energy itself presents difficult problems of management over the longer term. It is easy to deride the utilities for their efforts to stimulate consumption, but the truth is that most energy goes not into items like electric toothbrushes but rather for travel, heat, air conditioning, washing machines, refrigerators, and general industrial production. And all of this is without consideration of the energy requirements of extensive recycling, should we choose to follow that path. If we wish to economize on energy consumption, we must be willing to organize more rational systems of transportation; if we wish to control emissions and make sure of having really long-term energy supplies, there is no present alternative to advanced nuclear technology.

The Agricultural Economy

Output of food and other products deriving from current photosynthesis makes the most extensive use of the physical environment, alters natural systems drastically, and produces materials in a volume second only to the energy industries. Most agricultural and forest residuals generated on the land (such as manure and crop residues) have been readily assimilated by the environment, except where unusually concentrated. However, the use of chemical fertilizers and pesticides in the course of production imposes quite different and potentially more serious burdens. At the processing stage agricultural products also pose special problems, especially for water. Our problems on the land are aggravated by the growing specialization and concentration of agriculture and the more intensive use of land reflected both in commercial inputs and in the problem of disposing of large quantities of organic matter remaining after harvest.

The primary use of agricultural land is in food production. In the United States there has been no problem of adequacy. We have always been agricultural exporters and this remains true even at our higher population today. The story of our agricultural surpluses and adipose citizens is too familiar to need repetition, although in sheer pounds of food we consume less per person than in 1920 and per capita calorie intake is down about 5 percent, doubtless a reflection of our less strenuous existence. Although some Americans remain underfed, correction of their dietary deficiencies would not much alter the per capita consumption trend. Total calorie consumption will grow about in keeping with population.

The draft on the land has been somewhat greater than the calorie figures imply. We have demanded higher quality food and in particular have taken more of our calories as animal protein. The United States ranks among the highest countries in the world in this respect. Per capita consumption of wheat and potatoes has fallen, while the consumption of vegetables, meat, and poultry has increased. The shift to more animal protein is important because it makes more prodigal use of available resources: about six calories of food intake by animals is required to produce one calorie of meat for humans.

Even so, we have met the needs of a growing population at rising standards without increasing cultivated acreage. In fact, since World War I agricultural output has more than doubled, while the area of cropland has declined. Labor input has declined even more sharply to about one-third the peak level. These improvements in both production and productivity have been accomplished in the face of programs to restrain output and remove land from cultivation. If shortages were the concern and incentives or market forces were shifted to favor the expansion of output (for example, a long-term assurance of 100 percent parity) we probably could double production in a decade or so.

The United States can feed a population growing at present rates for a very long time. For the next generation or so this can be done from present cropland. During that time modestly higher real prices of agricultural commodities may be required to forestall the additional environmental damage which such expansion would threaten. At some later stage it probably will be necessary to expand cropland. We can approximately double the cultivated land area of the United States if we pay proper attention to erosion control. To be sure, much of this land would be costly to prepare, and yields would not match those on better soils. If population should go beyond the 500 to 800 million range we probably would have to shift back toward a cereal diet and away from animal protein; on such a basis we could feed a population still several times larger—perhaps more than the current world figure. The only point of this exercise is to put the danger of starvation in perspective—for the United States it is exceedingly remote.

The increase in current and potential production has been made possible by the use of agricultural chemicals, improved seeds, and mechanical energy. The elimination of draft animals in favor of tractors has released the significant amount of crop acreage formerly required to feed work stock and has caused little adverse environmental effect. Likewise, improved seed varieties are quite innocuous to the environment. The same cannot be said of chemicals.

Agricultural chemicals fall into two principal categories—fertilizers and pesticides. Total fertilizer use rose from an average of 22.5 million tons for 1950–54 to 38.9 million tons in 1968. Nutrient content rose even faster. Of the principal nutrients, nitrogen increased from 1.6 to 7.0 million tons, phosphate (P_2O_5) from 2.2 to 4.7 million, and potash (K_2O) from 1.7 to 3.9 million. Thus, total nutrient content about tripled over that span with the consumption of nitrogen recording the fastest growth. Even so, fertilizer application rates in the United States remain far below those of some other developed countries.[4] U.S. consumption is especially high in corn, tobacco, and cotton fields. If forced to guess, we would expect applications of nutrients in the United States to at least triple by the end of the century. (See Table 3, p. 44.)

Data on pesticides use are harder to come by. There are said to be over 900 chemicals used to formulate 60,000 different preparations in the United States. Recent growth in use has been at a rate of 15 percent per year. Most of this apparently is herbicides rather than the insecticides or fungicides which have been charged with more serious environmental consequences. Agriculture is variously estimated to use from one-half to two-thirds of all pesticides. Consumption of all sorts amounted to 350,000 tons in 1964. One guess (Table 3) anticipates 1.5 million tons of pesticides in agricultural uses by the end of the century.

In truth, there is little basis for long-term projections of consumption of either fertilizers or pesticides. We are only now beginning to understand the environmental consequences of these materials (see Chapter 4), and we cannot be sure that the past trend will be sustainable. However, expansion of agricultural output clearly will require increased use of fertilizers. Evidence from other countries where per acre applications are much higher gives hope that heavier use can be tolerated. We lack such reassuring evidence for pesticides and may need to resort to other measures that can be substituted for them. In both cases we are dealing with explosive growth rates that cannot be blithely extended.

Agriculture also produces a great volume of other residuals such as dust, sediment, manure, and organic residues. Cotton gins and alfalfa dehydrators

---

[4]For example, in the late 1960s consumption rates in kg. (2.2 lb.) per hectare (2.47 acres) of arable land were as follows:

	N	P_2O_5	K_2O
United States	30	22	18
The Netherlands	357	115	138
Japan	140	102	102
United Kingdom	102	59	61
U.S.S.R.	11	7	8

Data derived from *FAO Production Yearbook, 1969*, vol. 23 (Rome: Food and Agriculture Organization of the United Nations, 1970).

are important sources of particulates. Dust from wind erosion may be carried hundreds of miles. Waterborne sediments from farming dwarf all other pollutants for sheer volume, much of this material ending up behind reservoirs. But disposal of animal wastes may become the greater problem. Livestock produce about a billion tons of manure—an amount equivalent to a human population of around 2 billion.[5] Although some of the manure is dispersed over the fields, where it is not only harmless but useful, about one-half is concentrated in feedlots and dairies. When slaughterhouse refuse and carcasses are added, the animal wastes approach 2 billion tons a year. The trend is clearly in the direction of more beef production as an element in our diet and this production is most efficiently conducted in feedlots. About two-thirds of the cattle slaughtered now pass through feedlots in the United States. The concentrated generation of manure and other wastes is expected to about double by the year 2000.

The burning of plant residues on farms—a method frequently used to control plant diseases—adds to the particulate burden of the atmosphere, but it makes only a minor contribution to photochemical smog. Comprehensive estimates of these effects are hard to find; however, one guess (see Table 3) puts current particulates from this source in the United States at 2.3 million tons, increasing to 3.5 million by the year 2000. Forest fires are an even more important source of particulates; it is estimated that 5 to 7 million acres burn annually (including controlled burning).

Food and fiber processing industries also are a major source of organic residuals, especially those that create biochemical oxygen demand (BOD) in watercourses as wastes are broken down into their chemical constituents. About 25 percent of the carcass of meat animals is waste. While some can be incorporated in fertilizers and feeds, at least 10 percent is discharged to the environment, usually in urban areas. Tannery wastes are another problem and a source of particularly obnoxious water pollution. Canneries, milk processing plants, sugar mills, and soap manufacturing plants all produce organic residuals, although some of them are usable as animal feed or for other purposes. The one processing industry whose raw materials are based on current photosynthesis that dwarfs all others in burden on the environment is pulp and paper.[6]

All of the foregoing, except for pulp and paper, are more closely related to population than to other factors, so that explosive growth is not antici-

[5] Cecil H. Wadleigh, *Water in Relation to Agriculture and Forestry*, p. 41.
[6] *Ibid.*, p. 46.

pated. Moreover, since these are all industrial processes, there is greater hope of reducing their environmental effects through process change than is the case for on-farm residues, particularly those of pesticides and fertilizers.

Until now, agricultural producers often have been unaware of the environmental effects of their residuals, much like other producers and consumers. Substitute methods of pest control probably can be developed at no great increase in cost. The feedlot manure problem can be solved at tolerable costs as can the problems created by most agricultural processing industries. In some ways agriculture is more ecologically healthy than it was a generation ago, for major steps have been taken to improve soil conservation and range management practices. Forest resources also are probably better cared for than in the past. Despite current difficulties, one can be optimistic about the compatibility of environmental quality and a productive agriculture capable of meeting the country's needs well into the future.

Industry and Households

The other important residuals from human activity come from industry and households.[7] (Some of the agricultural processing activities already have been mentioned above.) Everything used in production or sold to households ultimately ends up on the junk pile, figuratively speaking, whether it is discharged to water, air, or land. It is difficult to portray the materials flow in industry. We lack direct information in many cases because industry has been too unconcerned about low-cost materials discharged to the environment during processing to record their use.

The extreme variety of industrial and household residuals also precludes any attempt here to project their future growth. One rough estimate of the future could be had simply by extending trends in the industrial production index. Even a modest 4 percent growth rate of this index would yield a total industrial output by the end of the century of well over three times the current figure. Whether this will translate into an equivalent increase in environmental burden is less certain. We can expect more intensive attention to process changes and to neutralization of damage, so that industrial growth may be achieved without the same multiple of damage. At the same time we are likely to see the introduction of ever more exotic materials into the environment and we may encounter thresholds of damage from some resid-

---

[7]Much of this discussion is drawn from Kneese, Ayres, and d'Arge, *Economics and the Environment*, pp. 30–68.

uals already present in lesser volume. The chemical and the mining and metallurgical industries contribute large amounts of the more troublesome
residuals.

The output of chemical industries is often an intermediate product.
Chemicals frequently are used or used up in the production of other goods.
Moreover, their use is often essentially dissipative and they only serve their
function in the course of being dispersed. A wide variety of chemicals share
this trait—pesticides, detergents, solvents, carriers, softeners, flotation agents,
bleaches, antichlors, lubricants, abrasives, fillers, explosives, etc. In addition,
unavoidable losses occur in the course of processing. Since chemical processes
often involve several stages, the opportunity for loss is magnified. Petroleum
products are especially subject to evaporative loss during processing.

The chemical industries generate some of the potentially most damaging
residuals. The environmental effects of many of them are not well understood, and, therefore, their rapid growth takes on added significance. There
are about 2 million known chemical compounds and the list grows rapidly. It
is estimated that 300 to 500 new compounds are introduced into commercial
use each year. Synthetic organic chemicals, of which 9,000 compounds are in
use, often defy natural processes of degradation and in some cases are particularly damaging to life systems. Production of synthetic organic chemicals
rose 125 percent between 1960 and 1968. Output of inorganics, including
most acids, generally did not rise as fast but is still impressive for some
categories.

Mining and metallurgical industries produce bulky residuals (for example,
slag), particulates, gaseous emissions, and liquid wastes (often acids). Slag has
become a valuable by-product used as road ballast, but the sulfur dioxide,
nitrogen oxides, and particulates released annually by industry, mostly from
primary metals, are a major source of air pollution. While the acids in spent
pickling liquors used in metallurgy can be neutralized, the metallic sulfates
they contain are not recovered at present.

Detailed studies of a few industries indicate that process changes can
greatly reduce waste discharge. For example, in the beet sugar industry such
changes introduced between 1949 and 1962 succeeded in reducing BOD
generation by over 60 percent. One cannot generalize across industry,
but it is clear that process changes are feasible in many branches. Under
a proper system of incentives, residuals generation need not rise as fast as
output.

Households are at the end of the line of the materials flow. Most of the
residuals generated in agriculture and power generation arise from activities to

satisfy household wants, but the actual goods delivered to households are a comparatively small part of the materials flow. However, the form and disposition of household residuals present special problems. In general we can expect body wastes to increase in proportion to population, and household chemical and solid wastes to grow no faster than industrial production. Thus, while the totals may be impressive, we are not talking of astronomical increases in the materials handled over the next few decades.

Sewage is a major form of household residual. In terms of dry weight, most of it consists of human excrement (about one-half pound per person daily). Use of a garbage disposal about doubles the dry weight of sewage per person. Also going into the sewage stream are various household soaps and cleaning compounds. The principal environmental effect of the organic materials in sewage is their demand on the dissolved oxygen (BOD) in the receiving watercourses. Although this can be removed or greatly reduced by simple treatment, removal of chemicals contained in cleaning compounds is far more difficult. Phosphates from sewage, along with nitrogen from the organic matter, are major burdens to water.

The remaining household residuals are solid wastes—garbage, combustible and noncombustible trash, ashes, etc. The daily average is a bit over 4 pounds per person. If industrial production indeed triples and the volume of trash increases proportionately, we could have severe problems. Of particular concern is that portion of the household trash that must be picked up by the garbage man or hauled to the dump. For households much solid waste is related to food consumption (remains and packages) and not therefore likely to increase with industrial output. Nevertheless, 50 percent increase in population and a similar increase in per capita waste would result in well over twice the present burden.

Roughly 80 percent of household solid wastes are combustible, but open burning contributes to air pollution. Decentralized incineration of refuse is poorly controlled and generates significant gaseous emissions and particulates. Central incinerators, which can reduce solid wastes to about one-fifth their original bulk, have much to commend them if gases are controlled. The chief drawback to centralized incineration is the cost of collection which frequently is 80 percent of all disposal costs.

Reclamation of solid wastes is comparatively low. Less than one-third of the 43 million tons of paper products manufactured each year is recycled. Few of the 48 billion cans or 26 billion bottles produced annually are reclaimed, and only about 10 percent of plastic and 15 percent of rubber products are reclaimed.

Junked automobiles also present special problems. Six million or so cars are scrapped each year. In 1965 we recovered almost 7 million tons of steel from these hulks. At present scrap prices and costs of separating the steel, not all auto bodies can be utilized as scrap because of the presence of other metals and nonmetallic impurities. Where scale permits, shredders can fragment auto bodies and allow magnetic separation of ferrous materials. If metal becomes more expensive or techniques for salvaging junked cars improve, nearly all of the metal content of the junked cars could be recycled, just as we salvage nearly all of the lead in batteries and reuse most tire casings at least once. However, there are about 2.5 million tons of nonmetallic materials in each year's crop of junked cars that must be disposed of and this will more than double by the year 2000.

In dealing with all kinds of residuals we have stressed that what goes in must come out. This is true in terms of mass and of the basic elements concerned. However, process change and recycling permit reduction of basic inputs for many types of desired output and treatment can alter the chemical form of residual materials to render them less harmful.

This is not to say that there is any prospect of total recycling. The cost in resources and energy required precludes this. If the materials concerned are renewable, then at some point it is preferable to rely on new supplies rather than to recapture everything that goes into the process. Even nonrenewable resources can be used sparingly or acquired from low-grade sources. But either of these measures calls for new inputs of energy and, as we shall see later, there are environmental limits to this possibility quite apart from the question of the adequacy of energy supply.

The Use of Space

The same natural environment that supplies our food and raw materials and absorbs our wastes also provides us space for living and for recreation. The way in which we organize the use of space has implications for almost every facet of life. In particular it greatly influences the amount of land needed for urban purposes, the convenience, efficiency, and aesthetic aspects of urban living, the transportation requirements of society, access to the out-of-doors, and the possibilities for preserving natural areas. It also helps to determine the amount of burden we place on the environment and our strategy for dealing with it. In this brief study we cannot treat these problems in any great detail. They are subjects of specialized study and there is no consensus among experts, not to mention the public, on how we should deal with them. However, we can trace some of the directions and dimensions involved.

Most land in the United States (89 percent of the contiguous 48 states) is devoted to three broad purposes—grazing (34 percent), forestry (32 percent), and cropland (23 percent). Urban use accounts for little over 1 percent of the total and recreation about two or three times this amount, although the market value of the land in these two uses outweighs all other land values combined. The remaining 7 percent of our land is in transportation arteries, airports, reservoirs, military reservations, marshes, deserts, bare rock, etc.

Over the past several decades crop acreage has fallen slightly as productivity has risen and we have sought to limit agricultural output. Except for land suitable as wilderness preserves, it is hard to see how we will be "short" of land far into the future. We may not perceive it this way, however, for most of us move in a constricted environment where congestion is part of our experience. For most urban dwellers the real question is not the gross availability of land on a national scale but how we organize the use of land for urban and recreational purposes.

Urbanization. Man is increasingly an urban animal. The trend to the city, though observable in all countries, is most advanced in the industrial countries. In the United States, while agriculture, forestry, and grazing occupy most of the land, farm employment is only 5 percent of the total labor force. Rural population is somewhat larger, but many who live in the country work in town or are retired from urban careers. Meanwhile, with improved transportation, and a high-technology agriculture, the distinction between urban and rural pursuits is blurred. A romantic back-to-the-land movement is favored by some elements of the counter culture, but it clearly is impractical as a panacea for the entire society and is not likely to affect either our land use or occupational patterns significantly.

Despite the popular image of a country becoming paved over and converted to urban use, cities occupy only a tiny part of our land area, even in the more densely populated East. Even if the United States urban population should double over a generation or so, urban land use would still reach only about 2 percent of the total.

Urban growth imposes a somewhat greater draft on agricultural land than the figures indicate, for city growth has tended to occur in areas that have had a productive agriculture and cities share agriculture's preference for level or gently sloping land, but so far we have not transferred enough land from agricultural to urban use to make much difference to our agricultural potential.

The sense of being cut off from the countryside and from nature arises from the fact that the majority of Americans spend most of their time within the area of their routine movements to work, to school, or to shops and may not have quick access to the open country. In part this is a reflection of our pattern of urbanization. Growth has been heavily concentrated in the metropolitan areas whose spread is increased as people move to the suburbs. Extensions of the suburbs have pushed the countryside still farther away. And just as the growth of agribusiness techniques has obscured the distinction between urban and rural employments, urban sprawl has blurred the physical boundary between city and country.

One may ask if we retain the advantages of either. The characteristic complaint of Americans is more apt to be crabgrass than asphalt; at least as many are exposed to suburban boredom as to the hazards of the city. They gain their private patch of grass, shade, and tranquility at the expense of a longer trip to work or store and more costly public utilities.

This pattern of urbanization has several consequences. One of the most nefarious has been the devitalization of the central city, which occurs not merely from loss of business and public revenue but perhaps even more from the relocation of capable people who once felt a stake in the city. Although they may continue to work there, their community life is apt to be centered in the suburbs. The city becomes the home of the poor, undiluted by the middle class; its deterioration becomes self-reinforcing.

From an efficiency standpoint our pattern of urbanization has obvious disadvantages centering on transportation and public utilities. The typical metropolitan pattern includes a central city not designed to accommodate auto traffic while suburban areas are too dispersed for efficient mass transit. If the road network is to feed into the city center, it can be built only at great financial and social cost. If both mass transit and road traffic are denied the city, new means of articulation, usually roads and private autos, will develop about the fringe. The unity of the city will be damaged as contacts of all sorts (the *raison d'être* of any city) become more difficult.

Perhaps in time activities will decentralize and the road grid will permit free movement over urban areas built to only moderate densities. But such a dispersed pattern carries implications for public services and waste disposal. The most obvious is the air pollution accompanying so much motor traffic. Also, if water, sewage, gas, power, and telephone lines and perhaps the coaxial cables of the future all are provided to householders over greatly extended street mileages, the costs will quickly mount. Since a dump or incinerator must be located away from built-up areas, the cost of disposing of solid wastes also rises.

From the standpoint of convenience and aesthetics the dispersed pattern presents a mixed picture. Tastes are very important in this area. Much of the

Solution

appeal of the suburbs is the escape they offer from the heat, noise, and sense of crowding that have characterized city living. To some extent these results could be achieved at much higher densities in high-rise apartments buffered by greenery, plantings, and common grounds. Architecturally such buildings can be attractive—perhaps more interesting than repetitive suburban builders' models. If grouped around a shopping mall or other focal point, they can offer a variety to neighborhood life not readily available to suburbanites. However, many prefer the limited yet private space of a suburban yard to the common space which might be available in well-designed urban clusters. Of course, compromises could be had, ranging from detached houses opening onto a common green on through a range of more intensive possibilities.

Although urban centers offer advantages in concentrated employment opportunities and in efficiency of production, consumption, and waste disposal, most Americans seem to yearn also for some assurance that nature is still there. The rural commune represents one extreme, rejecting the city and the material standard of life it makes possible. Contact with nature is preserved by dispersal. At the other extreme are such schemes as the visions of Paolo Soleri, who would carry concentration to its logical conclusion in massive work-living structures occupying only minimal surface despite their considerable cubic volume. By this plan, the uncluttered countryside would be only an elevator ride and a few strides away. Somewhere in between we have the city dweller sitting in the park and the suburbanite tending his garden.

In developing our land use pattern we have paid too little attention to the suitability of land for different purposes. On occasion we build a riverside park or preserve a strip of beach for public use, but generally short-term economics has governed land use. The stream may be canalized and the flood plain built over; the swamp or tideland drained or filled; good farmland converted to house lots; and the hills, if valuable enough, violated and left to erode. We have done this because generally we impose no standard other than that of the market on the use of land.

In the countryside, the urban influence continues in often displeasing ways. Generating plants, quarries, garbage dumps, and airports are visited upon the rural landscape. Careful planning can minimize the displeasure and inconvenience to those who live in or enjoy the country. There has been great progress in road design and many of our newer freeways harmonize with the landscape. So far no electric transmission line attains such harmony, though some designs are less objectionable than others.

Since urban land comprises so small a share of our total, the appearance and health of the land is far more dependent on agricultural and recreational pursuits than on urban uses. Agricultural land use practices and the way in which they may be damaging are discussed in Chapter 5. Over vast areas of the rural United States the population is declining. We make more intensive use of the cropland harvested through use of modern agricultural techniques, and we have improved range and forest practices so as to raise productivity and reduce damage to those lands as well. Though they are not left in their natural state, they offer habitat to many forms of wildlife and remain suitable for visual and physical enjoyment by men. The human tread is light in much of the countryside, although in only a few wilderness areas do we allow native life forms to work out their own balance apart from human intervention.

Outdoor Recreation. While the city is what we make it, the physical environment used in outdoor recreation depends to a much greater extent on what nature gives us. As population, income, and leisure all grow, are we likely to run out of the out-of-doors?

Plainly this is a problem only for modern man. Kenneth Clark assures us that prior to the 18th century the mountains and indeed nature in general were not highly valued or sought. Our ancestors had rather much of it and lacked the means we now have to take it in comfort. In any case, it now is in fashion. Nowadays we spend somewhere between $30 billion and $50 billion yearly for travel and paraphernalia for outdoor recreation and, as recreational spending rises, the proportion of it spent for the out-of-doors has been increasing.

In the years since 1910 attendance at national parks has increased 8 to 10 percent annually and as yet shows no signs of slackening. Data for national forests and state parks show a similar picture. Use of reservoirs managed by the Corps of Engineers has increased even faster—at a rate of 28 percent during part of the 1950s and early 1960s—and still grows rapidly although less spectacularly. Fragmentary evidence on attendance at local parks shows a slower rate of growth than for state or national parks.

Not much of the explosive growth in outdoor recreation can be attributed to population increase which, as we have seen, is 1 to 2 percent a year. The youthfulness of our population and rising income and leisure appear to be the chief causes. Also, improvements in transportation have made recreation areas accessible as never before. All of these factors will continue to operate. Already we celebrate Washington's birthday on Monday each year, and with the increased talk of a four-day week we may soon celebrate Friday on Thursday. Although it is clear that recent growth rates for outdoor recreation will not long continue—if they did people would have no time for anything but vacation—we still don't know just when the trend will level off.

Outdoor recreation is an important user of land and water resources and (for things like sail planing, kite flying, and bird watching) even a bit of the sky. The national park system occupies about 30 million acres and state and local parks and forests another 40 million. Substantial portions of the national forests and of reclamation and flood control acreage also are used for recreation. In addition to publicly owned areas, there are extensive private holdings. Some are commercial operations catering to vacationers, campers, and picnickers. Others are clubs or private vacation properties. Land owned by utilities and lumber companies often is entered for recreational purposes, and the Sunday drive in the country is still a popular pastime.

Rising intensity of use has physically damaged or reduced the attractiveness of some recreation areas. Yosemite Valley is threatened by the hordes of people trampling the earth. Crowding is often a psychological phenomenon, but at many campgrounds it is quite palpable. With it have come the ills of urban civilization, as parks suffer from increased vandalism and outbursts of disorder.

Quite distinct from most recreational uses of land is wilderness, a very restrictive and necessarily extensive use for which demand has been increasing. In one sense wilderness can be considered as an extremely specialized type of outdoor recreation land—large areas without roads or other "improvements" where small numbers of experienced back-packers can get back to nature. Wilderness can preserve its character only if it is lightly used; long before human wear and tear become evident it loses its appeal, for those who enjoy it most frequently love solitude.

But wilderness has other values. Persons who never expect to enter it take comfort from the fact that so much unspoiled land and water is *there*. And there is great scientific value, which perhaps will serve human well-being in the preservation of genetic stocks of plants and animals in their untouched natural habitat.

Interest in preserving natural areas is heightened by a growing recognition of the advantages of keeping options open. Unspoiled land, if some great emergency arises, can always be put to some other use, but once it has been so invaded it never can be restored to its pristine state.

On the World Scale

Although this study is focused on the United States, the significance of trends elsewhere on our shared planet cannot be ignored. As development proceeds in other countries, they in turn will contribute more heavily to pollution on a global scale.

Because of our high level of economic development, we serve in many respects as an indicator of what other parts of the world may experience later. In other respects, however, the United States is a poor indicator of problems elsewhere because of our modest population growth rate and density, our comparatively good resource base, and because our wealth, stock of skills, and institutions that allow us to tackle our problems are not typical of the world at large.

Population Trends. Our discussion of U.S. population trends touched briefly on the accelerating world growth. As recently as 300 years ago the world had only about .5 billion people compared to the 3.5 billion of today. Of these 1.5 billion have been added since 1930. At present rates of growth, world population doubles in 35 years. It is physically impossible for such rates to continue long, as human history is measured. A playful calculation shows that if they did it would require only 6½ centuries to cover the earth's land area solidly with a wriggling mass of humans. The best estimate of demographers is that rapid growth is sure to continue for some time, probably more than a hundred years, even on optimistic assumptions about controlling fertility rates.

The reason is the youthfulness of the population. In the United States, as we have seen, the problem arises in a context of moderate birth rates and only moderately youthful population. In the less-developed countries where the bulk of current population growth is occurring, birth rates often are twice the U.S. figure, and the age structure is warped even more sharply toward the younger ages. For example, about 41 percent of the population in less-developed countries is below 15 years of age. This age distribution represents not only a great current burden of dependent persons in relation to the working population but portends a long period of population pressure even if fertility rates fall. By the end of the century we can expect a world population of 6.5 to 7 billion, assuming some reduction in birth rates. Failing that reduction, we may have 7.5 billion. A continued decline in death rates and progress toward a net reproduction rate of one by the year 2040 (an optimistic assumption) would still yield a population leveling off at 15 billion late in the next century. Thus, considering demographic factors alone and leaving aside questions of resource adequacy or environmental tolerances, our best prospect would be for a stationary world population of between 15 and 20 billion.

In modern times population growth accelerated first in Europe and in countries of European settlement. These are the countries that nurtured the growth of modern science and technology which enabled them to produce and distribute goods on a much larger scale than before. For the less-developed countries the most spectacular population growth has come since World War II. In both cases the explanation for rapid growth is found in falling death rates rather than increased birth rates. The changes that allowed European peoples to check their death rates came over an extended period of time and were accompanied by falling birth rates as well; this was true even during the 19th and 20th centuries when the greatest population growth occurred.

In the less-developed countries the changes came abruptly when means of reducing disease by immunization and insect control were made available after World War II. As a consequence death rates fell much more sharply than they ever did in European countries, while birth rates were maintained. This combination has created the extremely youthful population, with its implications for still further growth in precisely those areas of the world already grimly poor. Projections to the end of the century anticipate that population growth in less-developed countries will be over five times that of developed countries, and by the end of the period about three-fourths of the world's population will live in countries that are now poor.

Heretofore, most of the world's poor have lived in rural areas. On the average, urban populations make up only one-fourth of the total in less-developed countries; in advanced countries the figure is nearer to two-thirds. Because productivity on the land is usually low in poor countries, development planners have viewed urbanization and the creation of nonagricultural jobs with favor. The process is in full swing in Latin America where many still poor countries are comparatively urbanized, and it is progressing in Asia and Africa as well. By now, however, this shift is seen with mixed feelings, for the provision of such essential urban services as water and sewer systems, basic public health services, not to mention housing and transportation, taxes the resources of poor countries (and even rich ones, as we know!). This growing concentration of population in countries that can ill afford to cope with the environmental effects of such congestion adds another dimension to the impact of general population growth.

Resource Adequacy. Given the demographic forces at work, will resources be adequate to allow the population growth to occur? What does this imply in turn for the environment? Much of the answer depends on what standard of living we assume. At standards approaching the U.S. or Western European levels, and with similar technology, it is very doubtful that the world can tolerate the environmental effects accompanying a population of 15 to 20 billion. The outlook for resource adequacy appears less disturbing, at least for a generation or more, although we cannot be sure that resources will prove sufficient to supply such a population for an indefinite period.

In terms of sheer availability of resource commodities—food, fuels, metals, water, etc.—the outlook for developed countries seems favorable for many years. It is less so for the densely populated and rapidly growing poor countries, but even in these cases commodity production is likely to increase enough to permit the projected growth of population. To some extent the future for the rich is also bound up with the plight of the poor, for rich countries are dependent on the poor for many resource commodities.

An effort to explore resource availability for major regions of the world was made at Resources for the Future by Joseph Fisher and Neal Potter.[8] They gathered information on per capita consumption and production of various resource commodities, and also data on labor productivity, price trends, and trends in international trade. While there are objections to any of these measures as a single indicator of resource availability, taken jointly they tell us something. Thus, higher per capita consumption, rising labor productivity, declining costs of resource commodities, and falling net imports describe a situation of good resource availability.

The conclusion for the United States is that continued technical progress should allow us to meet projected demands to the end of the century. There may be particular and temporary shortages, but, in general, supply problems can be met. Similar conclusions hold for Western European countries, although they are much more dependent on imported materials than we. For less-developed countries the picture is mixed. As a group they are well supplied with energy, but since this refers in large part to petroleum concentrated in a few countries, many of the less-developed countries may not have as good access to energy as the rich countries who are stronger traders. With regard to food, in some countries the race between population and sustenance will be very close. Much will depend on the rate at which technical advances can be adopted and on the extent of world trade in agricultural products.

In considering the adequacy of food supplies by the year 2000, on the basis of various demand assumptions and United Nations population projections, Fisher and Potter compared the world's calorie requirements at three

---

[8]"Natural Resource Adequacy in the United States and the World," in The American Assembly, *The Population Dilemma*, ed. Hauser.

levels: (1) extension of recent consumption trends, (2) the world at the U.S. per capita consumption level of 1965, and (3) the world at the per capita level of West Europe in 1965. Actual world consumption in 1965 was an estimated 7,800 billion calories a day. Attainment of level (1) at the end of the century would require 19,800 billion calories a day; of level (2), 22,100 billion; and of level (3), 21,100 billion. Projected world consumption at the 1965 U.S. level would be only about 11 percent higher than a simple trend extension.

To achieve any of the levels, world food output would have to be from 2½ to 3 times the 1965 figure. This would require an annual increase of about 3 percent, a rate that does not seem beyond the range of possibility. But these calculations concern only calories, with no allowance for correcting the serious protein and vitamin deficiencies that prevail in many countries. It is less likely that these dietary deficiencies can be made up by the end of the century. By attaining per acre yields already achieved in developed countries, the less developed can meet their basic calorie requirements; they will need to do better still if they are to have grains left over for animal feed to increase their protein consumption.

Achievement of these gains depends mostly upon the development and spread of advanced agricultural technology, although expansion of cultivated area also offers some promise in Africa and Latin America. Unlike medical and industrial technology, agricultural technology does not travel well. Local conditions, especially in tropical areas, require modifications of what has proved successful elsewhere and often entail a long and painful learning process. Moreover, the agricultural technology that we in the United States take for granted is supported by an enormous infrastructure of research, credit, and marketing facilities, as well as by a congenial institutional structure commonly absent in less-developed countries. The prognosis is only guardedly optimistic. In any case, success in achieving such levels, and indeed the very effort to reach them, requires a more than proportional increase in use of the agricultural pesticides and fertilizers whose use is creating some of the environmental problems in more advanced countries.

World energy supplies are quite sufficient over coming decades. It seems likely that total energy consumption will reach 4½ times the present level by the end of the century. This depends, however, on the maintenance of the world's trading and investment system, since energy resources are unevenly distributed and expensive to develop. Total world reserves of fossil fuels are estimated at 3 to 4 trillion tons of coal equivalent, or 500 times current consumption and 100 times the consumption projected for the year 2000.

This neglects the additional possibility of nuclear energy for which reserves are many times this amount, based on breeder reactors, and larger still if fusion reactors are realized.

For most of the metallic minerals (such as iron, aluminum, and copper) either the known resources are sufficient, or new discoveries, resort to lower grade ores, improvements in mining and processing, and conservation of metal should make it possible to support a growing population and increasing industrialization during the coming decades in various parts of the world. To realize this possibility, technological progress must continue, trade and investment channels must be kept open, and cheaper and more plentiful substitutes must be developed in some cases.

Forest products and water supplies present more difficult development and management problems. However, these should not prove insurmountable if technology and management institutions are developed and if the possibilities of substituting other inputs are fully utilized.

In sum, population growth is not likely to be restrained for the remainder of the century by famine or by shortage of minerals, energy, or other resources. We seem doomed to reach our 7 billion or so, along with the inevitability of more to come. The poor countries will have to strive hard to maintain and improve their standards. Even though their per capita levels will remain low, total output and consumption will be very large because of the vast number of people. The common wisdom that a relatively few developed countries are responsible for most of the draft on the world's resources and for the resulting environmental degradation is being overtaken by a new set of facts.

Moreover, as the world resorts to ever lower-grade resources, more material will have to be processed for each unit of usable output and more energy will be required to accomplish this. Thus, the generation of residuals from processing and energy use will tend to grow even faster than total consumption. In the absence of strong countermeasures, pressure on the environment will rise in both developed and less-developed countries. For developed countries the important change is rising per capita consumption magnified by still growing population. In less-developed countries, population plays a key role, and even modest increases in per capita consumption of energy and minerals imply huge absolute increases. The rapid urbanization of these countries under circumstances of poor sanitation, poor combustion, chaotic industrial and transport development, and very little regard for environmental control carries the potential for large-scale and acute human health problems. The often-expressed view that these problems can safely be postponed in favor of rapid growth is blind to the disastrous consequences likely to result.

We have tried to reduce some of these future environmental burdens to numbers in Table 3. These crude projections are instructive, but should not be taken literally. They are generally based on the assumption that the relation of wastes to economic activity will remain about constant. Although the projections do incorporate some technological changes (e.g., they allow a considerable shift to nuclear energy with attendant diminution in the proportion of SO_2 emissions), mostly they reflect what might happen in the absence of any serious efforts at control.

On this basis, emissions of gases and particulates would double or triple for the world as a whole. The effects on man would be still greater, for more people will be living under more congested conditions as urbanization spreads. In the categories of organic materials and plant nutrients the pattern is for doubling or tripling of present figures. For the most part, these pose a threat to water quality. Pesticide use could grow spectacularly, perhaps by a factor of 15 or so. It is hard to believe that this will be allowed to occur, but persistent pesticides are cheap, and the temptation to use them will be strong in poor countries. An even more spectacular increase is projected for the amount of high-level radioactive wastes as the world turns more to nuclear generation. There is no way the environment can assimilate or neutralize this—it must be permanently stored.

It is unlikely that the pollution levels implied by such projections will come to pass. If they do, there will be a great degradation of conditions for man, while for many other species the consequences will be fatal. In developed countries we have the wealth and are creating the institutional and technical skills needed to avoid many of these results if we show the will. The poor countries will find the problem more difficult in every respect. They have so little margin for environmental improvement and in quest of income will be inclined to risk serious damage.

Many of the environmental consequences of man's activities are quite local in nature. A few cross international boundaries where nations share common airsheds and watersheds. Those that are global in nature are fewer still: threats to the sea, residuals affecting the global climate, the dispersion of radioactive materials and persistent pesticides, damage to wide-ranging animal life. At the present stage of human consciousness it is fortunate that this is so, for it means that those of us who are able and willing can tend our own gardens without the arduous task of reaching international agreement on

Table 3. Selected Residuals from Production and Consumption, Estimated 197●
and Projected 2000

Residual	Source	Energy production[a]		Industry (excl. energy)	
		1970	2000	1970	2000
CO_2 (10^9 T)	U.S.	4	7		
	World	17	43		
SO_2 (10^6 T)	U.S.	21	32	6	17
	World	129	275	19	80
NO_x (10^6 T)	U.S.	20	38	.2	.●
	World	53	167	.6	2.3
CO (10^6 T)	U.S.	67	120	9	25
	World	144	538	27	144
Airborne particulates (10^6 T)[d]	U.S.	24	30	29	77
	World	133	284	91	382
Hydrocarbons (10^6 T)	U.S.	19	32	4.6	11.●
	World	42	140	14	57
Fecal matter (10^9 T wet)	U.S.				
	World				
Fixed nitrogen (10^6 T)	U.S.				
	World				
Potash, in KO_2 (10^6 T)	U.S.				
	World				
Phosphates, in P_2O_5 (10^6 T)	U.S.				
	World				
Organic wastes (10^9 T)	U.S.				
	World				
Insecticides, rodenticides (10^6 T)	U.S.				
	World				
Herbicides, fungicides (10^6 T)	U.S.				
	World				
Contaminated water (10^9 T)	U.S.	480[e]	100[e]	75	155
	World	1,600[e]	5,800[e]	225	1,000
Solid wastes (10^9 T)	U.S.			1.4[f]	3.●[f]
	World			4[f]	12[f]

Note: Table derived from work done for RFF by International Research and Technolo●
Corporation.

[a]Includes transportation. Excludes nuclear energy production, for which similar estimates

	United States		World	
	1970	2000	1970	2●
Mass of radioactive fission products (10^3 T)	0.013	0.84	0.04	
Mass of high-level radioactive wastewater (10^3 T)	0.47	30.0	1.4	1

Agriculture and pest control		Municipal waste and solid waste disposal		Municipal and rural domestic water use		Human biological functions	
1970	2000	1970	2000	1970	2000	1970	2000
0.22^b	0.33^b	0.15	0.5			0.02	0.03
1.4^b	3.6^b	.5	2			.35	.6
		.2	.4				
$.3^c$	$.4^c$	.5	1.4				
1.6^c	4.8^c	1.3	6.7				
10^c	15^c	7	21				
58^c	175^c	21	105				
2.3^c	3.5^c	.9	2.7				
14^c	42^c	2.7	13.5				
1.5^c	2.3^c	1.5	4.5				
9^c	27^c	4.5	20				
1	1.7					.01	.015
9.4	24					.18	.32
13	35					.05	.07
85	270					1	2
9	22					.05	.07
65	193					1	2
7	24					.003	.005
40	141					.5	1
.7	1					.002	.004
4.5	13					.03	.05
.2	.6						
.4	6						
.2	.9						
.4	9						
50	850			38	67		
00	8,000			220	470		
		.33	.7				
		1	3				

[b]Burning and livestock.
[c]Burning.
[d]Amounts generated; disregards current control of particulate matter.
[e]Electric power production; cooling water, assuming 15°F temperature rise.
[f]Includes mine tailings.

everything. In areas where agreement is necessary, it will be most difficult to achieve because of differing value systems.

Although we conclude that resources will permit the sort of population growth that demographers hold out as inevitable, and that the environmental consequences of this can be accommodated for the next generation or so (given a bit of technical help), the outlook is depressing. The world of the future does not sound like an exuberant place in which man will feel confident and secure. The expectation of a better life which the scientific revolution once offered is being dissipated by excess population growth in much of the world. Meanwhile, developed countries have not reconciled their insatiable demand for goods with the needs of their environment and, even as they remain the envy of their brethren elsewhere, they sense that the good life has somehow got lost in the smog.

Selected References

The American Assembly, Columbia University. *The Population Dilemma*. 2d ed. Edited by Philip M. Hauser. Englewood Cliffs, N.J.: Prentice-Hall, 1969.

American Chemical Society. *Cleaning Our Environment: The Chemical Basis for Action*. Report by the Subcommittee on Environmental Improvement, Committee on Chemistry and Public Affairs. Washington, D.C.: American Chemical Society, 1969.

Bollens, John C., and Henry J. Schmandt. *The Metropolis*. New York: Harper and Row, 1965.

Clawson, Marion. *America's Land and Its Uses*. Baltimore: Johns Hopkins Press for Resources for the Future, 1971.

––––. *Policy Directions for U.S. Agriculture*. Baltimore: Johns Hopkins Press for Resources for the Future, 1968.

––––; R. Burnell Held; and Charles H. Stoddard. *Land for the Future*. Baltimore: Johns Hopkins Press for Resources for the Future, 1960.

––––, and Jack L. Knetsch. *Economics of Outdoor Recreation*. Baltimore: Johns Hopkins Press for Resources for the Future, 1966.

Cochrane, Willard W. *The City Man's Guide to the Farm Problem*. Minneapolis: University of Minnesota Press, 1958.

Dana, Samuel T. *Forest and Range Policy: Its Development in the United States*. New York: McGraw-Hill, 1956.

Darmstadter, Joel. "Trends and Patterns in U.S. and Worldwide Energy Consumption: A Background Review." February 15, 1971. A revised version of this paper will appear in Sam H. Schurr, ed., *Energy, Economic*

Growth, and the Environment. Baltimore: Johns Hopkins Press for Resources for the Future, forthcoming.

Davis, Wayne H. "Overpopulated America." *New Republic,* January 10, 1970, pp. 13–15.

Frejka, Tomas. "Reflection on the Demographic Conditions Needed To Establish a U.S. Stationary Population Growth." *Population Studies,* vol. 22, no. 2 (November 1968), pp. 379–97.

Hall, Edward T. *The Hidden Dimension.* New York: Doubleday, 1966.

Halprin, Lawrence. *Cities.* New York: Reinhold, 1963.

Higbee, Edward. *Farms and Farmers in an Urban Age.* New York: Twentieth Century Fund, 1963.

Kneese, Allen V.; Robert U. Ayres; and Ralph C. d'Arge. *Economics and the Environment: A Materials Balance Approach.* Washington, D.C.: Resources for the Future, 1970.

Kormondy, Edward J. *Concepts of Ecology.* Concepts of Modern Biology Series. Englewood Cliffs, N.J.: Prentice-Hall, 1969.

Loehr, R. S. (Referee: S. A. Hart). "Changing Practices in Agriculture and Their Effect on the Environment." In Richard G. Bond and Conrad P. Straub, eds., *Critical Reviews in Environmental Control,* vol. 1, issue 1 (February 1970). Cleveland: The Chemical Rubber Company, 1970, pp. 69–99.

McHarg, Ian L. *Design with Nature.* Garden City: The Natural History Press for The American Museum of Natural History, 1969.

Meyerson, Martin; Barbara Terrett; and William L. K. Wheaton. *Housing, People, and Cities.* New York: McGraw-Hill, 1962.

Odum, E. *Ecology.* New York: Holt, Reinhart, 1969.

Rasmussen, Wayne D. *Readings in the History of American Agriculture.* Urbana: University of Illinois Press, 1960.

Storer, John H. *Man in the Web of Life: Civilization, Science, and Natural Law.* Signet Science Library Book. New York: New American Library, 1968.

Taylor, Lee, and Arthur R. Jones, Jr. *Rural Life and Urbanized Society.* New York: Oxford University Press, 1964.

Tunnard, Christopher, Boris Pushkarev, et al. *Man-Made America: Chaos or Control? An Inquiry into Selected Problems of Design in the Urbanized Landscape.* New Haven: Yale University Press, 1963.

U.S. Bureau of the Census. *Current Population Reports.* Population Estimates Series P-2S No. 381, December 18, 1967, and No. 448, August 6, 1970. Washington, D.C.: Government Printing Office, 1967, 1970.

U.S. Congress. *The Economy, Energy, and the Environment.* A Background Study Prepared for the Use of the Joint Economic Committee by the Environmental Policy Division, Legislative Reference Service, Library of Congress. Joint Committee Print. 91 Cong., 2 sess. Washington, D.C.: Government Printing Office, 1970.

————. *Environmental Effects of Producing Electric Power.* Hearings before the Joint Committee on Atomic Energy, 91 Cong., 2 sess. (January 27–30, February 24–26, 1970). Part 2 (vols. I and II).

————. *A Review of Energy Issues and the 91st Congress.* Committee Print Prepared by the Environmental Policy Division, Congressional Research

Service, Library of Congress, at the Request of Henry M. Jackson, Chairman, Senate Committee on Interior and Insular Affairs, 92 Cong., 1 sess. (January 29, 1971).

———. *Selected Materials on Environmental Effects of Producing Electric Power.* Washington, D.C.: Government Printing Office, 1969.

———. *Some Environmental Implications of National Fuels Policies.* Committee Print Prepared by the Staff of the Senate Committee on Public Works, 91 Cong., 2 sess. (December, 1970).

U.S. Forest Service, Department of Agriculture. *Timber Resources for America's Future.* Forest Resource Report No. 14. Washington, D.C.: Government Printing Office, 1958.

———. *Timber Trends in the United States.* Forest Resource Report No. 17. Washington, D.C.: Government Printing Office, 1964.

U.S. Office of Science and Technology. *Electric Power and the Environment.* A Report Sponsored by the Energy Policy Staff, Office of Science and Technology. Washington, D.C.: Government Printing Office, 1970.

U.S. Secretary of Agriculture and the Director of the Office of Science and Technology. *Control of Agriculture-Related Pollution.* Report submitted to the President. Washington, D.C.: Government Printing Office, January 1969.

Wadleigh, Cecil H. *Water in Relation to Agriculture and Forestry.* U.S. Department of Agriculture, Miscellaneous Publication No. 1065. Washington, D.C.: Government Printing Office, March 1968.

Wingo, Lowdon, ed. *Cities and Space.* Baltimore: Johns Hopkins Press for Resources for the Future, 1963.

THREE

ENVIRONMENTAL THREATS:
A Classification System

The magnitudes of human demographic and economic activity that generate most of the environmental burden have been reviewed in the previous chapter. The threats with which we are concerned arise from the activities of man. They are associated with his increasing numbers, his living arrangements, the changing volume and pattern of consumption, and with the technology and industry that make these possible. Plainly, there are almost no limits to the number and variety of these threats. Yet we ought to understand that the consequences of some environmental threats are more serious than others. To classify threats by order of gravity does not imply anything about either their scale or the immediacy; it refers simply to their potential consequences.

Much of the scientific and quasi-scientific discussion of the environment has pertained to possibly disastrous consequences. Present public concern, however, arises at least as much from a feeling that the general quality of the environment is declining as from more cataclysmic fears. Yet thinking of environmental effects in terms of their gravity is useful because our reactions may differ depending on this perception. A classification system that should be helpful in this regard is developed briefly below.

The largest, most immediate, most annoying, most manageable, and probably most costly category to deal with is what may be termed damage to amenities—the many inconveniences, nuisances, and aesthetic insults to which we are subjected. These are problems which, even if not cured, do not threaten health or survival but do diminish the quality of life. A second category concerns damage to human health. While health cannot be divorced entirely from amenity considerations, for many kinds of environmental threat it can be. Most of us would rank danger to health as a higher order threat than loss of amenity. Third, man is not exempt from the principle that a species survival is more important than individual life, so genetic damage or threat to human reproductive capacity must be considered as a still graver danger.

Fourth, the worst kind of damage that we can contemplate would be that which threatens the life-supportive capacity of the earth. Man individually and as a species is wholly dependent on other life for his own survival. A somewhat more ambiguous question arises when man, either to extend his own numbers or comforts, heedlessly extinguishes significant numbers of species. Those who take an exclusively man-centered view of the world would argue that this question should be viewed in terms of human values, although even they might question the wisdom of a single-minded pursuit of those values, or urge greater awareness of how today's irreplaceable sacrifice of genetic information might prove disastrous tomorrow. Others, who would maintain that man can find meaning only through recognizing himself as part of the natural order, would challenge any proposed action that would substantially alter the ecological balance. Thus, there will be dispute about the value of something like present ecological balance and the preservation of existing genetic material, but none about the importance of maintaining a gross ecological balance in which the earth's life-supportive capacity can function.

In considering environmental problems, a classification system based on order of gravity is not sufficient. It is also important to know which agents produce each type of damage, how these are related to economic activity, the kind of geographical area affected, the time scale over which damage occurs, whether it is irreversible or not, how responsive the problem would be to existing and prospective technology, at what cost, and perhaps other factors as well. These considerations can be arranged in a matrix that helps in appraising the situation. Such a matrix (Table 6) is presented in the last chapter after more of the necessary ingredients have been treated. Meanwhile the categories can be given more meaning by indicating some of the types of environmental insult which would fall within each.

Loss of Amenity

Loss of amenity is the first environmental result that most of us perceive. Air pollution is a nuisance first of all because it takes some of the zest from life. Our view of the scenery is impaired, eyes smart, we miss our breath of fresh air. To be sure, in this case as in many others (depending on the specific nature of the pollution) there may be other damage to health and to ecological balance. Thus air pollution occurs in more than one category; the pervasive interrelatedness of ecological phenomena strains any system of ordering. Similar characteristics are associated with many industrial odors, garbage dumps, foul-smelling water—they are unpleasant but may not be otherwise harmful.

Solid wastes provide the most ubiquitous type of environmental burden. The product of a high-income, style-conscious society that is often indifferent to quality, the discards—packaging, hulks, and garbage—are dispersed in street, field, and stream to yield a great aesthetic problem. Yet in most cases it is not more than that—it poses little threat to health or other life forms. Moreover, it is the kind of problem that can be managed at tolerable cost without surrender of much more than the right to casually disperse the trash. If we are buried in our own solid wastes this will not be due to any inexorable physical law but rather to failure to deal with the problem effectively. Noise is a growing problem of urban life, and may become more ubiquitous with development of the SST. While noise can have adverse physiological and perhaps psychological effects, in its most common form it is simply annoying.

Water pollution is far more complex, since it affects life at all stages and involves numerous possible agents. It is mentioned here as a loss of amenity mainly because it impairs recreational uses of water and the aesthetic pleasure we derive from proximity to water.

The way in which man has occupied space and laid out his public works and cities has profound implications for the amenity value of his environment. Here there would be less agreement on what is associated with diminished quality, but few commuters enjoy a lengthy trip to work; our failure to preserve urban open space is most widely lamented; and the inaccessibility of open country is accentuated by urban sprawl. Scant attention has been paid to the overall aesthetic aspects of either cityscape or landscape; most of us spend the greater part of our time in environments of no distinction and in wasteful combat with distance. Public works, utilities, and industrial plants, if not sensitively designed and located, impair enjoyment of our surroundings. Although social and economic factors—housing, school, personal security—are more important to the use and enjoyment of a city than its physical appearance and layout, the former are not entirely unrelated to the latter.

Finally, a major loss of amenity comes from the disappearance of natural areas and wilderness and many outdoor recreational opportunities. There is a psychic loss even on the part of those who have not used such opportunities but now lose their option to do so. Some would argue that the loss is more serious and that an occasional nature cure is essential for mental health, but in any case, the loss of amenity through the disappearance of natural areas is clear enough.

Human Health

The catalog of environmental problems that affect human health necessarily repeats some of the agents mentioned before. Air pollution, an aesthetic insult, also appears as a health hazard. In common with other environmental burdens, it affects general well-being, may shorten life expectancy, and can be fatal in concentrated forms where exposure is prolonged or where vulnerable individuals are involved. The aggravation of respiratory illness, impairment of lung capacity, and induction of cancer are the commonest effects of polluted air. Air is a medium by which we take in chemicals, lead, rubber, asbestos, and particulates, all of which may be hazardous. While localized concentrations of polluted air may be associated with chemical plants and metal refineries, the most pervasive source is from combustion.

Toxic agents taken up via the food chain pose another type of health hazard. The principal focus here has been on pesticides and their uncertain effects on health. Pesticides are a true case of environmental pollution because they are used for one purpose but have unfavorable side effects, are widely disseminated, and recur at unintended and essentially unavoidable points.

Most of the potentially harmful materials that man ingests are in a somewhat more nebulous category. We raise animals on hormones and antibiotics, load our food with preservatives and additives, flavor it with monosodium glutamate or sweeten it with cyclamate, swallow pep pills, depressants, hallucinogens, prescription drugs, and perhaps narcotics in quantity. In most cases we are ill-informed on the consequences of these agents aside from their primary effect. In a sense they are not environmental hazards because we have both social and individual options to forgo their use. In practice, however, the housewife must buy the frozen chicken at the supermarket and cannot know the conditions under which it was raised. Neither can she know the possible effects of (or perhaps even decipher) the chemicals listed as ingredients on the cake mix package nor argue with a harassed doctor about what the side effects of a prescription might be. Because the possible consequences of such inadequately considered decisions may be slow in appearing or may be obscured by the many complex exposures of modern life, they present an environmental hazard to health that may be great.

Analogously there are widespread public health and industrial safety threats over which, by the nature of our society, individuals have little personal control. We can reduce our individual exposure to auto accidents, mine disasters, textile plant dust, and the like by the way we organize our lives, but for society they remain part of the picture and must be confronted systematically.

While some public health hazards have been diminished by the use of insecticides, antibiotics, and sanitary engineering, these same measures have fostered new vectors—the resistant strain of virus replaces the vanquished bacteria, the malarial mosquito is gone from the recently drained swamp but the schistosomiasis-spreading snail moves into the newly irrigated field. The enormous amount of travel and international trade that we now take for granted makes geographic containment of human and animal diseases or crop pests difficult, and carries the risk that a new plague could sweep the world before defenses or immunities could be mustered. Of course, where there are known defenses, the speed of modern transportation is equally effective in containing disease.

Radioactivity poses a threat to human health, whether in peaceful or wartime use. In peaceful use the major health concern is its effect as a cancer-inducing agent. Direct radiation sickness from massive doses is to be expected only in cases of industrial accidents affecting few people (except in event of war), but sustained or sizable exposure to ionizing radiation is known to cause various forms of cancer.

Finally, the psychological effects of crowding and noise and the lack of contact with nature which were mentioned earlier as an aspect of amenity also have implications for health.

Genetic Damage

Environmental effects associated with genetic damage or impairment of man's reproductive capacity are harder to identify. In recent years it is not the failure of human fertility but rather its vigor that has caused most alarm.

Nonetheless, it can be assumed that if we are to limit reproduction we would prefer to do it deliberately rather than have it occur as the by-product of chemicals employed for other purposes. And if we are to toy with human genes, at least we should not do so in the spirit of Russian roulette.

Radioactivity is the environmental agent most clearly involved. The mutagenic effect of large doses is established, and even smaller exposures, such as those from natural background radiation, also are hazards. Man adds to this problem through medical use of X-rays and peaceful uses of nuclear energy. The role of other drugs and chemicals is more obscure. Pesticides, food additives, drugs, and hallucinogens have been called into suspicion or have proven harmful in some cases, but the extent and effect of exposure may not be known for some time.

It is sometimes suggested that there may be favorable mutations as well as harmful ones; indeed, background radiation may have introduced into the earth's biotic communities new genetic information, some of which has had survival value. Unlike earlier species, man himself could determine within limits which human mutations would survive, but we have neither the standards nor the social apparatus to do it with confidence.

Those who speculate about the genetic effects of radiation or chemicals on man's heredity might with equal profit turn their attention to the whole question of how modern society influences the composition of the gene pool. Whatever the factors that governed the natural selection of man throughout his biological history, they surely have been greatly modified in recent millennia and increasingly so as he became first a farmer and then a city dweller sheltered by public health and the welfare state from struggle with the natural environment. However, man as conscious manager of his own genetic nature will not find his problem easier if he is dealt a new hand of artificially produced wild genes with each new generation.

Ecological Balance

Our final category of environmental threat is damage to ecological balance and the life-supporting capacity of the earth. Most of the apocalyptic warnings that have become so frequent address this range of issues. They stress the delicacy or fragility of ecosystems and see human activity as interfering in a disastrous way with natural processes. This formulation masks some necessary distinctions.

Ecological systems are dynamic and have been in constant evolution since the beginning of life. They are altered in response to changing physical conditions and to new genetic information. At any moment in time the existing balance is delicate. Small variations in climate, weather, migrations from without, and so on, will affect species numbers and balance, but there will be a general tendency to revert to the original state unless the outside influences are permanent. The more complex the interrelationship within the system, the stronger this tendency toward stability will be. Some naturalists attribute value to the balance achieved in the absence of man, yet a dynamic view of ecological systems should be able to accommodate man's presence as well.

In truth, man is hard to accommodate. As a hunter he occupied a niche like any other life form and depended on the system. The survival of the predator requires the survival of the prey. Agriculture brought a revolutionary change. As an agriculturist man took a more active role, excluding unwanted species and preempting their niches for his own use. No longer dependent on the productivity of the natural system, he could increase his numbers, forcing out other life forms. Equipped with energy (animals, simple mechanical devices, fuels), weapons, and finally science and technology, industrial man overwhelms the natural system. Unlike any predecessor he now has the power to be the ecosystem manager. The question is whether he has the understanding, wisdom, and discipline for this role.

By his numbers and use of energy man gains dominance, tames and cultivates the earth. The very term "cultivate" is soothing, signifying control and mastery of the earth's fruitfulness. Yet man's genetic nature was not formed under these well-ordered conditions and perhaps it is unwise to destroy our past completely. In this connection, it is clear that only by control of his numbers and limitations on his occupancy of space can man leave room for many other species and for ecological preserves in which he can research his own past. Moreover, the value to man of maintaining the world's pool of genetic information against the possibilities of future use is well established. This can be done—even though many ecological systems, with their inherent balance in numbers, are eliminated—so long as environments are retained in which some of each species survive. Thus, man can sharply alter the ecological balance, as he has, provided that he understands the needs of his own nature and that he does not recklessly eliminate irretrievable genetic information that subsequently may prove useful. Both provisos are important, and Western man probably has given too little attention to the first.

In a dynamic system, life (and man as part of it) can survive amidst the great changes in ecological balance that man's role implies. Continuation of life requires continuation of reproduction, photosynthesis, and the recycling of minerals. In the case of terrestrial life there are added requirements of soil and water. These are generic requirements and stand apart from the particular ecosystem that may prevail.

The prophets of eco-catastrophe warn that man may be unwittingly intervening at this gross level, not merely to change the balance among species but also to damage in the largest way the entire web of life. They see the threat to photosynthesis as arising from air pollution, the use of pesticides and herbicides, and the spread of human occupation. Air pollution inhibits plant life, and human occupation precludes its growth (urban uses) or impairs its volume (destruction of forests). Moreover, since much photosynthesis occurs in the sea, it is feared that pesticides and herbicides accumulating there will destroy the phytoplankton on which marine life ultimately depends. On a geological time scale photosynthesis is responsible for the production of oxygen and assists in the maintenance of the carbon dioxide balance in the atmosphere, but its far more immediate importance is as an essential for the production of organic material for the support of life. It is hard to imagine a total cessation of photosynthesis; if it occurred it would be the ultimate catastrophe. It is easier to imagine that it may be reduced, in particular circumstances, with consequences that are harder to foresee. Climatic change, which is seen as a possible consequence of the use of fossil fuels, or other energy production, also has implications for photosynthesis, but its much greater import is simply for the kind of biotic communities that will be supported at any given spot on the earth.

In nature the cycling of minerals occurs through the decomposition of rock, the fixation of nitrogen by soil microbes, and the acquisition and release of carbon by means of photosynthesis and decay. Modern agriculture overdraws the natural supply of minerals and nitrogen, and it is feared that artificial applications contaminate water, impair the action of soil microbes, and reduce the tilth of the soil, leaving us vulnerable to unspecified agricultural disasters. Agriculture, along with man's engineering works, also is seen as responsible for the age-old problem of erosion. Since soil is essential for the production of nearly all terrestrial plant life and in turn is produced only over thousands of years by geological processes, its loss is of serious import. The close link between plant, soil, and water means that the problems of one are communicated to the others.

Reproductive capacity of certain life forms also may be impaired as an unintended consequence of the activities of man. The principal agents are radioactivity and pesticides. Although damage may not occur in the ecological system at all levels of the food chain, occurrence at any level will alter the ecological balance. This, however, need not be a disaster unless it affects the producers essential to other forms of life. The fear that it might, at least for aquatic environments, has attracted much of the attention of environmentalists.

Awareness of the idea of eco-catastrophe and doubts about the survival of man or other life have become marks of the sophisticated person. In the course of the popular discussion, scientific questions of the gravest sort have been batted about in unqualified terms by the unqualified. Why? Plainly these are matters that affect us all, but in most other matters we are willing to leave it to the experts. Perhaps what has been sensed is that the experts nearly always are expert in a narrowly defined area—that no one has devoted systematic attention to the interrelationships. It is the bias, the genius, and the despair of our science that this is so. Science enjoys prestige because it can understand and make things work at the problem level. It is unaccustomed to viewing things whole, and those who attempt that chore inevitably are "confused." But there is another reason why we have not left it to the experts— many of the questions now being asked are such that the expert simply cannot give answers with assurance. Thus we are compelled to ponder the voices in the wilderness warning us of our doom while lacking much of the information needed to evaluate the warnings properly. While we can aspire to repair some of this deficit over time, the speed of change promises that we will never catch up. Meanwhile we must act in ignorance. We must work to reduce the area of ignorance even while we devise strategies for action that take it for granted.

In Chapter 4 some of the technical information relating to the gravest environmental threats is reviewed, not in order to confirm the threats or lay them to rest, but simply to see how they operate and what the thresholds may be, and to gain appreciation of the state of knowledge and extent of agreement on facts. In Chapter 5 we shall examine the effects of these and other environmental threats upon the receiving media, principally water and air.

FOUR

ENVIRONMENTAL THREATS:
Five Major Hazards

We cannot pretend to know all of the ways in which human activities may alter the environment so as to threaten health, genetic inheritance or ecological balance, and the earth's life-support system. The list is potentially a very long one, but present knowledge does not allow us to speak confidently in many areas. Five of the hazards that have aroused major concern are examined in this chapter. They are man-made changes in global climate, radioactivity, use of pesticides, use of fertilizers, and soil erosion.

Man's Effect on Global Climate

Some of the most dramatic scenarios of environmental catastrophe have concerned man's effect on both the supply of oxygen and the climate. The suggestion that we may exhaust the earth's supply of oxygen is now discredited. However, we may be altering the earth's climate in uncertain but perhaps disastrous fashion through the discharge of CO_2 and of small airborne particles (aerosols) or through the emplacement of water vapor in the atmosphere, and this possibility deserves more serious consideration. Unfortunately, while scientists can discern the outlines of how they might proceed to learn the answers, they do not have them yet. For the longer term, if man continues to increase his use of stored energy as fast as at present, he may eventually encounter an apparently intractable (though still quite remote) problem of heat dissipation.

The fundamental physical processes determining climate are well understood. We can start with the principles of heat radiation. Any object cools off by radiating energy at a known rate. The sun, a hot object, emits energy rapidly, peaking in the shorter wavelengths of the spectrum. Its spectrum includes ultraviolet (shorter wavelengths than the visible spectrum) and extends through visible light far into the longer wave infrared scale. The earth, a cooler object, emits energy more slowly, peaked at the longer wavelengths. A simple model of an earth with no atmosphere would, at equilibrium, have a surface temperature just high enough to radiate away as much heat in infrared radiation as it received in the form of incoming solar radiation (insolation). We neglect here the small amount of heat reaching the earth's surface from its own interior.

If the earth's atmosphere did not interfere with insolation but absorbed infrared radiation, then it would be warmed by some of the outgoing infrared radiation from the surface. The warm atmosphere would itself become an infrared radiator, some of it directed toward the surface of the earth. This "greenhouse effect" clearly would cause the earth's temperature to rise.

Of course our real atmosphere is much more complicated than this. To begin with, it interferes with insolation. Oxygen in the upper atmosphere absorbs the ultraviolet radiation, some of the blue light is diffused and scattered by water molecules and dust particles, and all parts of the spectrum suffer some absorption and reflection by clouds and aerosols. Thus, the real atmosphere reduces and diffuses the solar beam and in turn is warmed by it both directly and by outgoing infrared from the earth's surface. The lower atmosphere is heated by contact with the surface of the earth and by the condensation of water vapor within it.

These effects are greatly complicated by the air circulation pattern. In the equatorial zone the sun comes from directly overhead, causing the surface and lower atmosphere there to become warmer. This warm air rises and spills out at the top. Its poleward motion provides the fundamental type of atmospheric circulation. However, as the earth spins on its axis and the poleward flow of air moves away from the equator and closer to the axis of rotation, the air is deflected relative to the surface by inertial forces into a circumpolar eastward flow. (This phenomenon is known as the Coriolis effect.) Thus, in the most simplistic form, we have a troposphere whose slow convective rising at the equator and sinking at the poles is superimposed on a vigorous eastward flow in both hemispheres.

This movement of the atmosphere is modified further by contact with the earth. The earth has extremely variable thermal and topographic characteristics. It is mostly covered by water deep enough to make ocean circulation patterns very complicated and of long duration. Land masses rise irregularly, and the polar regions are snow covered. The land absorbs more insolation than the sea, while snow reflects more, so the air circulation is carried over regions of vastly different surface temperature. In addition, mountains deflect the air flow to further complicate the simple picture of the circulation offered above.

Topographical and thermal anomalies of the surface, together with the Coriolis effect, cause air to pile up in some regions and thin out in others. Buoyancy of the air acts to restore uniformity, with regions of high pressure occurring at the bottom of a sinking column of air and regions of low pressure at the bottom of a rising column. Coriolis acceleration forces these columns into circular vortices which move across the earth's surface under the influence of the prevailing eastward flow. Major disturbances move thousands of tons of air containing large amounts of stored energy between regions of different temperature. Smaller disturbances (hurricanes, thunderstorms, dust devils) may be left in their wake.

Thus we may see the atmosphere as an enormous heat engine driven by the sun and dissipating heat into space. The heat is concentrated near the surface in the equatorial zone and is radiated into space at the top of the atmosphere. Moist air constantly transports heat upward and toward the poles while doing the work of producing the kinetic energy of circulating air.

Climate is further complicated by its relation to the sea and to polar ice. Ocean circulation is in response to wind and solar heating, but while atmospheric circulation occurs over a matter of weeks, deep ocean circulation takes hundreds of years. Melting the polar ice would absorb a very large amount of energy and might require similar lengths of time, although there is not full agreement on the latter point. All of this is important because seawater temperature greatly affects climate and the capacity of the sea to absorb CO_2 (greater at low temperature), while the extent of polar ice affects the earth's reflectivity and the surface available for air/sea interaction.

If we are to understand climate we must understand the detailed behavior of the atmosphere and its interaction with sea, land, and polar ice. Efforts have been made to analyze atmospheric dynamics through the use of mathematical models. The necessary simplification required in the models to fit them to available computers suppresses important synergistic effects and yields dubious results. Increases in computer speed and capacity should permit more realistic models in the future.

How, then, does pollution in the atmosphere affect climate? For the present there is far too much uncertainty to permit any definitive answer to the question. However, the principal effects are likely to be found among the following: aerosols, water vapor in the stratosphere, carbon dioxide, and heat from man's energy conversion, which are discussed below.

Aerosols. The effects of aerosols are the hardest to deal with, largely because these small airborne particles have such a variety of sizes, optical properties, and atmospheric residence times. Over most of the size range of interest here, aerosols make the atmosphere turbid or hazy. They also tend to scatter some of the light in the backward direction near 180°, and they tend to absorb some of it, both on the way down, and, if reflected from the earth's surface, on the way up again. This backscattering tends to reduce the amount of solar energy available to the earth's heat budget, while the absorption tends to warm up the atmospheric layer containing the aerosol. If this layer is high enough, cooling of the near surface environment results. Mitchell[1] points out that the recent global cooling trends may be caused by the umbrella of fine dust cast into the stratosphere by recent vulcanism. Bryson[2] thinks the cooling trend is due to man-generated turbidity, and cautions against the possibility of triggering another ice age, but a recent calculation by Mitchell shows that typical man-made aerosols in the lower layers of the troposphere lead to net heating of the near surface environment in most cases. The residence times of the most noticeable aerosols are short, and it seems that natural aerosols from vegetation, dust storms, and salt sea spray predominate in regions far from industrial areas.

Water Vapor in the Stratosphere. The question of increase of water vapor in the stratosphere has arisen during the controversy in the United States over the proposed supersonic transport (SST). Opponents of the program point out that the normal stratospheric water vapor content is very low, essentially because mixing of the troposphere with the stratosphere is weak and the

[1] J. M. Mitchell, "A Preliminary Evaluation of Atmospheric Pollution as a Cause of the Global Temperature Fluctuation of the Past Century."

[2] Reid A. Bryson and James T. Peterson, "Atmospheric Aerosols: Increased Concentrations During the Last Decade."

mixing process requires the water to pass through a very cold region in which the rising tropospheric air would presumably be dehumidified. It has been estimated that 400 SSTs each flying four flights a day would introduce 150,000 tons of water vapor to the stratosphere per day or 0.025 percent of the total amount naturally present in the altitude range in which the SSTs would fly. While there is a possibility that the vapor would have a relatively short residence time, this is at present a matter of some controversy. If the residence time is very long, the above rate in 10 years could lead to a doubling of the water vapor content. Manabe and Wetherald[3] calculate that if the water vapor of the whole stratosphere doubled, the greenhouse effect would raise the temperature of the air near the surface of the earth about ½°C while tending to cool the stratosphere. If the doubling took place only in the lower one-sixth of the stratosphere, we could expect a smaller effect. High cloud formation under specific circumstances has been suggested as another effect, but owing to the uncertain optical properties of such clouds, it is not clear whether this would tend to heat or cool the earth's surface. Recently the alarming suggestion was made that the regular operation of a fleet of SSTs in the stratosphere could quickly deplete the ozone supply which shields us from ultraviolet radiation. At the time of writing, that study had not been thoroughly evaluated. If any of the above concerns proves warranted, it should shoot down other SST programs as well as our own.

Carbon Dioxide. Carbon dioxide is a necessary product of the combustion of fossil fuels. Although it is considerably heavier than air, atmospheric circulation keeps it well mixed, so that its concentration is almost constant throughout the troposphere and stratosphere. It is an infrared absorber, and contributes to the earth's radiation balance through the greenhouse effect. Its absorption characteristics are known, and the effect of increasing the atmospheric concentration of CO_2 on the earth's surface temperature has been the subject of several numerical modeling experiments. World combustion of fossil fuels grows at about 4 percent per year (doubling every 17½ years), but fortunately not all the CO_2 we produce remains in the atmosphere. Much is taken up by the sea, where originally it is held in dissolved form near the surface. Later, some is precipitated as carbonates, which sink as sediments to the ocean floor. The present atmospheric concentration is about 320 parts per million by volume (ppmv). We currently produce another 2 ppmv each

---

[3]Syukuro Manabe and Richard T. Wetherald, "Thermal Equilibrium of the Atmosphere with a Given Distribution of Relative Humidity."

year of which about 50 percent remains airborne. It seems that over the long term the CO_2 concentration may be fairly well buffered chemically at the interface between the sea and the sea floor sediments, but, of course, the doubling time cited is far shorter than the ocean circulation time. For the short term it should be noted that since a gas like CO_2 is less soluble when water warms up, and since the oceanic reservoir is more than 50 times the atmospheric reservoir, the CO_2 dissolved in the surface layer of the ocean constitutes a destabilizing mechanism in climatic variation. Cautious extrapolation of present trends in the hope that 50 percent of the released CO_2 will continue to disappear still leads to about 380 ppmv by 2000 A.D., while combustion of all recoverable fossil fuels reserves might increase the level of CO_2 in the atmosphere by a factor of 4.

We must make every effort to understand the effect of rising concentration of CO_2 on our climate. We can expect energy use to continue to expand, and, since much of this can be economically derived from fossil fuels during coming decades, we must have reasonable assurance of the climatic consequences of this alternative.

Heat from Man's Energy Conversion. While most discussions of thermal pollution by the electric-power industry have centered on the rejection of waste heat to water or air, it is also necessary to consider all the energy produced, because virtually all of it is eventually converted into heat also.

In 1970 world energy use amounted to 5.7×10^{12} watts, continuously. By comparison, the sun provides a total of 1.76×10^{17} watts. Since about 50 percent of this is absorbed at the earth's surface, man's energy conversion now equals about 1/15,000 of the absorbed solar intensity. It has been argued by some that a 1/100 proportion of man-made conversion would have noticeable effects, and we will achieve this level in 130 years at our present 4 percent per year rate of growth in energy use. Even if this had no noticeable effect on climate, 17.6 years later we would have 2 percent of the present surface absorption of insolation, and so on, until 120 years later our energy conversion activities would equal the absorbed solar radiation.

Sellers has estimated that by the time we reach the 5 percent level we should have experienced global warming by more than $10°C$, and eventual melting of the polar ice caps.[4] The resultant climatic regimes presumably would be completely different from those we experience today. Such estimates are crude and likely only to indicate general tendencies. Response of

[4]W. D. Sellers, "A Global Climatic Model Based on the Energy Balance of the Earth-Atmosphere System."

the climate of the real atmosphere is likely to be more complicated than that of the simple model used by Sellers, and less extreme. Alvin Weinberg seems unperturbed by such possibilities as he discusses a hypothetical situation in which 20 billion people satisfy their energy and materials requirements from common rocks, air, and seawater to attain a living standard equal to the current U.S. level.[5] He figures per capita energy requirements for this at twice the current U.S. level and total man-made energy at only 1/300 of the earth's natural rate of heat loss. This in turn implies a minor effect on global temperature. It is not at all clear, however, why these population or per capita consumption figures should be accepted as ultimates. Indeed, in the United States we already appear headed for per capita energy figures several times as high without approach to reliance on common materials.

Climate remains a very complex subject and existing models are too simple to permit accurate predictions. Möller is the author of the often quoted "prediction" that doubling the atmospheric concentration of CO_2 would lead to an increase of $10°C$ in surface mean temperature.[6] Möller was making a first stab at describing the following synergistic process: concentration of CO_2 increases, causing increased greenhousing and increased temperature, increased temperature leads to increased evaporation from the sea, and thus to higher absolute humidity (assuming fixed relative humidity); and, since H_2O molecules are even more effective infrared absorbers than CO_2 molecules, the warming trend is reinforced. But in the same paper he makes a disclaimer to the effect that a 1 percent increase in general cloudiness in the same model would completely mask this effect.

We can easily see why he wanted to enter this reservation. The very increase in absolute humidity that reinforced the warming trend through infrared absorption might lead to increased cloudiness (or indeed to increased precipitation and winter snow cover) and thus, through reflection of insolation, considerably moderate the warming trend. Manabe and Wetherald using a radiative and convective atmosphere temperature adjustment scheme found that the same doubling of the CO_2 gave them only a $2.4°C$ temperature rise and that this could be masked by a 3 percent increase in low cloud.[7]

Oxygen. A word about oxygen is in order, if only to allay a fear that scholars no longer take seriously. Current production of oxygen is mostly owed to

---

[5] Alvin Weinberg, "Nuclear Energy and the Environment."

[6] F. Möller, "On the Influence of Changes in the CO_2 Concentration in Air on the Radiation Balance of the Earth's Surface and on the Climate."

[7] "Thermal Equilibrium of the Atmosphere."

photosynthesis, and, as nearly all of the oxygen is used up again when the plants rot, production only very slightly exceeds consumption. Fear has been expressed that excessive burning of fossil fuels might exhaust our supply, while the inhibition of photosynthesis would reduce new production. In fact, burning of all of the earth's biomass and fossil fuels would use up less than 3 percent of our oxygen supply—a reduction equivalent to moving from sea level to an elevation of 200 meters (656 feet). Of course, if photosynthesis were impaired, we would save the oxygen presently used in the decomposition of organic matter so the net effect on the oxygen supply would be negligible. We may take comfort: we would starve long before we asphyxiated. Oxygen depletion is not even a local problem in the atmosphere or in the deep ocean. It does of course occur in smaller bodies of water, but not because of any deficiency in global supply.

Conjectures and Next Steps. We are left with uncertainty whether over the short term (say the next 50 years) carbon dioxide and the greenhouse effect will raise the temperature significantly, or whether increased atmospheric turbidity due to man-made (or caused) aerosols will lower it significantly. There is also uncertainty about the effect of water vapor from SSTs in the stratosphere, but this does not seem to be so serious. There is even the possibility that climate may not be a unique function of the various forces at work and that "the flutter of a butterfly's wings" could trigger a large change from, say, a warm climate to an ice age (or to a much hotter era than the present one).

Over the longer term (say more than 100 years) we may have the problem of beginning to warm the climate directly with our own energy conversion. This problem will be with us (in slightly different degree at any one time) whether we derive our energy from coal fires, nuclear reactors, or from fusion generators. If we continue to double our energy conversion rate every 17½ years, in about 250 years it will equal the current rate at which we absorb solar radiation at the earth's surface. In order to double the rate at which it radiates heat away, a bare earth at a uniform temperature of $0°C$ would have to increase its temperature by approximately $50°C$. Our real earth with ocean and atmosphere would behave in a much more complicated way, but it is hard to see how it would not warm up considerably.

We have some time to grapple with these problems. We must use it to conduct research into many fundamental processes—for example, the nature and behavior of the ocean as a sink for carbon dioxide. We need to measure and then begin to monitor regularly the effects of various aerosols on atmospheric turbidity, and the effects of various kinds of clouds on atmospheric reflection of insolation (albedo). We need to monitor the behavior of the ocean-atmosphere system carefully, watching for long-term trends in temperature distribution, in the strength of circulation, in precipitation patterns, and in the concentrations of carbon dioxide, water vapor, and general cloudiness.

We must improve our general understanding of climate behavior, apparently by developing general circulation models to a higher level of sophistication and then using them to perform a more complete set of numerical experiments. Present general circulation models typically take hours to follow the simulation of one day's weather, and at least in some respects they are not sufficiently sophisticated. Even with the generation of computers currently under construction, we cannot afford to evolve a simulation of climate for hundreds of years by running a general circulation model while slowly adding man's pollutants. However, it may be possible to get from a model a working understanding of the long-term effects of our activities on climate by varying the input conditions of surface and atmospheric albedo, concentration of infrared-absorbing molecules in the atmosphere, level of solar activity, etc., in the general circulation model. Such studies might begin to yield some real understanding of what climate changes can be actually expected, rather than merely of the initial tendencies that will be caused by a particular facet of man's industrial activities. Estimates of climate changes resulting from this new understanding are expected to be less spectacular than those now obtainable from the simpler models, but on the other hand, they will be much more credible and therefore much more compelling.

However, it is clear that if the industrial revolution continues at the present rate, it is only a question of time until man's activities begin to change the earth's climate. We must understand the limits this imposes on us and act accordingly.

Radioactivity

As a general environmental threat, radioactivity is a creation of the past quarter century. Prior to the bomb only tiny amounts of radioactive materials were in the hands of men; and few but scientific workers, some medical personnel, and watch dial painters were conscious of any hazards. In that blissful age most of us viewed frequent X-rays as good for our health; we lived in contented ignorance of the possible effects of background radiation and faced no man-made isotopes. All that has changed. We are compelled to consider radioactivity, how it is generated, how it moves in the environment, its effects on man, and the magnitude of the problem of contamination over the coming years.

While the physics of radioactivity is well enough understood, the biological effects are less so. The radioactivity with which we are concerned here arises from the disintegration of unstable elements that emit particles capable of penetrating materials to varying distances. The particles ionize the materials through which they pass and then surrender their own energy. The effect of this on living tissue is not too well understood at a theoretical level, but at least some of the empirical results are well established. A chain of chemical reactions occurs that may bring critical damage to the cell. Consequences for the living organisms depend first on the way in which the radioactive materials move in the environment—how they become incorporated in, or perhaps concentrated in, living tissue and in particular organs. They also depend on the type of rays emitted—their strength and penetrating power. For present purposes it is unnecessary to delve into these complexities.

Most of our exposure to radioactivity is from natural sources.[8] About one-fifth of this is from natural radioisotopes incorporated within the body while the remainder is received from the ambient environment. Normal or background radiation arises from cosmic rays (emitted from the sun and from galactic sources) penetrating the earth's magnetic field and atmosphere, and from radioactive materials occurring naturally on the earth. These sources generally contribute 80-200 m/rem per capita each year. The amount varies, depending on the radioactivity of nearby rock, and increases with altitude. In

---

[8]The relative importance of background and medical radioactivity with that of nuclear industries and weapons sources at present can be compared in the table below which shows the average annual radiation exposure of the general population of the United States from various sources in 1970:

Sources	Dose[a] (m/rem)
Natural background	~120
Medical	
Diagnostic X-rays	~ 95
Therapeutic X-rays	~ 10
Nuclear energy industry	< 1.0
Fallout	< .8
All other	< .5

Source: Karl Z. Morgan, "Comments on Radiation Hazards and Risks," p. 6.

[a]These are genetically significant doses. Doses figured as total body dose or dose to critical organs would be at least twice as high. For definition of m/rem, see footnote 9, p. 69.

some places—parts of Brazil and India, for example—natural radioactivity may go as high as 1,000-5,000 m/rem.[9]

Weapons testing and use have contributed small amounts of radioactivity to the environment, and the processing of nuclear materials for weapons also produces by-products, some of which escape to the environment. These take the form of radioactive isotopes—i.e., radioactive species of naturally occurring elements. Except for China and France, testing is now restricted to underground shots and does not ordinarily release significant amounts of radioactivity to the surface.[10]

Peaceful use of nuclear explosives has been a negligible source of environmental radioactivity so far because the limited experimental work has been restricted to isolated areas. Where the explosion is contained underground (fracturing rock, creating cavities), it presents the smallest environmental hazard, although in some cases it is difficult to prevent the escape of gaseous isotopes, and other nuclides may migrate into groundwater if the geology favors it. The heat of the explosion causes glass to form in the bottom of the cavity and much of the radioactive material is fused into it. When mining is the intent, the product to be extracted may be too contaminated for use for a long period, thereby defeating the usefulness of the technique.

Large surface shots have not been used for major excavations, partly because of the difficulty in containing the fission products and activated dust generated and partly because of uncertainty about the role of the tritium (a radioactive form of hydrogen) that could be created in large amounts by the fusion reaction. Moreover, such shots would run afoul of the nuclear test ban treaty. Since alternative technology can be employed for nearly all types of engineering work and the consequences of nuclear shots remain uncertain, there has been no great compulsion to resort to nuclear excavation. It is likely, though controversial, that for large projects (for example, a second Panama Canal) this method would yield substantial savings in excavation cost. In the absence of much experience with the results and any strong commitment to employ nuclear explosives, there is little point in trying to detail the hazards involved. Most of the radioactivity from nuclear excavation could be contained in the area of the shot, but some inevitably would escape and contaminate the surrounding area.

[9] A rem (roentgen equivalent man) is the unit used to express human biological dose as a result of exposure to ionizing radiation. One m/rem is 1/1,000 of a rem.

[10] If a nuclear war should occur, the environmental consequences are beyond imagining, and anyway have been the subject of numerous other speculations. The possibility has too many imponderables to permit more than mention here.

Reactors and the attendant fuel preparation, reprocessing, and waste disposal are the focal points of concern about man-made radioactivity and the ones with the greatest potential for growth. This ignores medical uses of radiation, currently a far greater source of man-made exposure than all others but not environmental in character because nearly all such exposure is voluntary.

Power Reactors. All current power reactors use heat generated from controlled fission to operate conventional steam turbines. Standard models in the United States are either boiling water (BWR) or pressurized water reactors (PWR). In these models nuclear fuel elements encased in metal alloy tubes are immersed in water that is heated by the nuclear reaction. In the BWR the steam is run directly to the turbine, while in the PWR the water is contained in a closed system employing a heat transfer arrangement to produce steam for the turbine. Not yet beyond the prototype stage are breeder reactors capable of converting abundant but presently nonfissionable "fertile" materials into fissionable materials that can then be used as fuel. A successful breeder will generate more fuel than it consumes. In fuel and cooling design the breeder differs from existing reactors, but it still employs a steam turbine.

On the far horizon is the prospect of controlled fusion reactors. Recent scientific advance has raised the hope that these may prove feasible, although a present reading of possibilities indicates that they most likely will not become commercially important during the rest of the century. A fusion reactor is completely different in concept and would not present most of the hazards associated with fission reactors. According to one proposed variant it might even be possible to avoid the generation of much waste heat through a process of direct conversion to electricity.

In any discussion of the environmental effects of nuclear energy most of the attention must be on BWR or PWR plants, which are the prevalent technology in the United States. However, they are only an interim source of energy because low-cost fuel resources for such reactors are limited to a very few decades. Thereafter, we must turn either to breeders, for which there is ample fuel, or to fusion reactors, which have a virtually unlimited supply of potential fuel.

Radioactive isotopes are created in the present reactors in the fuel materials, in the structure of the reactor, and in the coolant. They may diffuse through imperfections or cracks in the metal cladding that contains the fuel or they may be generated by neutron or gamma ray activation in the coolant.

They may appear as gases (especially the noble gases krypton and xenon), or as radioelements such as iodine, cesium, or strontium, or they may be incorporated in the water as tritium. Most of the same materials appear at the reprocessing stage where spent fuel rods are sent for the extraction of plutonium and elimination of waste products. The amount of radioactive effluent released at this processing stage has been far greater than the releases from the normal operation of reactors, but there is no technical reason why it cannot be contained.

In normal operation, reactors release comparatively little radioactivity to their surroundings. Many isotopes are short-lived and can be dealt with by temporary containment. Available technology will permit the trapping of virtually all gaseous and liquid effluents so that near-zero release of radioactive materials to the local environment can be achieved. Moreover, of those which are released, some decay quickly, and others are so diffused as to cause little damage.

Increasing concern over reactor operation focuses on the accident hazard. The danger here is not from a nuclear explosion (which cannot occur) but rather from overheating and release of radioactive materials. In such an event the cooling liquids could become highly contaminated and be released along with gases in great volume. An accident could release water from the reactor core so that, unless emergency core-cooling devices work, the nuclear fuel would melt down, and it would become impossible to cool the molten mass. Such a melt-down could involve release of radioactivity from the core to the environment. Engineering safeguards are meant to preclude catastrophic accidents, but siting a power reactor close to a metropolitan population remains hazardous. That is why some experts feel that a distance factor must be included to provide an added margin of protection in the event of accident. Others favor putting the reactor underground or under water to diminish the hazard. It is contended that reactors could be placed underground without intolerable cost penalty, but this is not the current practice in the United States. So far as reactor accidents are concerned, the fusion reactor could be a godsend; it would have very little contained energy and would simply cease operation in case of malfunction.

Safety is a problem not merely in the operation of reactors, but also in the transportation of fuel, reprocessing, storage, and ultimate disposal of radioactive wastes. The potential for escape to the environment during these phases through ordinary accident will increase as the volumes transported and stored continue to grow. It has been suggested that giant reactors, which would permit fuel reprocessing at the site, would be one way of minimizing transport accidents. Indeed, the whole subject of the human error factor in nuclear safety deserves more attention. The excellent safety record compiled to date has occurred under hothouse conditions and under the surveillance of highly skilled personnel. As reactor technology becomes more routine and as it moves abroad to less-advanced countries, the levels of skill and supervision are likely to decline. Moreover, the possibility of losing track of some extant nuclear material (e.g., in times of civil disorder) will rise with the proliferation of sites and users, raising the specter of nuclear criminals.

Biological Effects. Apart from deliberate medical uses, the biological effects of radioactivity stem from the ionizing radiation associated with the escape of radionuclides to the environment. Acute radiation sickness in humans requires massive doses such as would be received only in industrial accidents or near the site of nuclear explosions. Ionizing radiation in the amounts likely to be received from peaceful uses of nuclear energy (emissions from reactors and fuel processing plants) would produce no immediately discernible clinical effects. Rather the effects are deferred in time, dispersed through the irradiated population and quite uncertain in extent and nature. They fall generally into two classes—genetic and somatic effects. The former involve changes in the germ cells—changes that are transmitted to offspring. Somatic effects involve mostly the induction of cancer. Radiation can produce mutations in any cell, but only those in the germ cells are transmitted to other generations. While results differ depending on whether germ cells or other cells are affected, the way in which radiation operates within the cell appears similar in the two cases. However, it is not well understood just how the ionization alters the cells or how, in the case of ordinary cells, it confuses the genetic message and causes the cell to go wild.

Our information on the effects of radiation comes from statistical studies of exposed human populations, especially survivors of World War II bombings in Japan, painters of radium watch dials, uranium miners, children irradiated *in utero*, and from studies of laboratory animals deliberately exposed. These data indicate that at doses somewhere between 25 and 100 rads,[11] induction of cancer can be established for certain types of cancer, especially thyroid cancer and leukemia. Other forms of cancer also are assumed to be induced by such doses, but because of the extended latency period for some types

---

[11] Rads measure energy per gram of target. They can be considered equivalent to rems for this discussion.

of cancer the resulting frequency is less clearly established. Genetic damage, albeit very infrequent, also occurs at these doses and apparently below.

Whether there is a threshold below which exposure to radioactivity has no somatic effects has been a major uncertainty. Data from which the effects of radiation have been established pertain to ranges of comparatively heavy exposure. If the relationship between exposure and cancer induction can be extrapolated back to the very light exposure to which the general population could be subjected under existing radiation standards, even though only a small percentage of the population would be affected, the absolute number could be significant. Two scientists, John Gofman and Arthur Tamplin, in highly publicized reports, have computed that exposure of our entire population to radiation in the amount permitted by present U.S. standards would result in somewhere between 9,400 and 104,000 cancer deaths per year based on our present population.[12] Even on this hypothetical basis other scientists, including Karl Z. Morgan, arrive at figures at or below the low end of this range.

All such conclusions assume: (1) a direct linear relationship between exposure and cancer induction, and (2) far more widespread exposure at maximum levels than we are likely to incur. They do not allow for any threshold below which effects disappear nor do they allow for a relative tapering off of effects at low doses. Moreover, they make no allowance for the effect of the rate at which radiation is received. While there is no proof regarding the existence or nonexistence of a threshold, radiation standards long have been set on the conservative assumption that there is no threshold. The tendency of the scientific community is further to assume that effects are directly related to size of dose. There is still much dispute about the effect of dose rate and the reparability of damage. Some evidence suggests that under favorable circumstances body tissues are able to repair radiation damage and that a given dose received at a slower rate will not have as severe a consequence as a more concentrated dose.

[12] See, for example, U.S. Congress, Senate, *Underground Uses of Nuclear Energy*, and John W. Gofman, "Calculation of Radiation Hazards," p. 5. In any realistic situation their numbers appear extravagant. Instead of the entire population, few if any people would be exposed to the maximum permissible dose. Reactors are expected to operate at a small fraction of the permissible level of releases, and recent revisions in emissions standards for reactors would mean that even persons at the edge of the reactor site could be exposed to only a small fraction of the allowable standard for general human exposure. Since dose is a function of distance from the reactor, few would receive even this dose from reactor operation.

Genetic effects seem somewhat better established. Experiments on mice have shown germ cells much more sensitive to concentrated doses of radiation than to the same amount received over an extended period. At low dose rates female cells appear to suffer no measurable genetic damage, although the same cannot be said for male cells. In both cases the damage falls sharply (or even disappears for females) if mating is delayed for a period after radiation exposure. These findings suggest that germ cells at earlier stages of development may be less vulnerable, or that they can repair the damage. In any case, the genetic hazard appears small, for massive doses of radiation are required to produce detectable evidence of it in mice. According to present standards men will be subjected only to tiny fractions of such amounts over their life span and at much lower rates. For example, the standard allows the general population to be subjected to 5,000 m/rem over a 30-year period, a dose rate 27,000 times smaller than the lowest rate used in the mice experiments in which no damage in female cells was detected even when a dose of 400 rads was used, and 3,000 times smaller than the lowest rate used for males.

Mice are not men, but there is nothing in these experiments to raise alarm about the likelihood of major genetic damage at radiation levels to which we will be exposed from reactor operation. At the same time we must recognize that any radiation, including normal background levels, is assumed to cause mutations. It is a question of balancing some genetic damage, however minor, against the value to us of nuclear energy.

Present standards for radiation exposure to man-made sources in the United States allow 170 m/rem per year for the general population with more permitted for occupational exposure. The standards were set with an eye to genetic effects in the population as a whole, allowing a 30-year total exposure of 5,000 m/rem plus an equal amount for medical radiation. By way of comparison a dose fatal in half of the cases amounts to 450,000 m/rem. As we have seen, background radiation amounts to 80–200 m/rem per year. A single chest X-ray delivers about 200 m/rem, while a G-I tract examination is 27,000–35,000 m/rem. The average annual genetically significant dose in the United States from diagnostic X-rays is estimated at 90–100 m/rem, making it by far our largest source of exposure to man-made radiation.

By contrast, exposure of the general population from the normal operation of reactors will be very light. Plant emissions standards have recently been revised, so that even those persons near the site are to receive no more than 5 m/rem. Already nuclear reactors and fuel-processing plants annually discharge only a tiny fraction of the allowable radiation and even near the station the dose received is under 5 m/rem. For the general population exposure from these sources is to be held below 1 percent of the natural background level. Because the genetic standards have been shown to have been conservatively estimated, some have argued that the emissions standards need not be as stringent as at present on those grounds.

If the concern is with cancer, acceptance of all of the most cautious assumptions (absence of threshold, linearity, and independence of dose rate) can lead to the conclusion that in large populations an impressive number of deaths would be attributable to man-made radiation if the permissible levels were reached for everyone. In fact we will not approach those levels from reactor operation. Our far greater exposure is from medical X-rays, a source amenable to drastic reduction by very simple procedures and in any case one under our personal control to some degree.

There are various types of radiation hazard other than nuclear industries and medical X-rays. Television sets, especially color TVs, allow the escape of some X-rays. Proper shielding can virtually eliminate this hazard. Ionizing radiation also comes from high-voltage vacuum switches and industrial X-ray equipment. Non-ionizing radiation, such as that from microwaves, is suspected as a cause of cataracts, nervous disorders, and other problems, but this hazard has not been well evaluated.

Future Prospects. Whatever the conclusions about human tolerance of radiation, it is clear that we will have to cope with increasing amounts of radioactive waste. Much of the radioactivity that escapes to the environment is comparatively immobile and is retained near the site where it does not threaten the general population. The noble gases and tritium will venture into the atmosphere and hydrosphere, their subsequent dispersal becoming a function of the often irregular movements of these media. The gases are rather inert, however, and they do not become concentrated. Other isotopes may be of particular interest because they have long half-lives, and hence accumulate in the environment, lodge in specialized tissues, or are concentrated by natural processes and passed along the food chain. In combination, such possibilities could result in damage even though overall environmental levels of radiation are low. Classical cases include the affinity of strontium for bone, where it lives out its lengthy half-life within the body, the iodine isotope (I^{131}) which has a short half-life but is concentrated in the thyroid where it can induce cancer, and the arctic lichen which absorbs its nutrients from air rather than soil and has transmitted radioactivity from test fallout to caribou and reindeer and thence to the unsuspecting Eskimo and Lapp.

Although it is not a simple matter, it is possible to relate the effective exposure of man (measured in rems) to the projected growth of nuclear reactors. To make such an estimate of future radiation hazards for man it is necessary to project the growth of nuclear power by type of reactor, to relate this to the escape of various isotopes, and, through assumptions about their movement in the environment and knowledge of their biological characteristics, to arrive at the effect on man.[13] However, the technology is so certain to change that any projection of radioactive emissions as far away as the year 2000 is sure to be superseded. For any near-term period the hazard from normal operation appears small. Moreover, it is far from certain that exposure levels ever will approach the levels set by current standards. Even with present technology, exposure at the site boundary can be held to 5 m/rem, and future developments promise to reduce this further. The experience with breeders is too short to allow a useful statement, but breeders will use a contained system like pressurized water reactors. Fusion reactors, still only a hope, offer promise of even better environmental performance.

So long as we depend on fission reactors we will have the problem of disposing of fuel-processing wastes. Current practice is to detain and dilute low-level wastes, discharging them to groundwater. High-level wastes have been stored. Because of the long half-lives involved, much of this requires permanent storage. A number of schemes have been advanced to provide such storage, but none has been finally adopted. The most appealing at present is for storage (in various containers) in salt mines where groundwater does not penetrate. Progress in reducing the intermediate and high-level waste to concentrated solid form promises that the cubic volume of waste will not grow as rapidly as power output, and studies indicate that acceptable costs can be obtained. It is harder to contemplate the human institutions necessary to safeguard the stored wastes for a few thousand years.

Radiation damage to nonhuman life forms does not appear to be a major hazard. For radiation to do important damage to other populations would require mechanisms for concentrating radioactive isotopes systematically in them. There is little evidence that this occurs.[14] In the absence of strong tendencies to concentrate radioactive isotopes, other life forms will be subjected to them in much the same proportion as man. Society's concern for the effect on man reflects the fact that we value individual human life. Race

---

[13] Some have argued that the quota of allowable man-made radiation exposure should be allocated among various purposes such as the power industry, medicine, fallout, and the like, with emissions of each to conform to appropriate totals. So far this has not been done.

[14] An exception may be in certain aquatic environments where filter feeders concentrate minerals, among them radioactive isotopes, and in turn pass them up the food chain. However, there seems to be little evidence of damage anywhere along the chain.

survival is not in question. We do not show the same concern for individuals of other species. In view of the statistically small effects on the human population, the same effects projected to other life forms represent no great threat to them as species.

How do we summarize this hazard? Owing to the circumstances of its early history, nuclear energy has been morally suspect. Incomprehensible to the layman, surrounded by technical jargon, invisible and mysterious, radioactivity is an "outsider," easy to cast in the role of a villain. The managers of nuclear development have responded by giving more attention to the dangers and engaging in more environmental research and monitoring than is accorded in most other fields. The safety record is good, especially in view of the novelty of the technology. Exposure at the levels permitted by existing standards would at worst produce a relatively small number of cancer deaths per year and a small number of mutations. Both effects are substantially deferred; even a greatly expanded nuclear industry could confine exposure far below currently allowable standards, and technical progress could reduce it further. Fusion reactors carry the hope of greatly expanded nuclear energy with negligible environmental cost. (They would still generate heat, however; and at some point that could prove a limiting factor on expansion, as noted in the Global Climate section of this chapter.)

These prospects fall well below the range that we have been willing to accept for many other types of environmental hazard (air pollution and auto accidents, for example). The risks in fact are better known and probably much lower than those of generating electricity in fossil fuel plants. The possibility of accidents in fission reactors is harder to evaluate; however, locating them away from population centers might alleviate this concern at tolerable cost. This possibility deserves more study. The risks inherent in the transport of nuclear materials also need more careful study. Perhaps the most disquieting consideration is whether we can devise stable and enduring institutions that will enable man to live in eternal intimacy with the atom. We will have to increase our understanding of it and maintain our control in perpetuity, for nuclear energy is the essential long-range energy source for a technical civilization. There is nothing in the nature of the beast that makes it an uncontrollable environmental hazard, but its management and control present a great challenge to human institutions.

Recent environmental discussion has called into question two of the principal technical bases of modern agriculture, namely the use of chemical pesticides and the application of nutrients. In the following two sections we shall examine the principal hazards attributed to these two agricultural inputs. The final section of the chapter is devoted to another hazard that is related to agriculture—the ancient problem of erosion.

Pesticides

Pesticides are one of the technical inputs central to high-productivity agriculture. Dating at least from the publication of Rachel Carson's *Silent Spring* there has been a growing sense of disquiet about the environmental consequences of using pesticides. They have had unintended and deleterious effects on some forms of wildlife, and there are many unanswered questions concerning their effects on man. The persistence of some pesticides in the environment and their wide dispersion, along with our fragmentary knowledge of the consequences, all favor great caution in their use. As with many environmental problems, however, there is no simple response to these considerations. Farmers and timber growers have come to depend on pesticides. Public health authorities here and abroad defend the use of insecticides for malarial control and other special purposes. It is hard to fault less-developed countries for giving a higher priority to production than to environmental quality when they are struggling to feed their people. Finally, pesticides are not all of a piece—they vary in characteristics, in method of application, in circumstances under which they are best used, in the nature of side effects, and so on.

"Pesticides" is a generic term referring to all kinds of chemicals used to kill organisms inimical to human purposes. They can be classified by chemical composition, by the kind of organism they aim to destroy (herbicides, insecticides, rodenticides, for example), or by other characteristics such as persistence or toxicity.

Degrees of Persistence. Much of the concern about pesticides is related to their persistence. Some are composed of tightly bonded molecules which degrade only slowly in the environment. This has led to the fear that with increasing use the level of residual chemicals will increase. It is sometimes suggested that this may cause irreversible damage by leaving in soil or water an amount of residual poisons sufficient to reduce numbers or to cause extinction of desired species. Also, it is feared that pesticide residuals may halt the vital photosynthetic activity occurring in water or attack the eggs and young of fish and shellfish and thereby destroy aquatic life.

Statements about persistence are often imprecise or ambiguous. First, for the most persistent pesticides, degradability varies greatly depending on conditions. They may be very slow to break down in colder climates, in clay, in dry soils, or in soils that are high in organic matter. They also persist when contained in body fat. Second, what we generally measure is application and disappearance from the immediate environment. Disappearance does not necessarily imply degradation—some of the material may simply be dispersed or it may be relocated in sediments far from the point of application. Thus measurements of persistence really are minima and they offer no assurance that under some conditions or in different places the chemicals do not survive. With this caveat in mind we may look at the principal chemicals in order of persistence.

Nonpersistent pesticides are short-lived, losing their toxicity within a single growing season under normal conditions. This class includes the organophosphorous compounds such as malathion, methyl-parathion, and parathion. It also includes the carbamates, of which carbaryl is the most widely used. Although targeted mostly on insects, these classes also are toxic in varying degree to other species. Their toxicity to mammals, especially in the case of the parathions, is often higher than that of the more persistent types. Likewise, the organic phosphorous Azodrin has proved deadly to doves and related birds, while carbaryl is very toxic to bees. Strong synergistic effects have been observed with some of the organophosphorous compounds whereby their toxicity greatly increases when used together. To gain degradability we may have to accept other undesired effects.

Moderately persistent pesticides lose their potency in one to eighteen months under normal environmental conditions. This class includes most herbicides as well as some insecticides. Atrazine and 2,4-D together accounted for over half of total agricultural herbicides used in 1964.

Persistent pesticides slowly lose their activity but may retain half their strength for two to five years or under certain conditions for much longer. The most important of these are the chlorinated hydrocarbons, most notably DDT. The cyclodiene organochlorines are another group of importance and include aldrin, dieldrin, endrin, heptachlor, and toxaphene. Moderately toxic to animals, some of these are especially damaging to fish and shellfish. Even the persistent organic chemicals do not build up indefinitely. They are degradable, albeit slowly, and tend to reach a maximum concentration under conditions of repeated application.

Finally, we have a group of permanent pesticides of virtually nondegradable toxins. They include compounds of mercury, arsenic, and lead which have very low water solubility.[15] Once applied they remain in the environment unless physically removed. If taken into the body these are very injurious to human beings because they accumulate and cause insidious damage or, in sufficient concentration, prove lethal. However, they tend to be rather immobile and their unwanted effects are therefore easier to avoid (except perhaps in seafood).

The Evidence on Damage. Pesticides are designed to kill living things and frequently they kill more than intended. In doing so they may reduce the biological diversity of the ecosystem in which they are distributed. Agriculture itself is the original simplification of the ecosystem in replacing many species with a single plant. Modern agriculture carries this to an extreme with entire regions often given over to a single crop. This effect is accentuated by such practices as clean cultivation, and the elimination of hedgerows, which further reduce diversity. Overly simplified biotic communities are less stable and are subject to rapid changes when a species multiplies free of competitors or outruns food supply. The introduction of pesticides into this system simplifies it further by eliminating many competing species, often including those which prey on the pests. With the natural system of control of numbers so completely disturbed, pest control becomes dependent on the use of chemicals. We become addicted to them.

As with most kinds of addiction, increased doses are needed to give the same effect. With pesticides this is the result of the development of resistant strains. Those individuals most susceptible to the chemicals die out, while hardier individuals or mutants survive and multiply to fill the empty biological space. The combination of resistance and the disappearance of natural enemies may compel spectacular increases in dosage. As an example, the resistance of the bollworm in the Texas Rio Grande Valley to insecticides used in its control increased 30,000 times between 1960 and 1965. A steadily growing list of species has developed a degree of immunity, and in some cases this extends to different types of insecticides.

Pesticides vary greatly in their effect on their unintended victims. Some pesticides have immediate toxic effects on species we value, such as birds or bees. Generally speaking, vertebrates are unlikely to suffer acute poisoning unless they are caught in the spray of the more toxic pesticides or, as with fish, in a concentrated solution of chemicals. For most vertebrates the effects

---

[15] Their presence in the environment, especially in the cases of mercury and lead, is mostly due to sources other than agriculture. Mercury has the added disadvantage that it can assume organic form and become biologically concentrated.

usually occur at later stages and in more subtle ways. Insects commonly are less fortunate; and the destruction of natural predators that are beneficial to man is one cause of the addiction to insecticides mentioned above. The most readily observed effect on vertebrates other than man is the impairment of reproductive success, especially in birds and fish. This stems from the incorporation of persistent pesticides in body tissues, especially fat, where they resist degradation. In the case of birds, DDT may cause eggshells to be too thin, leading to breakage and loss of the embryo during hatching. Among the most affected species are the ones at the end of the food chain where pesticide residues have concentrated, but even with them no clear pattern is apparent. For example, herons carry a heavy residue load but appear to maintain their numbers, while certain other carnivorous birds (kingfishers, falcons, petrels, golden eagles) are declining. Some fish in the Mississippi delta have acquired a degree of pesticide immunity which makes them lethal to their own predators.

The delayed effects on fish and birds illustrate a recurrent environmental phenomenon—the way in which natural processes may concentrate a very dispersed residue. In Clear Lake, California, a plankton-fish-bird chain concentrated DDT by a factor of 100,000. In another instance an oyster in 40 days of activity achieved a concentration of DDT 70,000 times above that of the surrounding water. In the case of chlorinated hydrocarbons, concentration may be traced to several food chains. Common ones include leaf-litter-earthworm-robin, lake plankton-fish-grebe, or lake plankton-small fish-lake trout. Some pesticides that are rather insoluble in water but are easily adsorbed to soil particles and very persistent in muck contaminate especially the fertile waters at the edge of lakes or streams and are passed on up the food chain where they lodge in fatty tissue. Since the yolks of eggs (birds, fish, shellfish) are composed in large degree of fat that provides food for the growing embryo, the chemicals reach the organism at its most vulnerable stage.

Much of the alarm about pesticides arises from the possibility that they will inhibit photosynthetic activity in the water by destroying the phytoplankton, which is responsible for a major share of the world's photosynthesis. Laboratory experiments have shown that photosynthesis is reduced by 70–94 percent by the presence of 1 part per million (ppm) of various chlorinated hydrocarbons and by 50–90 percent by 100 parts per billion (ppb) of DDT; even lesser concentrations have also been shown to reduce photosynthesis. In evaluating these data, however, one must recognize that ordinarily water will not contain concentrations approaching this magnitude.

Water generally has less than 0.1 ppb of DDT, or a tiny fraction of the amount used in the experiments,[16] although in local situations and especially near the point of application the concentration may reach damaging levels.

During handling or application some pesticides carry the hazard of acute toxicity. Deaths attributable to pesticides at this stage are distressingly frequent, in part because farm workers sometimes are not able to read labels or may not understand the warnings. However, the danger of accident is no greater than for many things found in the medicine cabinet. The need for extreme care in handling the most toxic varieties must be stressed.

Apart from the acute toxicity of exposure to spray or liquid chemicals, the effects of pesticides on human beings are largely speculative. There are formidable difficulties in trying to separate the long-term consequences of exposure to low concentrations of pesticides from the many other risks to human health. In addition, the physiological effects are quite different for different types of chemicals. Most attention has gone to DDT because of its persistence, mobility, and tendency to be stored in fat and also because it has been in use longer than many. There is no evidence that the general population has been harmed by its accumulation; on the other hand, it is impossible to prove the absence of damage. All we know for sure is that we all have accumulated a measurable amount of DDT and its derivatives. There is some evidence that at given rates of exposure the body does not accumulate beyond a certain level and there is no evidence that the equilibrium level, even when comparatively high, is harmful. Even the ingestion of more concentrated doses amounting to 200–1,000 times the rate found in restaurant meals in the United States produced no detectable results over a 21-month period. While these results cannot be extrapolated to a lifetime or extended to the other chemicals, epidemiological data for the years 1945–65, when DDT came into civilian use, show no deviation from earlier trends.

Experimental work on laboratory animals has been undertaken to ascertain the mutagenic, carcinogenic, and teratogenic (fetal malformation) effects of pesticides. It is all rather inconclusive. At doses well above those to which we are normally exposed, carcinogenic and teratogenic effects can be induced

---

[16] DDT occurs in such low concentrations that in rain and surface water it is usually measured in parts per trillion (Gordon Conway et al., "DDT on Balance," *Environment*, vol. 11, no. 7, p. 2). U.S. drinking water contains an estimated 0.02 ppb of DDT (U.S. Department of Health, Education, and Welfare, *Report of the Secretary's Commission on Pesticides and Their Relationship to Environmental Health*, p. 384). After treatment for gnats, Clear Lake had 0.02 ppm. Big Bear Lake was deliberately poisoned at a level of 0.2 ppm. In Lake Michigan, muck was found to have 0.014 ppm (National Academy of Sciences–National Research Council, *Scientific Aspects of Pest Control*, pp. 252–55).

in animals by some pesticides. However, the same is true of countless other chemicals, including some that are widespread in nature, and there is always some difference between effects on animals and men. Mutagenesis has not been shown, but many pesticides have not been tested for this. It must be remembered that man's longer life span subjects him to long-term carcinogenic effects not easily determined in animal studies. After all of these qualifications are considered, we must return to the fact that, while deaths can be attributed to improper handling of pesticides, none have been known to result from their residuals in the environment.

Although pesticide residuals have not been shown to be damaging to man, some evidence of effects on other warmblooded animals, especially birds, suggests the need for continued caution. The rapid metabolization of fat during periods of hunger releases stored pesticides. This may affect hormonal balance and be reflected both in decreased general vitality and in reduced mating activity. These effects also have been noted in mammals but so far they have not been detected in man. Man's lesser reliance on stored fat offers some protection. However, the possibility of impairment should not be ignored, for such a result would present a threat to race survival and therefore be more disastrous than mere damage to individual human health.[17] Meanwhile we are inventing and disseminating new compounds constantly—much faster than we can test them for all possible effects.[18] "While there is little ground for forebodings of disaster, there is even less for complacency."[19]

Patterns of Use. Pesticides are not an entirely new environmental hazard, but their massive use dates from World War II. Prior to that time plant extracts and metallic compounds, particularly arsenic, were employed along with cyanide and sulfur in special uses. However, DDT, used first by the military for malaria control during World War II, opened the new era. Most pesticides are used in agriculture, although DDT and some others retain important public health functions as well. Overall it has been estimated that pesticide use will increase in years immediately ahead at a rate of 15 percent per year

[17] A recent report has connected anovulation in mice with exposure to DDT under laboratory conditions. The same researchers note increased epidemiological evidence of this difficulty in humans. They connect it to damage done in the fetal stage. If this suggestion withstands scientific scrutiny, it will dramatically tilt the balance toward more extreme care in pesticide use (*Washington Post*, April 4, 1971).

[18] American Chemical Society, *Cleaning Our Environment: The Chemical Basis for Action*, p. 233.

[19] U.S. Department of Health, Education, and Welfare, *Report of the Secretary's Commission on Pesticides and Their Relationship to Environmental Health*, p. 236.

in the United States, with the herbicide component growing even faster. Long continued growth at this rate could have frightening implications.

DDT use has declined since 1963. U.S. production of 103 million pounds in 1967 was down about 25 percent from the 1966 figure. In 1967 exports of 82 million pounds (down approximately 10 percent from the preceding year) went primarily to five countries: India, Thailand, Brazil, Nepal, and Mexico.

There is an uneven pattern of regional pesticide application within the United States. Heaviest application is in the Southern Plains and the Corn Belt. In the Southern Plains, the primary purpose of application is insect and disease control, while in the Corn Belt it is for weed and brush control. The principal crops on which pesticides are used are cotton, fruit and nut trees, small grains, and corn.

Although chlorinated hydrocarbons are still fairly widely used domestically, they are not increasing. For the world as a whole, increasing amounts of pesticides are being used for agricultural purposes in the developing countries. Chlorinated hydrocarbons are dominant among the pesticides so used, for both agricultural and public health purposes.

Some Pros and Cons. What do we gain from the use of pesticides? In agriculture they are used to increase the yields and quality of produce as well as to reduce the uncertainty of crop yields. Obviously their value varies depending on the crop and on local conditions. Results on some USDA test plots have suggested that dramatic yield increases are associated with pesticide use. For example, cotton yields may increase 50 percent if the crop is protected from the boll weevil. Corn sheltered from the corn borer and root worm increased its yield by 20-100 percent, or about 60 percent on the average. Small grains—oats, wheat, barley—showed increases ranging from 24 percent to over 1,000 percent; potatoes, 70 percent; and alfalfa, 40-90 percent.[20] While these results exaggerate the benefit to the total farm economy, they do indicate that pesticide use can bring substantial increases in crop yield in many situations.

There also may be sizable benefits to the individual farmer because, with less uncertainty, he enjoys easier credit, freedom from the need to diversify so much, and opportunity to take advantage of larger-scale production of the chosen crop. He may also save on labor and water costs if weed control through the use of herbicides proves cheaper than cultivation.

---

[20]See J. C. Headley and J. N. Lewis, *The Pesticide Problem: An Economic Approach to Public Policy*, pp. 62 ff.

All of these factors convince agricultural economists of the economic rationality of pesticide use. One estimate showed a return of $4 for each $1 spent on farm pesticides.[21]

Increasingly, however, there are cases in which these benefits cannot be claimed, even at the point of application. In some instances chemicals are applied to control insects that in fact do not impair output. In other cases they may control one pest but decimate the predators of another pest, which is then released from control. Beyond this, they increase the tolerance of target species to the chemical and thus compel ever larger applications. A classic example is that of the Cañete Valley of Peru where a regime of chemical treatment of cotton fields was begun in 1949.[22] Initial success raised yields per acre from 440 pounds in 1950 to 648 pounds in 1954. As immunity increased and new pests appeared, the rate of application was increased, and new chemicals were introduced. Despite this, yields declined to 296 pounds in 1956. When these practices were halted and a new approach used, yields subsequently recovered, and the story has an instructive message. Evidence from Central America also has shown that massive pesticide applications can be counterproductive, impairing output and contaminating untreated fields and cattle so as to damage still wider parts of the agricultural economy.

Public health authorities would be very reluctant to forgo the use of pesticides, since they have been of great help in controlling malaria, cholera, typhus, and other diseases. The amounts used for these purposes are, at least in principle, subject to close control. There can hardly be any doubt that the public health benefits of chemical pest control efforts throughout the world have been enormous and have saved many millions of lives.

Must we poison ourselves in order to eat? For the United States the answer is surely "no." The fact that pesticides sometimes become counterproductive when improperly used suggests that we may even be spared the choice. As we have seen, use of DDT is already on the decline—a drop that will accelerate as new government regulations come into play. While part of this change represents merely a shift to other organochlorides of long persistence, much of it is a shift to organophosphorous compounds, which are more toxic to vertebrates at the time of application but less persistent in the environment.

---

[21] J. C. Headley and A. V. Kneese, "Economic Implications of Pesticide Use," p. 37.
[22] See Ray F. Smith, "Integrated Control of Insects, a Challenge for Scientists," p. 2.

Things That Can Be Done. We often can do with fewer chemicals or with less damaging ones. Decimating relatively harmless bugs or routinely spraying harmful pests present in only modest numbers and under control by predators places a needless burden on the environment. One promising approach is the use of integrated pest control programs where chemical agents are used sparingly together with biological controls. This was the technique adopted in the Cañete Valley example mentioned above. We also could exercise greater care in application. Present techniques, especially the use of cropdusting planes, result in very uneven application and place much of the material in the atmosphere where its dispersion may be global rather than confined to neighboring fields and water. Greater care in the selection of the material would spare the environment; often broad-spectrum formulas or persistent compounds are used where more limited or shorter-lived types would serve as well. There is the hope that more specific toxins can be developed to strike only at target species. However, this frequently is difficult not only on scientific grounds but even more so economically because such chemicals would have a very restricted market. One of the chief reasons for continued high use of popular compounds is their widespread effectiveness and their low cost when produced in volume.

There are various other ways to control pests. Biological controls are one. Predators may be introduced to restrain pest numbers; pathogens or diseases affecting the pests also may be spread. One difficulty with the introduction of new predators is that their full ecological consequences often cannot be foreseen. In some cases cultivation practices are important; cover for predators can be provided while that essential to pests is removed. A natural system likely would require greater crop diversity or separation of stands with some loss in efficiency. Any system of biological control will not be 100 percent effective.

The famous case of the screwworm fly demonstrates yet another technique of insect control. Releasing a large number of sterilized males to mate with normal females achieved complete eradication of the species in some areas at a cost far below the expense of spraying. Another possibility is to modify insect behavior through physical or chemical stimuli so as to attract them to concentrated poisons or to confuse their reproductive signals. So far this is not well advanced. The same is true of attempts at genetic manipulation of insect populations. Plants could also be bred to resist insects more effectively. The history of agriculture has been in large part a quest for resistant varieties, but if other qualities are impaired the new variety may be less attractive to man.

Finally, we could learn to live with the insects. This would imply some loss of yield—how much is unclear—and compel an increase in crop acreage. It has been suggested that the effects of a 70-80 percent reduction in insecticide use could be offset by a 12 percent increase in cropland in the United States. Another accommodation would be to modify our grading standards for agricultural commodities to allow greater variation. If we insist on almost total insect control in food crops we are committed to much higher use of insecticides. It takes more insecticide to move from 98 percent to 99 percent insect eradication than from an 80 percent to an 85 percent level.

Conclusions. Although reassuring to a degree, the evidence indicates a need for great caution in pesticide use. No disastrous and permanent environmental consequences have been successfully attributed to pesticide use. Acute poisoning at the time of application is a hazard to many species and it can destroy the balance of their local populations. As the Cañete Valley story illustrates, recovery is possible even at the site of severe abuse and the damage may not be permanent. This conclusion cannot be extended to every situation and every species—some of the more fragile ecosystems are less easily restored and for certain species the penalty is severe. So far, long-term accumulation of persistent pesticides has been limited, and catastrophic damage has not occurred. The absence of discernible long-term effects on man also is encouraging. But we do not know enough about how toxins are degraded or dispersed to accept with confidence a manyfold increase in their application, and the observed effects of pesticide residuals on some species should give us pause both regarding implications for the ecological system and for human health. In effect we are conducting a large-scale experiment on ourselves (and all other living things) without sufficient controls to make it a very good one. These uncertainties, while they provide little of real substance for horror stories, argue strongly for caution.

Some simple and obvious steps should be taken—to restrain the amount of application, select the chemicals more carefully, and apply them so as to minimize dispersal. If we desire greater specificity or wish to develop other means of control, a research program of considerable magnitude will have to be planned and funded. If we are determined to restrict use at the expense of output and quality of product, then we face the problem of allocating the cost. These various approaches are not mutually exclusive. We have every reason to hope that we can restrict the use of long-lived pesticides without severe economic penalty.

Fertilizers

Despite its primary effect of favoring plant growth, fertilizer use has occasioned much concern as a possible threat to the environment. Attention has centered in particular on the role of nitrogen and phosphate fertilizers in contributing to an excess of plant nutrients in water (eutrophication). Other more calamitous warnings have concerned nitrate poisoning of infants (methemoglobinemia) from excessive concentrations in water and the fear that heavy use of nitrogen fertilizer adversely affects the porosity and tilth of the soil and impairs its natural fertility by destroying the soil bacteria needed to fix nitrogen or to convert organic matter into the form of nitrogen required by growing plants.

Not much evidence is adduced to support the latter two warnings. The most frequently cited report attributing infant deaths to methemoglobinemia from nitrate in well water pertains to the years 1947-50 when 14 deaths were recorded in Minnesota. It is interesting that this occurred at a time when rates of fertilizer application were far below current rates, suggesting that other sources of nitrate may have been to blame. More recent reports are sparse and poorly documented. It is clear enough that many rural wells have unsafe nitrate levels, at least during parts of the year, and that this has been true for some time. It is not at all clear that this is to be associated with fertilizer use; livestock operations are more suspect.[23] In local situations the nitrate content of drinking water is a proper concern and one that should be monitored, but the hazard does not appear to be general.

As for the nitrogen-fixing soil microbes, they have survived all kinds of tortures under laboratory conditions. They can be relied on to do their duty when they have organic material to work on or when symbiotic plants, such as legumes, are present. It is true that under sustained cropping the humus content of the soil and its natural supply of nitrogen declines. Tilth is diminished and we do become dependent on artificial nitrogen supply for satisfactory yields. However, by no means all soil structures are fatally damaged by this process, and the microbes remain. At existing dietary standards and population levels we cannot contemplate a large-scale reliance on natural fertility, so the issue is whether in the long run we can continue to rely on

[23] Douglas H. K. Lee, *Nitrates, Nitrites, and Methemoglobinemia.*

our current practices of plant nutrition. So far there is no evidence that we cannot, at least so far as the provision and availability of nitrogen are concerned. Any contrary indication is not likely to appear as a sudden crisis.

Effects on Aquatic Plant Growth. Let us turn then to the more plausible and immediate concern about the effect of fertilizers and manure on aquatic plant life. The agents involved include both nitrogen and phosphate. Overfertilization of water speeds the growth of aquatic plants and may overburden its supply of dissolved oxygen (DO), bringing putrescence in its wake. Aquatic plant growth can be limited by shortage of any of the essential nutrients. The sudden appearance of algal blooms or aquatic weeds indicates a more generous supply of the formerly limiting nutrient. Only a detailed analysis of the local situation can pinpoint the cause. (It should be borne in mind throughout that the added nutrients may derive from sewage, detergents, or other sources as well as from fertilizers.)

If one looks at the increasing consumption of fertilizers (Chapter 2), laboratory evidence concerning the effect of such nutrients in water, and the growing problem of eutrophication, it is plausible enough to connect them. Very small quantities of nutrients in water can have very large effects on plant growth. For example, only 15 parts per billion of phosphorus or 0.09 pounds of P_2O_5 per acre-foot of water are required to support algal blooms. Thus even a 1 percent loss of P_2O_5 in runoff from a field treated with 40 pounds of phosphate per acre would support a noxious bloom in five acre-feet of water. In the farmer's account books this kind of disappearance of fertilizer would represent a loss of about 5 cents. For nitrogen the situation is comparable. Only 0.3 ppm of inorganic nitrogen in water are required to support algal bloom. If the nitrogen is applied at a rate of 160 pounds per acre, a 1 percent loss in runoff and percolation would support algal bloom in two acre-feet of water at a loss to the grower of 6 to 10 cents.

The farmer, of course, is interested only in supplying the amount of fertilizer that will be taken up by plants. However, fertilizer is cheap and its use an inexact science. Over some range it pays to overfertilize to ensure timely availability of nutrients. As we have seen, only tiny applications beyond plant uptake could cause severe problems if transported to lakes and streams. Since we share with the farmer an interest in low-cost food production, we cannot lightly suggest that penalty taxes be placed on the consumption of fertilizer.

Before impaling ourselves on this dilemma, however, we should look at the evidence linking fertilizer use and aquatic plant growth. The crucial link is the leaching or erosion of fertilizer from the field into stream or lake. Our understanding of that process is deficient, and evidence is circumstantial rather than direct. There are no experiments that have measured nutrient balance over a long time, especially the amount of nutrients lost to water via runoff or percolation. Nor are there any recorded data on the loss of nutrients to the air. Instead, these losses to the environment have been calculated as residuals only after known destinations—such as recovery in crops—have been determined. In the case of nitrogen, known destinations account for about 80 percent of added nutrients. The fate of the remaining 20 percent—whether it is denitrified and lost as gas, or is carried off into the water—has not been experimentally determined, although work is now under way in a number of locations to find the answer.

How complex these processes can be and how many variables may affect them is shown in experiments conducted by the U.S. Department of Agriculture and reported in 1967.[24] Twenty-foot core drillings were made in Colorado's South Platte Valley. The soil cores were analyzed, as was the groundwater that percolated into them when the water table was reached. Nitrate levels in the soil ranged from as little as 80 to 90 pounds per acre for irrigated alfalfa and for virgin grassland to 500 pounds per acre of irrigated land (other than alfalfa) and nearly 1,500 pounds for feedlots.[25] Compared to these differences in the soil profiles, the mean nitrate content in the water table ranged only from 7.4 ppm (for dryland) to 13.4 ppm for feedlots. It averaged higher in virgin grassland (11.5 ppm) than in irrigated non-alfalfa land (11.1 ppm) that probably had received 100 pounds of nitrogen per year per acre for several decades. The lowest findings in any of the coreholes were 5 ppm in dryland and zero in irrigated land.

Obviously, there was much nitrate in the grassland that had not been put there by man. Experience tells us that a good deal of it would disappear once the land was put to the plow, but in what proportion it would go into crops, into the air, into surface water or groundwater, or stay in the soil is not predictable.

Gaps in Present Knowledge. There is, of course, good reason why we have such inadequate knowledge of the routes of nutrients into and out of the cultivated soil. In the past, interest was lodged exclusively in the relation of nutrient input to plant growth: up to what rate of fertilizer use would mar-

---

[24] B. A. Stewart et al., *Distribution of Nitrates and Other Water Pollutants Under Fields and Corrals in the Middle South Platte Valley of Colorado.*

[25] Interestingly, the cores from dryland, which had never been fertilized, had nearly three times the nitrate content of virgin grassland which also had never been fertilized.

ginal returns exceed marginal costs? Efforts were concentrated on having farmers use more, not less, fertilizer, and on convincing them that there was ample room for increased application that would earn them a return on their outlay.

Such an interest is not apt to yield answers to the totally different inquiry: given a specified input of nutrient, where does it go? That is why we have not had systematic input-output or material balance studies that would trace the flow of inputs from inorganic fertilizer, manure, original soil fertility, and precipitation to the outputs in the form of crop removal, crop residuals, runoff in surface water, deep percolation, volatilization, and changes in the quantity of nutrients fixed in the soil, i.e., "inventory" changes.

Nitrate has always been a ubiquitous component of our biotic surroundings. When a forest is cleared, the leaf mat, partially decomposed litter, organic matter, and the roots are decomposed by micro-organisms. One of the products of this process, known as mineralization, is nitrate. Studies of the type cited above have shown that nitrate is quite high in the water issuing from logged or cut-over areas. It was this nitrogen that nourished the early food crops for the pioneers in the wooded area of the eastern portion of the United States.

In the grassland areas to the west, the decomposition of the plowed-up sod furnished the nitrate for crop production. The prairie portion of the corn- and wheat-producing areas had a large reserve of soil organic matter built up over a long period of time, which served as a bank of nitrogen for continuous crop production. This enabled farmers in the Midwest to sustain relatively high grain production much longer than was possible farther east.

Cultivation stimulated mineralization and made nutrients available far in excess of crop requirements, entailing large losses to water, and probably to air. This greatly diminished the original soil content of organic matter, long before there was any concern over the disposition of fertilizer.

With long-continued cultivation and with the advent of high-yielding hybrid corn requiring higher levels of soil nutrients, the nutrient supply from organic matter and animal manures became inadequate to sustain the higher levels of production.

Calculations made in 1936 put the annual net loss of nitrogen for the United States at nearly 7 million tons.[26] There were gross losses of 4 million tons of leached soil nitrogen, 5 million tons lost by soil erosion, and just over

[26] J. G. Lipman and A. B. Conybeare, "Preliminary Note on the Inventory and Balance Sheet of Plant Nutrients in the United States."

4.5 million tons removed by harvested crops. About half the total losses were compensated for by manure, nitrogen fixation by plants, chemical fertilizers, below-soil portions of crops, rainfall, etc.

Principal nitrogen losses in earlier years, then, were caused by leaching and erosion. There is now less leaching, and erosion control practices have reduced nutrient loss via erosion. Plant uptake is now the major fate of the available nitrogen for any crop year.[27] Thus, it has been estimated that in the United States loss of nitrogen in the soil now is perhaps only half of what it was 40 years ago, while removal by harvested crops may have doubled. On balance, then, removal has remained roughly unchanged, and the new element—added fertilizer—has made up for the previous net loss of several million tons per year. The unknown variable is the fraction of added fertilizer that is removed by leaching or is immobilized by reaction with the soil. Under current practices, one need make only very conservative estimates of denitrification and immobilization to account for all the nitrogen that is not removed in the crop. This would leave no nitrogen to be accounted for by leaching.

The weakness of the argument lies in its indirectness. It is not based on observation and measurement except to the extent that recent tests of well water (in surveys carried out in Nebraska in the early 1960s) show no clear relation between nutrient content and agricultural practices or soil amendments.[28] The best one can say is that there is a fairly good *prima facie* case for doubting that fertilizer use at present levels of application, except possibly in isolated instances, represents a threat to water quality. The key term here is "present levels of application." As pointed out, rates have been rising continuously and steeply. The higher the fertilization level, the greater the opportunity for losses. There is, on the other hand, the experience of European countries where high rates over long periods have not been shown to have produced ill effects on water quality. Again, this is only circumstantial evidence: it may be due to different farming systems or to failure to pursue this particular inquiry. The relationship between crop uptake and residual disposition of nutrients as rates of application increase needs more study.

More specifically, two problems deserve study. One is associated with the limits of crop uptake as such. Most crops have a limited uptake of nitrogen

[27] Actual physical removal depends on the crop and on how it is harvested. For example, in corn, which is one of the major users of fertilizer nitrogen, the grain alone may contain only about one-half of the aboveground portion of the plants. Corn removed from a field for silage for a dairy farm removes more of the plant and more nitrogen than does a corn crop harvested as grain only.

[28] B. A. Stewart et al., "Nitrate and Other Water Pollutants Under Fields and Feedlots."

and do not use excessive amounts even if they are present, although there are some vegetables that use larger amounts if available.

Second, application practices are a very large factor in controlling disposition. Time of application in relation to temperature, rainfall, aeration, plant growth stage, and, obviously, rate of application are important. No leaching to groundwater will occur when the water-holding capacity of the soil is below saturation. That capacity is, in turn, a function of porosity, texture, depth, and various biological and physical characteristics. Overirrigation and heavy rainfalls will promote downward leaching. Plants, through both foliage and roots, influence water flow, interacting with the elements noted above. Uptake is greatest during the "grand period" of growth. Therefore, application just before that period will minimize losses to the soil, to the atmosphere, to runoff, or to groundwater. But economics and convenience suggest different timing patterns (fall application helps to smooth seasonal fluctuations for both the fertilizer producer and the farmer). The more desirable split applications that are timed to accommodate crop needs raise cost to the farmers. The loss of nutrients occasioned by single applications at less efficient moments can be overcome through higher rates, and the farmer is tempted to follow that path.

The above considerations suggest that what is economically an optimum rate and method of application is not necessarily, and perhaps not usually, an optimum practice for minimizing losses of nutrients to the environment. Current rates of application in the United States are still low relative to what the aboveground portions of the plant can take up, so the environmental problem is not as yet acute. However, we must study the hitherto neglected question of disposition of added nutrients and we should promote fertilizer practices that maximize plant uptake. To the extent that this involves added cost to the farmer, it raises, as in other areas of production, problems of providing incentives for him to adopt these practices.

So far, we have dealt principally with the role of possible adverse consequences of nitrogen additions to the cultivated areas. The role of chemical fertilizer in waters found unduly high in nitrate is not clear, but the evidence at this time points more to other organic sources (such as sewage or feedlots). The role and source of phosphate in the eutrophication of lakes and streams is a far more controversial subject. In most of the grassland or mixed grassland and timbered lands of the United States, runoff and drainage have enough nitrogen and phosphorus not made by man to cause eutrophication if other conditions are favorable. (Bottom sediments are an ample source of phosphorus as well.) While the conditions favorable to eutrophication are not

well defined, it has been suggested that a biologically active carbon source
such as that from sewage and other organic wastes may be necessary in
addition to adequate amounts of phosphorus and nitrate. Much of the controversy over the role of the various substances involved centers on two
questions: (a) what is the origin of the phosphate? and (b) what are the
limiting elements in a given situation?

In contrast to nitrate, phosphate is rather tightly bound to soil particles;
little or no fertilizer phosphate added to the soil is lost by leaching and none
by volatilization. Instead, fertilizer phosphate is lost as a part of eroding soils.
The erosion sediments added to streams and lakes have enough phosphorus
when released by microbial action to support algal blooms, provided again
that other conditions are favorable. Thus the greatest hazard from cultivated
lands is soil erosion, and the most direct route to amelioration is erosion
control. Even so, other sources of phosphate may be sufficient to stimulate
undesired plant growth.

The Feedlot Problem. Total farm animal wastes in the United States are the
equivalent of those of about 2 billion people.[29] A cow produces over 16
times the body waste of a human being, and a pig or a sheep from 2 to 2½
times as much.

In earlier times animal manure was applied to the land as a source of
nutrients, but today it is largely waste. The farmer can often meet his needs
at less cost by purchasing commercial fertilizers. This may be true for manure
generated on the farm as well as on feedlots because collection and spreading
is more costly than the mechanized application of commercial fertilizer,
which is available in the desirable mix and can be applied at the chosen time.

Feedlots present a special problem because of concentration; feedlot
cattle may be allowed only 50 square feet of space per animal and large-scale
feeding is for the most part confined to few areas. Even at a less dense rate,
say, 150 square feet per animal, annual excretion of nitrogen per animal
amounts to about 20 tons per acre of feedlot. The fact that feedlots often are
on sloping ground favors disposal into watercourses.

Feedlots are a clear pollution threat. Pollution of the air always results.
Though probably not a health hazard, it is unpleasant. Runoff from lots into
streams and lakes and the downward leaching into underground water supplies are common occurrences in areas of heavy cattle feeding. In many rural
areas water sources have been contaminated to levels far above those safe for
domestic use.

---

[29] Cecil H. Wadleigh, *Water in Relation to Agriculture and Forestry* (Washington,
D.C.: Government Printing Office, March 1968), p. 41.

The best disposition of animal manure would be to return it to the soil where it would help supply nutrients and improve soil structure.[30] This is not economically attractive and will be resisted until the environmental hazards become more generalized and more sharply defined and the chains of cause and effect are more persuasively demonstrated.

The feedlot problem contrasts with the broader issue of levels of fertilizer application for maximum crop production. While the feedlots are highly concentrated and the problem is severe locally, the increased level of fertilizer application for high crop production is general. This upward trend will undoubtedly continue and will be extended to areas now using little or no fertilizer, so that the contamination of water becomes a lively possibility. Greater efforts to keep soil erosion to a minimum would at least keep phosphorus out of the waters issuing from heavily fertilized areas, but more complete control of nutrients presents very difficult technical problems.

Erosion

Soil erosion—long a concern of the conservation movement—has been rediscovered by the new environmentalists who see population growth, the resulting demand for food, and a materialistic social system all combining to despoil the land.

The environmentalists' worries commonly pertain both to the loss of the soil itself and to the loss of its natural nutrients. As we have seen, nutrients can be supplied readily enough to cropland; even if our understanding of the requirements for plant growth is incomplete, the problem (cycling minerals) is one that we should be able to master.

Soil loss is another matter. We need the soil as a medium to support roots, expose plants to the sun, and hold water and nutrients within reach. Loss of topsoil at a rate of 1 percent per year (a figure often bandied about) would doom our agriculture in a surprisingly short while, for soil formation is a process requiring thousands of years.

We have plenty of evidence of how other civilizations have perished through failure to protect the land from erosion and siltation. Indeed, the record of successful agriculture practiced continuously at the same site over really extended periods is mostly limited to flood plains and deltas whose fertility is owed precisely to erosion elsewhere. The potential threat posed by

---

[30] Special problems are created when the ground is frozen, for manure distributed at this time cannot be absorbed into the soil and may be washed into watercourses.

erosion is therefore a grave one—a threat to the viability of plant and associated life in the affected area. Erosion can also cause siltation of reservoirs and navigation channels, and can impair the amenity uses of water by making it muddy and adding nutrients.

Calling the potential threat grave does not mean that it is immediate or severe. In the United States it is a diminishing problem. While erosion is a process accelerated by human activity, we know how to reduce it and have made much progress in doing so. The worst abuses of the past were predicated upon the availability of cheap land elsewhere and are no longer rational by economic standards. There may be renewed concern in the future, for as pressure for food production grows we may be tempted to bring erosion-prone lands into crop production. While our aim should be to diminish soil losses to a rate no faster than the rate of soil formation, this goal does not appear to deserve the highest priority in the light of all the environmental and other problems that confront us.

The erosion hazard depends in large measure upon the climate. Rainfall (not the absolute amount as much as the volume in a given time and impact with which it falls) is a major factor. The British Isles, with their frequent but rather gentle rains and climate favorable to grass, have little erosion problem. In most parts of the United States, where rain falls more heavily, erosion presents a vastly greater hazard. There are sharp contrasts, however, within the country. In the northern Lake States conditions are somewhat similar to Britain's; in the Southwest, at the other extreme, the infrequent rains usually fall with great intensity and impact. Wind also greatly affects erosion; the southern Great Plains have a vastly greater hazard of this kind than, for example, New England.

Topography also affects the erosion hazard. All other factors being equal, steep lands erode more easily and more rapidly than do flat or gently sloping ones. In some areas of the United States, the land is so nearly flat that water erosion is nearly impossible. Erosion also varies markedly with soil type or texture (clay, loam, sand, etc.), and the finer textured soils are generally more susceptible.

In many situations, virtually any attempt at crop production will lead to increased erosion, sometimes in spite of protective measures. Elsewhere, normal cropping practices may accelerate erosion little or not at all, and such hazard as exists may be easily met by special conservation measures.

Some Historical Background. Soil erosion was taking place within the United States when white men first came. Early explorers remarked upon the silt-laden streamflow of some rivers. The Missouri River was known, almost from the beginning, as the Big Muddy; the Colorado was early described as too thin to plow, too thick to drink. Dust storms swept the Great Plains from the time of earliest exploration and settlement, long before there was any significant cropping.

The American Indians had only a modest impact upon the soil and its vegetation. Their numbers were too few and their technology too feeble to damage the environment very much. They did have fire, however, and they used it to influence grass growth and game movement, with the result that extensive areas that otherwise would have been forested were kept in prairie.

White settlement led everywhere to major changes in vegetation and to increased erosion. Permanent settlements were initially almost always based on agriculture and this necessitated clearing the forests or plowing the prairies. In the process, the natural ecosystem was destroyed and the settlers established their own vegetative pattern on the land—a monoculture of crops. Soil erosion was serious in the Colonies in the 17th and 18th centuries. When the natural fertility of the soil became too depleted, or the erosion was too severe, the land was abandoned and new land was cleared farther west.

Accelerated soil erosion was especially severe in much of the South during the 19th century and in the first quarter of the 20th century. The one-crop cotton economy left the land bare and exposed to rain all winter. In the Plains, dust storms were common and accelerated or increased damage was frequent as more land was plowed and left nearly defenseless against the wind. Still farther west, there was much accelerated erosion resulting from improper irrigation developments and practices, from poor road construction and drainage, and from overgrazing. Throughout the country, forests were cut with little or no concern for restocking; fires were generally uncontrolled. There was a common belief that forested land would be converted into farm land; hence it was an advantage to prevent the regrowth of trees. The exploitation process reached its peak and the condition of the soil and the vegetation reached its low point around the 1920s.

Those responsible for the depletion of resources often failed to realize the long-term consequences of their actions. Particularly as settlement moved into the drier western areas, there was a tendency to apply standards of land use more suitable to wetter eastern areas. Grazing land was plowed for crops in the mistaken belief that it could be cropped indefinitely.

In many cases, the adverse consequences were not apparent at once. Even when they were, farmers, ranchers, and lumbermen often did not know how to prevent the resource damage they were creating. Above all, during the exploitative period the conservation of soil and vegetative resources simply did not pay by conventional economic standards—all too often it still does not pay. Given the supply of cropland, grass, and trees, there was little economic gain from conserving them. The consuming public was happy to have low-priced products from the land. There was neither the knowledge nor the incentive to conserve the soil.

The past two generations have seen a marked improvement in conservation of the soil and of vegetation. During the late 1920s and early 1930s, an effective soil conservation movement was launched. Soil conservation districts, an institutional innovation, were begun and by now include almost all farmland in the United States. A federal program of financial aid to farmers to encourage soil conservation has funneled substantial sums to farmers. The achievement of these efforts has been considerable. Also, the health of the forests and rangelands has improved substantially in recent years.

The Present Situation. In thus emphasizing the great improvements of the past generation, one should not suggest that all is now perfect. Conditions on some land are still poor, and some will argue that the overall situation is still intolerable. We can do much more, if we choose, and if we really think this is a high priority task.

Of the 438 million acres classed as cropland in 1967, 51 percent had erosion hazards of varying seriousness. Such threatened land would benefit from terracing, strip-cropping, contour plowing, grassed waterways, and other devices or practices aimed at reducing erosion. In 1967, the Soil Conservation Service estimated that 151 million acres of cropland had been "adequately treated" from a conservation viewpoint. About one-third of the land that was used for crops and needed some treatment was adequately treated. We do not know whether the adequately treated lands represent those most in need of treatment or those less in need.

Although substantial progress has been made in reducing erosion, some lands are still eroding seriously. What would happen if present soil erosion rates in the United States continued indefinitely? Is it really true that billions of tons of precious topsoil or millions of acres of good cropland are "destroyed" by erosion each year? Most such statistics originated three decades or more ago when the losses were higher, and they have always been seriously inflated. Nonetheless, an accurate estimate of the current erosion situation would reveal millions of acres of land on which soil materials are being removed faster than new soil is being formed. We simply do not know for how large an area this would be true.[31]

Based on this loss, one can make a set of assumptions that point to a serious lack of cropland in the United States in the future: continued soil erosion on at least some land, proceeding to the point where the land is no longer usable; a progression to land not now seriously eroding as demand increases; and absence of effective measures to control erosion. But the mere statement of these conditions raises great doubts as to their probability.

A contrary assumption would be that the clear trend toward reduced soil erosion of the past 35 years would continue. At some date, all cropland, actual and potential, would be "adequately treated" according to Soil Conservation Service criteria. This assumption is as unrealistic as the first. It is most improbable that every acre experiencing erosion will ever be treated to the point where all erosion is stopped. Land opened for building sites, for example, usually goes through a stage of accelerated erosion. In other cases, considerations of cost would surely enter. At present levels of demand for land the most practical way to "treat" many easily eroded areas is to stop using them for crops.

In the United States, soil erosion is not one of the major environmental hazards. If we should choose to give soil erosion a high priority, the present imperfect situation could be greatly improved in a relatively few years. It is doubtful that we shall give it a priority much higher than it has had over the past three decades in which substantial progress has been achieved.

Other Parts of the World. The situation varies greatly in other parts of the world. For example, in the British Isles and northern Europe there is very little erosion, while in the Mediterranean Basin it is mostly severe. Throughout most of the lower-income countries, there has been little concern about erosion and vegetative depletion, and even less effort to control them. Some countries, it is true, have set up special soil conservation, forestry, or wildlife organizations, often modeled more or less after the U.S. counterparts. However, most peasants in poor countries are either uninformed on conservation practices or so concerned with eking out a livelihood that they can spare no

---

[31] One writer suggests that sediment losses of 4 billion tons or the equivalent of 4 million acres of topsoil occur yearly. One-fourth of this is carried out to sea and another one-quarter is said to be deposited behind reservoirs. Presumably the rest is deposited in flood plains (Wadleigh, *Water in Relation to Agriculture and Forestry*, pp. 24, 35–36).

energy or resources to control erosion. In addition, they often face an institutional structure that makes efforts in this direction difficult or impossible.

In parts of West Africa, clearing and burning-over the land, followed by cropping and then abandonment, has long been practiced as a land use rotation system, and with a good pragmatic base. Now, however, an increasing population dependent upon the land is forcing a shortening of the recuperative part of the rotation, with ultimately bad, if not disastrous, results. Here landowners might respond to a land management program that keeps land in crops permanently and maintains or improves the soil at the same time, but only if they understand the technical aspects and have the means to establish and maintain such a program. They are likely to be unmoved by exhortation against the only things they have known how to do to feed themselves and their families.

The less-developed countries do not see erosion as one of their most pressing problems. Farmers and other land users in a low-income country will respond to land management practices that improve the resource base if they also raise current income. Warnings about future ill consequences accomplish little or nothing.

Selected References

Climate

Bryson, Reid A., and James T. Peterson. "Atmospheric Aerosols: Increased Concentration During the Last Decade." *Science*, vol. 162 (October 4, 1968).

Fletcher, J. O. "Controlling the Planet's Climate." *Impact of Science on Society* (UNESCO), vol. 19, no. 2 (April–June 1969), pp. 151–68.

Frisken, W. R. "Extended Industrial Revolution and Climate Change." *Eos*, vol. 52, no. 7 (July 1971).

Manabe, Syukuro, and Richard T. Wetherald. "Thermal Equilibrium of the Atmosphere with a Given Distribution of Relative Humidity." *Journal of the Atmospheric Sciences*, vol. 24 (May 1967).

Mitchell, J. M. "A Preliminary Evaluation of Atmospheric Pollution as a Cause of the Global Temperature Fluctuation of the Past Century." In Singer, ed., *Global Effects of Environmental Pollution*. Reidel (Holland), 1970.

Möller, F. "On the Influence of Changes in the CO_2 Concentration in Air on the Radiation Balance of the Earth's Surface and on the Climate." *Journal of Geophysics Research*, vol. 68 (July 1, 1963).

Peterson, Eugene K. "Carbon Dioxide Affects Global Ecology." *Environmental Science and Technology*, vol. 3, no. 11 (November 1969), pp. 1162–69.

Robinson, G. D. "Long-Term Effects of Air Pollution–A Survey." CEM 4029-400 (June 1970). The Center for the Environment and Man, 250 Constitution Plaza, Hartford, Conn. 06103.

SCEP. *Man's Impact on the Global Environment. Assessment and Recommendations for Action*. Report of the Study of Critical Environmental Problems (SCEP) Sponsored by the Massachusetts Institute of Technology. Cambridge, Mass.: MIT Press, 1970.

Sellers, W. D. "A Global Climatic Model Based on the Energy Balance of the Earth-Atmosphere System." *Journal of Applied Meteorology*, vol. 8 (June 1969).

Weinberg, Alvin M. "Nuclear Energy and the Environment." *Bulletin of the Atomic Scientists* (June 1970), pp. 69–74.

Radioactivity

Curtis, Richard, and Elizabeth Hogan. *Perils of the Peaceful Atom*. New York: Doubleday and Ballantine Books, 1970.

Gofman, John W. "Calculation of Radiation Hazards." Paper presented at meeting of the American Physical Society, Washington, April 26–29, 1971.

Holcomb, Robert W. "Radiation Risk: A Scientific Problem?" *Science*, vol. 167 (February 6, 1970), pp. 853–55.

Lieberman, Joseph A., and Walter G. Belter. "Waste Management and Environmental Aspects of Nuclear Power." *Environmental Science and Technology*, vol. 1, no. 6 (June 1967), pp. 466–75.

Little, John B. "Environmental Hazards: Ionizing Radiation." *The New England Journal of Medicine*, vol. 275, no. 17 (October 27, 1966), pp. 929–38.

Logsden, Joe E., et al. *Radioactive Waste Discharges to the Environment from Nuclear Power Facilities*. U.S. Public Health Service, Rockville, Md., March 1970, Clearinghouse Document No. PB 190–717.

Morgan, Karl Z. "Comments on Radiation Hazards and Risks." Paper presented at meeting of American Physics Society, Washington, D.C., April 29, 1971.

———. "Maximum Permissible Levels of Exposure to Ionizing Radiation." Lecture for International Summer School on Radiation Protection, Boris Kidric Institute of Nuclear Sciences, Cavtat, Yugoslavia, September 20-30, 1970.

Novick, Sheldon. *The Careless Atom*. Boston: Houghton Mifflin, 1969.

Rose, David J. "Controlled Nuclear Fusion: Status and Outlook." *Science*, vol. 172, no. 3985 (May 21, 1971), pp. 797–808.

Shapley, Deborah. "Plutonium: Reactor Proliferation Threatens a Nuclear Black Market." *Science*, vol. 172 (April 9, 1971), pp. 143–46.

U.S. Congress. Senate. *Underground Uses of Nuclear Energy*. Hearings before the Subcommittee on Air and Water Pollution of the Senate Committee on Public Works on S. 3042, 91 Cong., 1 sess., November 18–20, 1969. Washington, D.C.: Government Printing Office, 1970.

Pesticides

American Chemical Society. *Cleaning Our Environment: The Chemical Basis for Action.* A report by the Subcommittee on Environmental Improvement, Committee on Chemistry and Public Affairs. Washington, D.C.: American Chemical Society, 1969.

Edwards, C. A. (Referee: R. S. Adams). "Persistent Pesticides in the Environment." In Richard G. Bond and Conrad P. Straub, eds., *Critical Reviews in Environmental Control*, vol. 1, issue 1. Cleveland: The Chemical Rubber Company, 1970.

Environment, vol. 11, no. 7 (September 1969). See articles on pesticides, pp. 2ff.

Headley, J. C., and A. V. Kneese. "Economic Implications of Pesticide Use." *Annals of the New York Academy of Sciences*, vol. 160 (June 23, 1969), pp. 30-39.

Headley, J. C., and J. N. Lewis. *The Pesticide Problem: An Economic Approach to Public Policy.* Washington, D.C.: Resources for the Future, Inc., 1967.

Heinrichs, W. L., et al. "Persistent Estrous Syndrome Following DDT Administration to Neonatal Rats." Abstract in *Clinical Research*, vol. 19, no. 1 (January 1971), p. 171.

National Academy of Sciences. *Chlorinated Hydrocarbons in the Marine Environment.* A Report Prepared by the Panel on Monitoring Persistent Pesticides in the Marine Environment of the Committee on Oceanography. Washington, D.C., 1971.

National Academy of Sciences–National Research Council. *Scientific Aspects of Pest Control.* A symposium arranged and conducted by the National Academy of Sciences–National Research Council at Washington, D.C., February 1-3, 1966. National Academy of Sciences–National Research Council Publication 1402. Washington, D.C., 1966.

Rudd, Robert L. *Pesticides and the Living Landscape.* Madison: University of Wisconsin Press, 1964.

Scientists' Institute for Public Information. *Pesticides.* A Scientists' Institute for Public Information Workbook. New York, 1970.

Smith, Ray F. "Integrated Control of Insects, a Challenge for Scientists." *Agricultural Science Review*, vol. 7, no. 1 (First quarter 1969).

Stickel, Lucille F. *Organochlorine Pesticides in the Environment.* U.S. Bureau of Sport Fisheries and Wildlife, Special Scientific Report—Wildlife no. 119. Washington, D.C.: Government Printing Office, October 1968.

U.S. Department of Health, Education, and Welfare. *Report of the Secretary's Commission on Pesticides and Their Relationship to Environmental Health.* Parts I and II. Washington, D.C.: Government Printing Office, October 1968.

Wurster, Charles F., Jr. "DDT Reduces Photosynthesis by Marine Phytoplankton." *Science*, March 29, 1968, pp. 1474-75.

Fertilizers

Commoner, Barry. "Can We Survive?" *Washington Monthly*, December 1969, pp. 12-21.

Lee, Douglas H. K. *Nitrates, Nitrites, and Methemoglobinemia.* Clearinghouse Publication PB 192-779, National Institute of Environmental Health Sciences, Research Triangle Park, North Carolina, May 18, 1970.

Lipman, J. A., and A. B. Conybeare. "Preliminary Note on the Inventory and Balance Sheet of Plant Nutrients in the United States." New Jersey Agricultural Experiment Station Bulletin 607, 1936.

Stanford, George; C. B. England; and A. W. Taylor. *Fertilizer Use and Water Quality.* United States Department of Agriculture, Agricultural Research Service, ARS 41-168. Washington, D.C.: Government Printing Office, October 1970.

Stewart, B. A., et al. *Distribution of Nitrates and Other Water Pollutants Under Fields and Corrals in the Middle South Platte Valley of Colorado.* United States Department of Agriculture, Agricultural Research Service, ARS 41-134. Washington, D.C.: Government Printing Office, December 1967.

Stewart, B. A., et al. "Nitrate and Other Water Pollutants Under Fields and Feedlots." *Environmental Science and Technology,* vol. 1 (September 1967), pp. 736–39.

Erosion

Held, R. Burnell, and Marion Clawson. *Soil Conservation in Perspective.* Baltimore: Johns Hopkins Press for Resources for the Future, 1965.

FIVE

BURDENS
ON THE RECEIVING MEDIA

The review in the preceding chapter of some of the gravest threats to environmental quality inevitably included a good deal of discussion of present or potential effects upon the receiving media. Many other influences, however, affect the quality of water and air. In this chapter we shall take a general look at conditions and prospects for each of these two categories including the property, health, and ecological damage that results from their pollution. Also, to round out the picture, brief mention will be made of solid wastes, which are chiefly a burden on land, and of some other, harder to classify, consequences of environmental burdens, of which noise is perhaps the leading example.

Water Pollution

Lakes, streams, underground aquifers, estuaries and other in-shore waters, and the high seas all provide us with varied and useful services. Frequently the many uses of water do not seriously conflict among themselves or threaten water quality, but when water is used to carry off industrial, farm, and human waste products it may become unsuitable for drinking, recreational use, and some industrial purposes. The direct threat is mostly to amenity or convenience, although in some instances there may also be effects on human health, or there may be long-term ecological consequences.

It is sometimes hard to remember that natural waters are the home of an active and diversified biotic community that is closely linked with nonaquatic forms. This is true even in clean fresh water—a complex mixture of suspended solids, dissolved salts and chemicals, and microorganisms. Pollution of fresh water alters and may destroy aquatic life that should be valued for its own sake as well as for its contribution to human purposes.

The principal burdens on water quality come from industry, agriculture, and households. Industry discharges organic matter, inorganic chemicals and suspended solids, the chief offenders being the chemical, paper, food, and primary metals industries (see Table 4). Energy use is the principal source of thermal pollution. Agriculture discharges mostly organic matter, largely in the form of animal wastes from feedlots. Agriculture also is the source of most pesticide residues and chemical fertilizers, and it generates a major portion of the soil sediment. Human waste consists of organic matter and various suspended solids, while households also discharge chemicals, chiefly detergents.

Some of these contaminants can be eliminated or neutralized by natural processes occurring in the water. Organic matter, heat, and bacteria fall in this category of degradable pollutants. Others, particularly mineral salts, heavy metals, silt, and some chemicals are not readily removed from the water by natural processes, although some may be precipitated to the bottom. The fact that some pollutants are naturally degradable does not diminish their harmfulness to aquatic life or to human uses of water when they are present in excessive concentrations.

Degradable Pollutants. The best-known degradable pollutant is domestic sewage, but in the aggregate both industry and agriculture produce greater amounts of organic waste. Some industrial plants are huge producers of organic pollution: a single pulp mill, for example, can produce wastes equivalent to the sewage flow of a large city. Table 4, in addition to breaking down the components of industrial wastes, compares the total industrial load with estimates for all domestic sewage.

When an effluent bearing a substantial load of organic wastes is expelled into otherwise clean water, a process known as "aerobic degradation" begins immediately. Aquatic biota, primarily bacteria, feed on the wastes and break them down into their inorganic components (nitrogen, phosphorus, and car-

Table 4. Estimated Volume of Industrial Wastes Before Treatment, 1964

Industry	Waste-water volume (billion gallons)	Process water intake (billion gallons)	BOD (million pounds)	Suspended solids (million pounds)
Food and kindred products	690	260	4,300	6,600
Meat products	99	52	640	640
Dairy products	58	13	400	230
Canned and frozen food	87	51	1,200	600
Sugar refining	220	110	1,400	5,000
All other	220	43	670	110
Textile mill products	140	110	890	N.E.
Paper and allied products	1,900	1,300	5,900	3,000
Chemical and allied products	3,700	560	9,700	1,900
Petroleum and coal	1,300	88	500	460
Rubber and plastics	160	19	40	50
Primary metals	4,300	1,000	480	4,700
Blast furnaces and steel mills	3,600	870	160	4,300
All other	740	130	320	430
Machinery	150	23	60	50
Electrical machinery	91	28	70	20
Transportation equipment	240	58	120	N.E.
All other manufacturing	450	190	390	930
All manufacturing	13,100	3,700	22,000	18,000
For comparison: sewered population of United States	5,300[a]	–	7,300[b]	8,800[c]

Source: Environmental Quality, The First Annual Report of the Council on Environmental Quality, Transmitted to the Congress August 1970 (Washington: Government Printing Office, 1970), p. 32. Data derived from T. J. Powers, National Industrial Waste Assessment, 1967.

Note: Columns may not add, due to rounding.

[a] 120,000,000 persons times 120 gallons times 365 days.

[b] 120,000,000 persons times 1/6 pound times 365 days.

[c] 120,000,000 persons times 0.2 pound times 365 days.

bon) which are basic plant nutrients. In the breaking down of organic material some of the oxygen which is always dissolved in clean water is consumed. This depletion tends to be offset by reoxygenation which occurs at the surface and as a consequence of photosynthesis by the plants in the water. If the waste load is not too heavy, dissolved oxygen in the water first will drop to a limited extent (say, to 4 or 5 parts per million from a saturation level of perhaps 8-10 ppm, depending upon temperature) and then rise again. The drain upon oxygen which this process entails is known as biochemical oxygen demand (BOD). The term is commonly used as a measure of the effects of organic wastes upon fresh water.

If the proportion of organic waste in the water becomes great enough, however, the process of degradation may exhaust the dissolved oxygen. In such cases degradation is still carried forward but it takes place anaerobically, that is, through the action of bacteria that do not use free oxygen but organically or inorganically bound oxygen, common sources of which are nitrates and sulfates. Gaseous by-products result, among them methane and hydrogen sulfide. Water in which wastes are being degraded anaerobically emits foul odors, looks black and bubbly, and aesthetically is altogether offensive. Although rare, this condition is by no means unknown. For example, a lake near São Paulo, Brazil, is largely anaerobic and most of the streams in the Japanese papermaking city, Fuji City, likewise lack oxygen. Levels of dissolved oxygen low enough to kill fish and cause other ecological changes are a much more frequent and widespread problem.

High temperatures accelerate degradation, so a waste load that would not deplete dissolved oxygen at low temperature may do so if the temperature of the water rises. In such circumstances heat may be considered a pollutant. Huge amounts of heat are put into streams by the cooling water effluents of industry. Steam electric power plants, whose output (as discussed elsewhere) is increasing rapidly, pose a special problem; even now they use more water than all industries and municipalities combined. Nuclear power, which rejects more heat per kilowatt-hour generated than fossil fuel plants, aggravates this problem.

There is increased concern about the impact of heat residuals. One response to this situation has been increasing use of cooling towers to relieve the burden on water by transferring residual heat energy to the air instead of to the water.

One author has discussed what might happen over the central region of the United States if we used once-through cooling and discharged waterborne heat to the Missouri and the Mississippi rivers. Assuming that about 540 million kilowatts of fossil-fuel burning capacity are installed and operating in this region by the year 2000, he writes:

Imposing the requirement of at least 10 miles separation between stations and noting that such a generating capacity will raise the water temperature by about 20 deg F, we find approximately 3000 miles of river spreading over the central region of the United States with a temperature 20 deg F higher than normal. This temperature change would double the evaporation rate on this massive river network, resulting in: a great deal more water available to the atmosphere for clouds and precipitation in this region; a considerable increase in the thermal energy available to drive the large storm systems in the area;

and even a possible thermal anomaly over a large enough area for a long enough time so as to produce a climatic variation.[1]

The ecological effects of such a large-scale heat discharge to our streams can only be speculated about at this time. If there were a substantial discharge of organic wastes to these streams at the same time, they would almost certainly become anaerobic in the summertime and the fresh water life forms we are accustomed to would be lost.

The ordinary sewage treatment plant that processes organic waste uses the same biochemical processes that occur naturally in a stream, but by careful control they are greatly speeded up. Under most circumstances standard sewage treatment plants are capable of reducing the BOD in waste effluent by perhaps 90 percent. As with degradation occurring in a watercourse, plant nutrients are the end product of the process.

Where levels of free oxygen are low (but not zero), a stream can be usable for a variety of purposes. Aesthetic quality largely governs the utility of water-based recreation; low levels of dissolved oxygen need not prevent people from enjoying some activities, such as boating and swimming. However, the ecological effect may be profound, and extensive stretches of streams that persistently carry less than 4 or 5 ppm of oxygen will not support the higher forms of fish life. Reduced levels of oxygen, even where they are not lethal, increase the sensitivity of fish to toxins. Water in which the organic waste has not been completely stabilized is more costly to treat for public or industrial supplies. Finally, the plant nutrients produced by bacterial degradation of organic wastes may cause algae blooms. Up to a certain level algae growth in a stream is not harmful and may even increase fish food, but larger amounts can be toxic, produce odors, reduce the river's aesthetic appeal, and increase treatment problems.

Problems of this kind are particularly important in comparatively quiet waters such as lakes and tidal estuaries. In recent years certain Swiss and American lakes have changed their character radically because of the buildup of plant nutrients. The most widely known example is Lake Erie, although many other lakes are going through this accelerated process of eutrophication. The possibility of excessive algae growth is one of the unresolved problems in planning for pollution abatement in the Potomac and other estuaries, for effective treatment processes today carry a high price tag. Two extremely important challenges to research are to find improved means of removing

[1] S. M. Greenfield, *Science and the Natural Environment of Man*, p. 3.

plant nutrients from sewage effluent and to predict with more accuracy the conditions under which algae grow and the effects they have on water.

The magnitude of our present and future water pollution problem is imperfectly indicated by historical records of BOD and by some BOD load projections into the future. The figures on BOD from industry are extremely undependable, and the projections typically neglect all means of reduction (like industrial process and product changes) except treatment. What will happen to BOD in the years to come obviously depends largely on the extent to which wastes are treated before they enter streams. Over the past half-century BOD load has increased by considerably more than 2 percent per year. Continuation of present rates of construction of treatment facilities would result in an estimated growth of BOD of about 3.5 percent per year while plant nutrient discharges would grow even faster. However, on another set of assumptions, involving considerable growth in treatment facilities, BOD could actually decline at about 2 percent per year.

Bacteria can for most purposes be considered along with what we have called the degradable pollutants since those of the enteric infectious type die off rather quickly in a stream, and treatment with chlorine is highly effective against them. Thus the traditional scourges of polluted water—typhoid, para-typhoid, dysentery, gastroenteritis—have become almost unknown in municipal areas in this country. Public health engineers were so successful in devising effective water supply treatment that attention to pollution lapsed until its recent upsurge.

Viruses, some of which are more viable than bacteria outside the body environment, are apparently less susceptible to treatment and have become a source of concern to public health officials. Some believe that viruses in water supplies are associated with the spread of certain diseases at less than epidemic levels, rather than being epidemiological problems, as some bacteria once were.

Nondegradable Pollutants. Nondegradable pollutants are not attacked by aquatic biota and undergo no great change once they get into a stream; the stream does not "purify itself" of them. This category includes inorganic substances—such materials as inorganic colloidal matter, ordinary salt, and the salts of numerous heavy metals. When these substances are present in fairly large quantities they result in toxicity, unpleasant taste, and hardness. It is these pollutants that are partially or wholly responsible for corrosion, scaling, and pitting of industrial equipment such as pipes, water heaters, boilers, and rollers in steel rolling mills. They necessitate the use of water softeners, distilled water, and extra soap, and add considerably to the expense of treating industrial water supplies. To take care of them, we rely heavily on the dilution capacity of receiving waters. These pollutants are also a public health problem—usually when they enter into food chains. Two particularly bad instances of poisoning by heavy metals have stirred the population of Japan. These are mercury poisoning through eating contaminated fish and cadmium poisoning through eating rice contaminated by irrigation water. Several hundred people have been affected and more than a hundred have died.

Persistent Pollutants. A third group of pollutants, mostly of relatively recent origin, does not fit into either the degradable or nondegradable category. These persistent or exotic pollutants are best exemplified by the synthetic organic chemicals produced in profusion by the modern chemical industry. They enter watercourses as effluent of industry and also as waste residuals from many household and agricultural uses. These substances are termed persistent because stream biota cannot effectively attack their complex molecular chains. Some degradation does take place, but usually so slowly that the persistents travel long distances in virtually unchanged form. The older detergents, pesticides such as DDT, and phenols that result from the distillation of petroleum and coal products are among the most common of these pollutants. Fortunately, the recent development and successful manu-facture of degradable detergents has opened the way toward reduction or elimination of some of the problems associated with them, especially that of foaming. The dry detergents, whether degradable or not, present another problem. They contain phosphate fillers that aggravate the nutrients problem.

Some of the persistent organics, like phenols and hard detergents, present primarily aesthetic problems. The phenols, for example, can cause an un-pleasant taste in water, especially when it is treated with chlorine to kill bacteria. Other organics are under suspicion as possible public health prob-lems and are associated with periodic fish kills in streams.

Some of the chemical insecticides are almost unbelievably toxic. Endrin, which until recently was commonly used as an insecticide and rodenticide, kills fish in minute concentrations. It has been calculated, for example, that 0.005 pound of endrin in three acre-feet of water is acutely toxic to fish.[2]

Concentrations of the persistent organic substances in public water sup-plies have seldom if ever risen to levels high enough to present an acute danger to public health. The public health problem centers around the possible chronic effects of prolonged exposure to very low concentrations. Similarly, even in concentrations too low to be acutely poisonous to fish,

[2] Robert P. Rudd, *Pesticides and the Living Landscape*, p. 105.

these pollutants may have profound effects on stream ecology; higher creatures of other kinds—especially birds of prey—are now being seriously affected because persistent pesticides have entered their food chains.

No solid evidence implicates present concentrations of organic chemicals in water supplies as a cause of health problems, but some experts are suspicious of them. Several public health officials feel they may be linked to cancer, and the late Nobel prize-winning geneticist H. J. Muller asked whether they might not be involved in genetic mutations. It has been demonstrated that concentrated raw and finished water supplies have carcinogenic effects when injected into test animals, but the truth is that we do not know enough about the effects of these chemicals. This knowledge is very difficult and very expensive to come by.

There are at least one-half million known organic chemicals, most of them synthetically produced. Even in treated water supplies, hundreds of organic chemicals are present at low concentrations. Identification is costly, and with few exceptions no one knows what chemicals in what concentrations are present. Chronic toxicity tests are very expensive—reported figures run from $50,000 to $250,000 per compound. The U.S. Public Health Service drinking water standards contain an aggregate standard for all synthetic dissolved organic substances that can be extracted from the water by a carbon filter. However, this standard, which is 200 parts per billion (higher than concentrations currently found in public supplies), has little meaning with respect to chronic toxicity since it is based upon the threshold where tastes and odors become apparent. Toxic effects may occur at lower levels.

Possible Countermeasures. The degradation of our aquatic environments has been one of the most offensive kinds of damage that we have incurred. For the most part, however, except for the unknown possibility of chronic toxicity from low concentration discussed above, it does not represent the kind of irreversible or intractable problem that forces us to question our entire direction. Although agriculture presents some stubborn difficulties, nearly every kind of industrial or domestic discharge could be treated or reduced at costs that are within the range of consideration.

The technical possibilities are legion. Just three major industry groups—food, paper, and chemicals—generate 90 percent of the BOD originating in industry.[3] In such industries as beet sugar and paper, simple extension of best

---

[3] American Chemical Society, *Cleaning Our Environment: The Chemical Basis for Action* (Washington, D.C.: American Chemical Society, 1969), p. 97.

practice would go far to reduce the problem. Minor compromises in public taste (less refined products) would also be a great help. And industry, which heretofore has enjoyed free use of the water for waste discharge, has only begun to explore the possibilities of reducing effluent. Even now it is contended that most industrial waste water could be treated at costs of under 1 percent of gross sales.[4]

It lies within our power to produce potable water from sewage effluent.[5] In most cases this would not be warranted on economic grounds because such high water standards are unnecessary, and we can cope with conditions in the stream by other means such as dilution or aeration. However, we can remove 90 percent of BOD and suspended solids by primary and secondary treatment at costs of 5-10 cents per 1,000 gallons, and we could strip out phosphorus, nitrogen, salts, and bacteria at about four times that figure.[6] In other words, nearly complete renovation of water is feasible at mentionable prices if we want to do it.

In few cases is it reasonable to treat water to a very high standard prior to discharge into watercourses. We might do it if we aimed at closed circuit reuse. However, constant reuse would allow for the buildup of unidentified chemicals. At present we do not know what enters the water or the full consequences of unidentified contaminants for health. Futhermore, reuse might allow the concentration of viruses which may escape present treatment methods. In most cases, treatment would be used simply to reduce the burden on natural water rather than as a source of water supply. In terms of social cost, reducing the volume of effluent may prove to be one of the lowest-cost ways of cleaning up our water. While viruses have eluded present treatment methods, even they can be destroyed if necessary by irradiation.

Most water pollution is not necessarily permanent since, if we reduce or stop the additions, natural forces will act to restore quality. The problem of maintaining water quality is permanent, however, because we must continually manage the water resources that we use to ensure against overloading. The presence of too many plant nutrients, leading to eutrophication, is one type of damage that may be difficult to reverse, especially in lakes. Even here solutions may yet be found, and the industrial and municipal origins of the problem can be controlled. The contribution of agriculture is far more diffi-

---

[4]*Environmental Quality, The First Annual Report of the Council on Environmental Quality, Transmitted to the Congress August 1970,* p. 33.

[5]American Chemical Society, *Cleaning Our Environment: The Chemical Basis for Action,* pp. 124-25.

[6]*Ibid.,* pp. 124-25, 136.

cult to manage. Pesticides can be regulated at the point of manufacture or sale. Animal waste from feedlots carries a burden of nutrients and microorganisms that can be diverted (and used) at some cost. The flow of nutrients from artificial fertilizers and from range lands into water can be limited by good practice but would be very hard to control completely.

Apart from agriculture, we could treat all liquid wastes to the point where we discharge little other than H_2O if that suits our purpose. It will not suit us on economic grounds. Management of fresh water is possible to the extent that we want to plan and pay for it.

The most serious possibility of disaster is that we may flush too much to the sea and in our ignorance do unforeseen damage to it. We must learn more of the ocean's capacity to sustain insult and to restore itself before we can congratulate ourselves on running well-managed sewers into it.

The Oceans. The sea is a significant and expandable source of food. It is also important to photosynthetic activity, absorption of CO_2 from the atmosphere, and regulation of the earth's climate. We know all too little of how the sea and its biotic communities impinge on global ecology, but there is every reason to treat this relationship with great respect. Instead we utilize the sea thoughtlessly as the ultimate sink for all sorts of debris and chemicals generated on land and transported by air and water. A major threat to life in the sea presently discernible (but apparently not imminent) appears to come from pesticides. Alteration of nutrient balance and oxygen content as a consequence of industrial pollution has been observed in local situations or in restricted waters. Oil spills thus far have a localized effect, but are disastrous for sea birds and some other marine species caught in them. However, with increasing ocean traffic there is a risk of marine accidents that could disperse highly toxic materials and lay waste vast areas of the ocean as accidental discharges already have done in the inland waters. The ocean's capacity to degrade oil, already taxed by routine tank cleaning and spills, will be severely tested if supertankers of the future break apart at sea. This problem, along with many others concerning the ocean, needs further study.

Air Pollution

Air pollution is principally a threat to human health and amenity, although as we have seen, it has a potential effect on climate (and thereby on global ecology) through the growth of CO_2 and particulates in the atmosphere. Air also is a medium through which pesticides and some types of radioactive residues may be diffused. In terms of annoyance and demand for curative measures air pollution probably excites the public more than any other environmental problem.

Energy use is the source of most air pollution. As we saw in Chapter 2 (Table 2), most discharges to the atmosphere in the United States come from automobiles and electricity generation, while space heating and industry contribute diverse gases and particulates (fly ash). The chief pollutants derived from energy use are CO, CO_2, SO_2, NO_x, hydrocarbons, and particulates. The same materials may be generated by other industrial processes, especially in the chemical industries and the preparation of ores for smelting. Fluorides also may be released by industrial processes.

The air has the capacity to purify itself when relieved of new burdens; thus we apparently do not face irreversible damage from the usual kinds of bad air. But if we continually overload it we spend most of our time in a chronically contaminated environment at considerable risk to health. Moreover, even though most of what we put into air does not reside there permanently, it must either be transformed or pass to land and water, and we may encounter it again.

The Anatomy of Air Pollution. Now, let us review what happens to the various air pollutants after discharge, their effects on receptors, and what we know about the economics of air pollution.

We have noted the capacity of the atmosphere to assimilate discharges without acute damage. This varies with timing, concentration within a given space, and the nature of the materials being discharged. To maintain a desired level of air quality in a given area, we must know the time and location pattern of discharges and understand how it results in a particular temporal and spatial pattern of atmospheric pollution. We also must consider the mutual and reinforcing interactions of residuals in the environment and the physical and chemical reactions in the atmosphere after discharge (smog is an example). In most cases there are multiple sources of discharges, with variations in type, quantity, and timing. We can make reasonably accurate predictions only under fairly simple meteorological and topographic conditions and for a limited area.

Many complicating factors affect the dispersion, modification, transformation, and accumulation of gaseous residuals in the atmosphere. At the local scale, one of the most important of these is the effect of urban areas, not only in generating large volumes of gaseous residuals, but also (in combination with local meteorological conditions) in impeding their dispersion. Urban areas tend to impair wind velocity and favor the development of inversion layers that block the diffusion that normally takes place when warm air rises. This, in turn, may result in the generalized "heat dome" effect of cities.

Precipitation is the primary cleansing mechanism for airborne gases and fine particles. A gas such as sulfur dioxide, which is highly soluble in water, is absorbed by raindrops or snowflakes as they fall, and wide areas may be affected. For example, the high stacks that are used on power plants in England to reduce the local impact of air pollution are said to be causing "acid rain" in Scandinavia. And atmospheric scavenging is believed to be contributing to the deterioration of water quality in the Great Lakes Basin, at least with respect to the presence of trace elements in the lakes.

The geographical extent of the atmospheric scavenging phenomenon is illustrated by data from Europe relating to the acidity and sulfur contents of precipitation and the consequences on soils, surface waters, and biological systems. In 1958 pH values (pH is a measure of acidity—the lower the pH the higher the acidity) below 5 were found only in limited areas over the Netherlands. In 1966, values below 5 were found in an area that spreads over Central Europe, and pH values in the Netherlands were less than 4.

An additional complicating aspect is the variable and random nature of air quality. The assimilative capacity of the atmosphere varies over time—diurnally, weekly, seasonally, and from year to year—as a result of varying meteorological conditions. Different combinations of varying time patterns of discharge and of meteorological conditions yield various levels of air quality. Thus, in New York City for the 1955-58 period, winter concentrations of SO_2 averaged three times the summer concentrations. During inversion periods SO_2 concentrations ranged from 0.56 to 0.80 ppm; at other times from 0.01 to 0.07 ppm. The concentration of CO in the atmosphere rises almost exactly with traffic volume. Better understanding of the effects of time variation of concentrations in the atmosphere may be the key to deciding on appropriate action. Frequently it is much cheaper to reduce peak concentrations than it is to reduce substantially the total volume of discharge over time; and our control policies are based on cutting peaks. Still we really do not know whether the worst effects of air pollution come from the peak concentration or an accumulated amount of exposure over time.

Effects on Human Health. Air pollution probably has the greatest potential among the various types of environmental threat for producing identifiable disasters in the near future. Already there have been several recorded instances in which it has reached deadly levels. One was in the Meuse Valley in Belgium, where in 1930 a hundred persons were made ill and sixty-three died. A similar situation occurred in the United States in 1948 when fog and low-level temperature inversion covered the horseshoe-shaped valley of the Monongahela River around the town of Donora, Pennsylvania; nearly half the population became ill and twenty people died. In London during two weeks of December 1952 an estimated 4,000 deaths were recorded beyond those normal for the period. London suffered again in December 1962, when more than 300 people died from the effects of air pollution. Smogs producing very severe illness have also hit several Japanese cities—notably Yokkaichi.

However, occasional instances of deadly gases and particulates engulfing a city do not begin to define the magnitude of the problem. The greatest health problems appear to arise from persistent exposure at levels that do not cause acute illness. Thousands of American communities are affected by air pollution. While air pollution in its most acute form is a highly local phenomenon, in densely settled industrial areas some effects are becoming regional in scope.

Except for extreme incidents like those noted above, fatalities are not traceable individually to the impact of air pollution. This is primarily because most of the effects are synergistic. Air pollution is a stress which, in concert with a number of other physiological stresses, tends to increase the incidence and the seriousness of a variety of pulmonary diseases, including lung cancer, emphysema, tuberculosis, pneumonia, bronchitis, asthma, and even the common cold.

The preponderance of evidence suggests that the relationship between such pollutants as SO_2, CO, particulates, and heavy metals and disease is real and large. But one should not underrate the difficulties of establishing such relationships with certainty; the physical relationships between frequency, duration, level of exposure, and health impacts are not fully established. Because adverse air quality is particularly an urban phenomenon, and because there are so many other factors which affect mortality (and morbidity) in urban areas, the establishment of specific cause and effect is extremely difficult.

Among other complications is the fact that the response to adverse air quality conditions is not distributed evenly among the respective populations. Both exposure and susceptibility to adverse conditions vary. The mean ambient concentration in the center city or the mean for the entire urban area does not give any real index of the combination of exposures in the three primary environments of the individual—residence, work, and transportation to and from work. Contrast the center city residents who walk on city streets, inhale fumes from buses, and do not have air-conditioned houses or work places with suburbanites in their air-conditioned houses, cars, and work places.

Susceptibility to a given level and duration of concentration varies with such factors as age and physiological condition of individuals. Diet and use of tobacco and drugs, for example, affect the response to air quality conditions.

Even when damage to health can be established, it often is hard to say how much of the harm should be attributed to air pollution. It might also come from water or food. Although there are differences in the way the body reacts to a substance received through different media, the impact of damage to the human system may in part be additive. Depending also on the degree of physical stress from general environmental conditions, the result may be, in some cases, acute physical illness, chronic illness, or mutagenic or teratogenic effects on man.

Odors are an especially complex manifestation of air pollution. They can simply be objectionable to most people, or they can actually make people ill. The currently available evidence suggests that it is impossible to characterize odor intensity on a purely analytical basis. And there are other complexities as well. One is that the sensing of weak or faint odors is impossible in the presence of strong odors. Another is that odor sensations of similar intensity can have an antagonistic effect when they occur simultaneously, which seemingly reduces the intensity of the individual components. This is the case with respect to kraft pulp mills, where several odorous compounds occur simultaneously.

Atmospheric conditions are still another factor affecting the impact of odors. Wind velocity, wind direction, temperature, and humidity all are involved. Finally, it seems that many individuals generally can become accustomed very rapidly to sensations of constant odor intensity, as they can to those of noise. To the extent that this is more than loss of sensory capacity it raises the very profound question of how we should regard human adaptability in the analysis of environmental problems.

Economists are now making a serious effort to assess the cost of air pollution effects on human health. In one major study two researchers correlated differences in mortality and morbidity in different geographical areas with indices of air pollution, also taking into account differences in social class and population density.[7] The most striking relationship they found was between air pollution and the bronchitis death rate. While air pollution was

---

[7] Lester B. Lave and Eugene P. Seskin, "Air Pollution and Human Health."

less strongly correlated with other ailments, significant relationships nonetheless were established for lung cancer, stomach cancer, heart disease, emphysema, and infant mortality. According to these calculations, cleaning the air to the same level as that enjoyed by the area with the best air would reduce the bronchitis death rate alone by 40-70 percent.

In view of the strong association between air pollution and respiratory disease, the researchers concluded that about 25 percent of the direct costs of such disease (medical costs and forgone earnings) could be avoided by a 50 percent abatement of air pollution levels. If the other diseases studied are included in the calculation, the savings in health costs from a 50 percent abatement of air pollution would have run over $2 billion in 1963. According to the authors, these figures are very conservatively estimated; not all of the health effects of air pollution were included and direct medical costs and forgone earnings do not reflect what people would be willing to pay to avoid the human suffering associated with disease. Also, the figures say nothing of the generalized sense of ill-being or discomfort that air pollution brings.

Effects on Animals and Plants. Animals and plants also suffer from air pollution, particularly those in or near cities. Livestock and wildlife are generally apart from cities, so effects on them are usually minor. Effects on pets almost certainly exist, although they have not been much documented.

Much the same situation holds for plants. Crops are mostly some distance away from cities, and hazards are likely to be rather special in nature (e.g., fluorides from superphosphate plants, or sulfur oxides from copper smelters). However, in some districts truck crops—mostly fruits and vegetables—are grown in close juxtaposition to major cities. Agricultural damage in the citrus belt of southern California seems to be due mainly to oxidants, such as ozone and peroxy-acyl-nitrate, which are produced by the interaction of unburned hydrocarbons, oxides of nitrogen, and strong sunlight. In the mixed truck-farming region of the Middle Atlantic states (potatoes, tomatoes, leafy vegetables, green peas, sweet corn, apples, peaches, dairy and poultry farming), the major cause of damage seems to be sulfur, which often causes leaf-spotting and discoloration and sometimes stunted growth or worse. There are deleterious effects on shrubs, flowers, and shade trees in suburban gardens and city parks and on forests downwind from cities.

As with direct effects on human health, it is difficult to trace a given symptom or a case of stunted plant growth to a particular air pollutant. Again, air pollution is an environmental stress, along with drought, extremes of temperature, and pest outbreaks. A healthy organism may withstand a single moderate stress but not two or three different stresses at the same time. There are no satisfactory methods of allocating the observed damage when a number of causes interact synergistically, nor can the damages themselves be adequately measured and reduced to economic terms.

Considerable work has been done on agricultural damage from gaseous residuals, primarily in the laboratory, yet there appear to be no definitive data that show relationships between dollar damages and the frequency, duration, and level of exposure. Presumably, if the physical effects on crop yields could be defined, these could be translated into dollar damages. The problem is that outside the laboratory, air quality is only one of the variables that affect crop yield.

Damage to Property. A third category of effects comprises damage to property. Here again, sulfur and oxidants are perhaps equally potent. Sulfur oxides combine with water to form sulfurous acid (H_2SO_3) and the much more corrosive sulfuric acid (H_2SO_4). These acids will damage virtually any exposed metal surface and will react especially strongly with limestone or marble (calcium carbonate). Thus many historic buildings and objects (like Cleopatra's Needle in New York or the ancient stones of Venice) have suffered extremely rapid deterioration in modern times.

Sulfur oxides will cause discoloration, hardening, and embrittlement of rubber, plastic, paper, and other materials. Oxidants such as ozone will also produce the latter type of effect. Of course, the most widespread and noticeable of all forms of property damage comes from soot, which has some secondary effects of its own. Airborne dirt affects clothing, furniture, carpets, draperies, exterior paintwork, and automobiles. It leads to extra washing, dry cleaning, and painting; and, of course, all of these activities do not entirely eliminate the dirt, so that people also must live in grimier surroundings.

Because the physical, chemical, biological, and economic effects of air pollution are so ill understood, most estimates of pollution damage are elaborate guesses. For example, the most frequently quoted figure for total annual property damage from air pollution in the United States—$11 billion—is really an estimate of cleaning costs derived from smoke damage data for Pittsburgh in 1913. Many years later, the original figure was adjusted to 1959 prices on the basis of the commodity price index. The updated per capita damage estimate for Pittsburgh was then multiplied by the 1958 U.S. population to arrive at $11 billion.

Some researchers have argued that part of the damages associated with air pollution are reflected in property values. The potential home buyer perceives

and evaluates many of the effects of air pollution on residential property—
ailing shrubbery, off-color paint, sooty surfaces, unpleasant odors, hazy view,
for example. Whether or not he connects these with air pollution, the buyer
will take them into account in his offer price.

Residential property values have been analyzed in this connection in three
cities—St. Louis, Washington, and Kansas City.[8] Variations in sales prices and
rents were correlated with two pollution variables—sulfur trioxide and suspended particulates—along with such other factors as age and condition of
property, distance from the center of the city, racial composition of the
neighborhood, and family income and general educational level. Higher air
pollution levels were significantly related to lower property values: in all
three cities even a 5-15 percent decrease in air quality correlated with a
significant decrease in property values. Each 1 percent increase in either of
the pollution variables was associated with an 8 percent decline in property
price or in rental value.

It seems likely that the marginal benefits of a major reduction in air
pollution would far exceed the marginal costs. Drawing on a number of
published and unpublished studies, Paul Gerhardt of the Environmental Protection Agency offers a figure of $15-$20 billion as the annual cost of
damage from air pollution in the United States, of which about $6 billion is
damage to health.[9] Since he figures that an added $4-$5 billion per year over
the present $500 million would suffice to reduce various pollutants by 60-90
percent, it is plain that there is a strong economic case for air pollution
abatement.

Current technology provides fewer means of dealing with air pollution
than with water pollution. In part this is because it is easier for man to
control the quality of the water he uses than that of the air he breathes. In
part it is because air is not delivered to users in pipes as water frequently is, so
that it is only to a limited extent that polluted air is treatable before it is
consumed. Accordingly, control of air pollution is largely a matter of prevent-
ing pollutants from escaping from their source, eliminating the source, or
shifting the location of the source or the recipient. Water pollution, on the
other hand, is in general subject to a larger array of control measures. Nevertheless, both present intricate problems of devising optimal control systems.

---

[8]R. J. Anderson, Jr., and T. D. Crocker, "Air Pollution and Housing: Some Findings."

[9]Communication to author, May 24, 1971.

Other Burdens

An attempt to cover all kinds of environmental threat is as frustrating as chasing an electric rabbit. The rate at which we create new substances, multiply the output of old ones to damaging levels, or discover harmful potential where it was unsuspected before has been accelerating. We can do no more here than mention a few others.

Solid Waste. Solid waste may wander as fly ash from stacks or as sediment from farms and mills, but most of it occurs on the land surface to be burned, compacted, buried, or recycled. It presents a fairly minor health hazard—mostly it is an aesthetic burden to be managed in the least objectionable way consistent with our willingness to pay. The ecological consequences are few. While disposal sites may be hard to come by for political reasons, we do not face early natural limits on the landscape's ability to absorb waste. (For one thing, we can simply pile it up!) Therefore, our interest is in efficient management of the burden consistent with standards of taste and cost. Emphasis on handling what we generate should not preclude efforts to reduce its volume where this is the more efficient.

Paper products—cardboard, newspaper, and miscellaneous—make up about half of the refuse at sampled municipal dumps. Clearly much of this is a candidate for reuse. Metals, a much smaller share, also could be reused if economical collection and sorting can be devised. We may have to wait until some future scarcity compels it. Lately two types of containers, nonreturnable bottles and aluminum cans, have attracted attention because of their nondegradability in the environment and low salvage value. Junked automobiles can be reduced to scrap by improved techniques, but the scale required is generally large and the entire process subject to the vagaries of the scrap metal market.

Disposal of household wastes follows fairly standard routines of burning or burial after collection. Improvements in these techniques must be pursued in order to minimize the burden on other media (e.g., air pollution from burning), to minimize health danger (rats, flies), or to find ways of using residual products. In fact, more efficient incinerators (including use of by-product heat) could greatly reduce volume and simplify the disposal problem.

Noise. Aircraft are becoming a significant factor as a source of noise as well as in air pollution. Noise from existing planes in the vicinity of airfields already is the subject of frequent citizen complaint and numerous lawsuits.

The question of the SST has become a *cause célèbre*, for it threatens damage to property and wildlife as well as to peace of mind.

The whole problem of noise has attracted growing attention. It is well established that severe or sustained exposure to loud noise can impair hearing. At much lower levels, many people suffer from loss of sleep or nervousness. Other biological species may be even less tolerant than humans. Comparatively few emitters of noise pose the danger of acute damage to health at the distances from which we hear them and we should be able to restrict the location of those. It is in the more subtle area of ill-defined or difficult-to-measure damage to hearing and health and in the varying tolerance of noise (or preference for it) among individuals that we encounter our problem. The noise threat of most interest to us comes from urban, industrial, airport, and highway sources that are often quite diverse and difficult to control except by broad spectrum regulation. Design of equipment also offers possibilities for reducing noise levels.

Accidents. Accidents of all kinds are a part of the world we live in and their effects cannot always be confined to the site. We have already discussed the possibility of accident at a nuclear power plant, which could affect large numbers of people, and the environmental consequences of the escape of pesticides. The increased use and transport of radioactive materials, pesticides, poisonous chemicals, etc., make it certain that accidents will occur, on both land and sea.

The line between environmental hazard and industrial accident is hard to draw. If a uranium miner incurs lung cancer from exposure to radon daughters we are quick to note the environmental cause. But the chances are that his work is replacing that of a coal miner who is regularly exposed to more familiar but no less lethal hazards. We probably should distinguish between industrial hazards relating directly to the work environment and those that escape the site. Presumably the industrial risk can be defined and the worker can take his chances on the job if he feels well-enough compensated. In practice many lack alternatives or are ill-informed concerning work hazards. By the same token, many of us may tolerate environmental hazards properly defined because we are tied to a job in an area where they prevail.

Poisoning. Exposure to lead and mercury poisoning has attracted much recent attention. More recently cadmium and vanadium also have been accused, although little is known of their dispersion or effects. Lead poisoning has a history dating back to Roman times and in the modern era it has been associated mostly with paint. Our principal exposure to lead now comes from its use in gasoline and subsequent discharge into the environment. Some is inhaled and additional amounts move through food into body tissue. Lead is not highly mobile and is found in much greater concentrations in the air and plants near roads and freeways, and in the bodies of people who frequent those areas. So far damage has not been established at the levels to which we are customarily exposed, but there is no assurance that we escape it, either. Some argue that there may be a threshold below which we suffer no damage. No one claims that it is good for you. Present intentions are to remove lead from fuel or greatly reduce the amount, not merely to avoid possible damage to health but also to reduce air pollution from automobiles.

Mercury is far more damaging. Even in very small amounts it does irreparable damage to the brain. Environmental sources have been seed grains treated with mercury fungicides and improperly used for human or animal consumption, and diverse uses in the chemical, paper, and other industries. Industrial discharges of mercury to water have led to its incorporation in aquatic food from which it is passed to humans. The most spectacular case to date is in Japan where many have been affected. In the United States fish from several inland waters as well as ocean swordfish have been declared unsafe because of mercury contamination. Although so far we know little of its extent, plainly this is a threat to be taken seriously. Since mercury is not a common material it should be possible to control its use on land, but its presence in ocean species suggests possible natural sources or types of biological magnification which are very disquieting.

The list of threats could be extended to drugs, food additives, and other materials over which we have little individual control. In all too many of these cases we know little of the possible long-term effects. Witness the parade of suspects—cyclamates, cleaning enzymes, asbestos dust from brake linings, rubber particles from tires, monosodium glutamate, Orinase, and so on. Many who are disproportionately concerned about well-publicized environmental hazards blithely continue to expose themselves, willingly or no, to countless other insults which in time may prove equally damaging.

Selected References

Anderson, R. J., Jr., and T. D. Crocker. "Air Pollution and Housing: Some Findings." Paper 264 presented at Institute for Research in the Behavioral, Economic and Management Sciences, Krannert Graduate School of Industrial Administration, Purdue University, December 1969.

Bower, Blair T. "The Economics of Water Quality Management." Remarks prepared for presentation at the International Scientific Symposium on Computers and Water Resources Management, Montpellier, France, May 27-29, 1970.
Council on Environmental Quality. *Ocean Dumping: A National Policy.* A Report to the President. Washington, D.C.: Government Printing Office, October 1970.
──────. *Toxic Substances.* Washington, D.C.: Government Printing Office, 1971.
Environment, vol. 13, no. 4 (May 1971). Articles on mercury, pp. 2 ff.
Greenfield, S. M. *Science and the Natural Environment of Man.* Santa Monica: The Rand Corporation, February 17, 1969.
Kneese, Allen V. "Economics and the Quality of the Environment: Some Empirical Experiences." In *Social Sciences and the Environment.* Boulder: University of Colorado Press, 1968.
Kneese, Allen V., and Blair T. Bower. *Managing Water Quality: Economics, Technology, Institutions.* Baltimore: Johns Hopkins Press for Resources for the Future, 1968.
Lave, Lester B., and Eugene P. Seskin. "Air Pollution and Human Health." *Science,* vol. 169, no. 3947 (August 21, 1970), pp. 723-33.
"Lead in the Air." *Environmental Science and Technology,* vol. 3, no. 6 (June 1969), p. 529.
Löf, George O. G., and John C. Ward. "Economics of Thermal Pollution Control." *Journal, Water Pollution Control Federation,* December 1970, pp. 2102-16.
Marx, Wesley. *The Frail Ocean.* New York: Ballantine Books, 1969.
Parker, F. L., and P. A. Krenkel. (Referee: D. B. Stevens). "Physical and Engineering Aspects of Thermal Pollution." In Richard G. Bond and Conrad P. Straub, eds., *Critical Reviews in Environmental Control,* vol. 1, issue 1. Cleveland: The Chemical Rubber Company, 1970.
Rudd, Robert P. *Pesticides and the Living Landscape.* Madison: University of Wisconsin Press, 1964.
Shacklette, Hansford T., Josephine G. Boerngen, and Robert L. Turner. *Mercury in the Environment: Surficial Materials of the Conterminous United States.* U.S. Geological Survey Circular 644. Washington, D.C.: Government Printing Office, 1971.
Shurcliff, William A. *S/S/T and Sonic Boom Handbook.* New York: Ballantine Books, 1970.
United Nations Economic and Social Council Committee on Natural Resources. "Natural Resources Development and Policies, Including Environmental Considerations. Report of the Secretary-General. Addendum: River Discharge and Marine Pollution." E/C.7/2/Add. 8/Rev. 1. January 27, 1971.
U.S. Department of Health, Education, and Welfare, Public Health Service/Environmental Health Service. *Danger in the Air: Sulfur Oxides and Particulates.* National Air Pollution Control Administration Publication no. 1. Washington, D.C.: Government Printing Office, 1970.
Vellentyne, J. R. "Phosphorus and the Control of Eutrophication." *Canadian Research and Development,* May-June 1970, pp. 36-49.
Woodwell, George M. "Toxic Substances and Ecological Cycles." *Scientific American,* vol. 216, no. 3 (March 1967), pp. 24-31.

SIX

COPING WITH
ENVIRONMENTAL PROBLEMS

As we have seen in reviewing the causes, nature, and extent of environmental threats, the serious problems that we already face are small compared to those we can expect in the future if present trends continue. What can we do to head off further deterioration, or perhaps disaster?

In trying to answer this question it is helpful to split it into its long-term and its more immediate aspects. The long view goes into the whole range of human aspirations, values, and ways of thinking about population, income and its distribution, use of materials, man's place in the balance of nature, and other elusive profundities. We shall look at some of these questions—no work of this scope could attempt to explore them thoroughly—in the next chapter. Here we shall consider some of the things that can be done now.

Some of the technological possibilities for dealing with specific problems have been noted in the two preceding chapters. In this chapter we shall be concerned with possible directions for technological advance and with incentives and institutional practices that will help us alleviate the problems. Attention is weighted on the side of amenity and health considerations of more immediate concern to us, of shorter-term or continuing problems rather than irreversible or cumulative ones, of local or national rather than global concerns. Within this range, however, we confront a large share of the problems that give us most annoyance, and success in dealing with them may postpone the arrival of more serious environmental congestion or of global effects that would present us with difficulties of a different order.

Broad Approaches

Consequently, our concern here is with situations in which foreseeable technical research, definable regulations, economic incentives, and systems of organization can make a real difference. Such measures have the potential of allowing us to meet most of our problems over the next 20 or 30 years without incurring serious degradation of the environment. At least this is true for advanced countries like the United States where population growth is moderate and rising income can be diverted to environmental correction. The prospect of truly intractable problems lies farther down the path of exponential growth.

No one can lay out policies sufficiently comprehensive to deal with the problems of today and tomorrow. At best we can offer some indication of the kinds of choices we face and the sorts of considerations that might govern choice. If the rules and the technology that we now have are ill-suited to our changed circumstances, the constructive response is to amend them rather than seek out scapegoats and flay them to no real purpose. Also, it must be clearly understood that even if we can eliminate all of the irrationalities and inefficiencies in the way we do things the consumer will pay the net cost of further measures to protect the environment.

Collective Decisions. In a democracy like the United States the first require-ment for policy formulation is widespread public awareness of the nature of the issues. While the technical complexities of environmental problems often are too much for the average citizen, the quality problem can be related in understandable terms to the nature and magnitude of our consumption, to the environmental standards we want to maintain, and to the kinds of trade-offs required to attain them. It would be helpful if we could discuss our alternatives more often in terms of dollars per month on the electric bill or cents per passenger mile traveled rather than in strictly emotional terms.

Our society has always been wary of compulsion; understanding and voluntary action will go part way toward correcting environmental ills. If the Woodstock generation would pick up its trash, the appearance of many a public place would be greatly improved. Yet while responsible individuals, firms, and government entities can do much to improve environmental quality, it remains true that in a competitive society those who set the lowest standards soon debase other people. We must make collective decisions on environmental standards. The very process of deciding on standards in a democratic society helps to attain the public understanding and willingness to cooperate that so greatly simplifies enforcement. Such decisions should be illuminated by awareness of economic considerations but need not be controlled by them. Within this framework the use of economic incentives often can do much to preserve individual options while still inducing the desired social performance.

Policy therefore should seek to arrive at necessary collective decisions based on widespread discussion and understanding while still striving to maintain options.

Major Objectives. A few general goals stand out. First, we want to avoid disaster, including piecemeal steps toward it. While this is most compelling with respect to human reproduction and genetics and the earth's life-support system, it is apt to be most immediate with respect to human health. The chief near-term threats are from air pollution, nuclear accident, and the numerous carcinogens that we ingest.

Health is often referred to as an absolute right—something that cannot be left to the marketplace. Although we do not leave it entirely to the market, it has an economic dimension nonetheless. To the extent that health is affected by the environment we should be prepared to take those meliorative measures whose cost is less than their economic return via reductions in morbidity and premature deaths. Most of us would go farther and demand that pollution should not seriously impair vitality or normal lifespan even if the economic cost of accomplishing this is greater than the economic value of the production gained. We would wonder at a value system that sets a pecuniary measure above life itself.

Even apart from disaster, we must give some thought to the long-run consequences of our activities. If what we do is cumulative and irreversible, then it must be weighed in a different balance than even severe ephemeral damage. Disturbance of ecological systems, extinction of species, build-up of long-lived poisons, major loss of soil, destruction of estuaries, threats to the sea, and alteration of earth heat budgets all partake of this characteristic. Even if they are not known to be disastrous, in most cases we lack assurance that they will not be, and we must be wary of incremental acts that leave us exposed to such hazard. We must take decent thought for the long run in all our actions. Again this is essentially a noneconomic decision even though attention to it will entail costs.

As a conscious long-term strategy we should emphasize recycling, partly in the interest of long-run resource adequacy in a finite world and partly to intercept residuals often harmfully discharged to the environment. Recycling is technically feasible in many areas and is economically practical at present in some—chiefly metals, chemicals, and fibers.

The recovery of dispersed materials that have reached consumers, like fabricated metals, wastepaper, and certain other residuals such as farm wastes, suffers from high costs of collection and classification. Industrial-process residuals are easier to recover, and active concern about discharge to the environment will promote more of this. In not a few cases it is discovered that with appropriate process changes, it is either economical to reclaim residuals or quite inexpensive. More systematic attention to the reclamation of metals, fibers, and farm wastes not arising from industrial plants might well reveal the same possibilities.

Recycling is not a panacea, however. The chief input that we cannot recycle is energy. Indeed, in its commonest present form as fossil fuels its use adds to the environmental burden. Extensive recycling may require much energy and, if we are dogmatic about it, the attainment of higher percentages of recovery will require disproportionately more energy. Thus recycling, apparently facilitated by cheap and abundant energy, strains against a limit. As we have seen (Chapter 4), ultimately the simple heat from energy conversion may impose a ceiling. If we sought complete reclamation of materials, this would compel stabilization of material throughput at a lower level than otherwise required. Such a view is based on the reasonable assumption that the acquisition of new materials continues to require less energy than complete recycling of the stock.

Another objective of policy is to deal rationally with the manageable. Most amenity considerations are in this class. They are not essential either in total or in particular. We can decide how much and what ones we want, and in what degree, and we must pay the price. Nonetheless, amenities are of great importance—their loss is probably what is bothering us most. While collective decisions are necessary to ensure that desired amenity levels will be available to us, we need much more sensitive means of determining what the public wants.

It is in this area in particular that the desirability of maintaining options becomes important. And it is here also that we can explore the uses of economic criteria to determine how much we want and how we shall allocate costs and benefits. Social benefits and costs are useful concepts for helping to set amenity standards and the market often is a useful allocator. Their proper role, and refinements in concept and measurement, are subtle matters which require detailed study. The admonition to "make the polluter pay" does not suffice until we know how his charge is arrived at and how those damaged by his acts fare in the outcome. In addition, the way always must remain open to determine policy on noneconomic grounds in response to considerations other than efficiency.

Finally, as an aspect of dealing rationally with the manageable, policy should aim to eliminate gratuitous environmental insults—those which have little economic rationale and are the result of inertia, antiquated practices, or lack of attention. It is hard to know how much burden of this sort we carry, but recent alertness to environmental consequences has unveiled many cases where by-product values have paid the cost of recovering pollutants and would have done so all along. It is not uncommon for added costs of only a few percentage points to be sufficient to eliminate most objectionable discharges. For example, it would cost comparatively little for slaughterhouses to refrain from dumping offal in the river or for cattle feeders to pond their manure or to arrange its transport and use. Stack particulates and slag have found markets, and strip mines often can be reclaimed at minor cost. It might even be suggested that reallocation of engineering talent in Detroit to concentrate on safer and less noxious cars could save us enormous social costs at hardly any added product cost.

A Congressional report offers some specific cost estimates for technical possibilities in the energy field: ponding or cooling towers for electrical plants may add a cost of $1-$10 per kw of capacity over present costs of $170-$200; much strip-mined land can be "reclaimed" at under 10¢ per ton of coal; and oil can be desulfurized at 25¢-50¢ per barrel, or 0.7 mills per kwh.[1] According to the same source sulfur can be captured from the stack at 0.4 mills per kwh; however, the technology for this has not been proven on a commercial basis.

These approaches are stated in general terms. Only an informed public making its wishes known can give them substance. To be effective, action will have to be focused on particular aspects of the environment—an airshed or watershed, a development project, an industrial plant or process, a major

---

[1] U.S. Congress. *The Economy, Energy, and the Environment*, A Background Study Prepared for the Use of the Joint Economic Committee by the Environmental Policy Division, Legislative Reference Service, Library of Congress, Joint Committee Print, 91 Cong., 2 sess. (Washington, D.C.: Government Printing Office, 1970), pp. 45, 100, 106–7.

technical decision, a class of products or pollutants. In specific policy situations it will be necessary to choose among technical and institutional alternatives.

The Role of Technology and Research. Let us look first at technology. Although environmentalists often view technology as part of the problem, it has another role as part of the solution. Technological advance is the basis for the economic growth that provides us with the means to attack environmental problems. Scientific talent and equipment are luxuries not available to poor countries. The very size and wealth of our economy gives us resources to study the nature of our ills. We benefit from economies of scale because much of the scientific work needed is unrelated to the size of the economy.

While technical decisions normally are within the control of industry, the public can influence the availability of technical solutions and the incentive to employ them both directly and through the sort of pressure that the institutional framework brings to bear on firms. Policy can shape the technical effort by organizing and funding work considered most critical. Government can undertake research directly where other institutions are unable or unwilling to do so. Research by government may be preferable by reason of the scale of the research or the need for tight interaction between scientists. It may also be required where existing technical competence is largely the captive of special interests who are unmotivated to explore alternatives or where private firms would be unable to capture the gains from their research and hence unwilling to undertake it. Government also has a role in stimulating, coordinating, and financing private research in universities and encouraging similar work in industry. The latter role is closely related to the establishment of environmental quality standards that give industry research efforts necessary direction. In any case, government must organize the necessary environmental monitoring and baseline studies that are required to give us early warning of adverse changes.

A systematic technological response to environmental threats must aim at reducing the amount of unwanted residuals, neutralizing those that occur, or insulating the environment from them where this is impossible. In some cases it may also be possible to enlarge the assimilative capacity of the environment and thereby reduce congestion.

The most fundamental technical approach—reduction in the amount of residuals generated—can be accomplished by changes in inputs and by process changes as well as by shifts in product mix. Recycling and the recovery of by-products may be important. Attention must be focused not only on final products but also on what is discharged along the way; such residuals cannot be treated as if they were nonexistent or their disposition costless. While economic incentives or other rules are required to provide the engineer with guides for trade-off between processes and inputs, the mere creation of a higher level of awareness of the relationship between physical throughput of materials and environmental impact may open up unforeseen possibilities for minimizing damage.

Awareness and responsibility must extend to what happens to products after they are placed in the hands of consumers. The automobile is the obvious example, but many other products, even if not contributing to environmental burden when in use, do so when discarded. It also would be appropriate to give renewed attention to the quality and durability of manufactured goods; usually the initial and terminal environmental burden of a durable product does not exceed that of a poorer quality product that needs more frequent replacement.

More systematic consideration of materials and processes used in industry would help. Where alternatives are available, their environmental consequences as well as their costs should be compared. Incentives then might be designed to favor those least offensive. Industry practice often is a matter of habit; processes used in one branch may be environmentally harmful while those used in other industries to handle analogous problems are less objectionable. Extension of best practice across the spectrum of industry could help to reduce the total problem.

When a residual is so toxic that even restricted discharge to the environment cannot be tolerated or when objectionable consequences are cumulative and irreversible, direct control of production, use, or application of the materials may be required rather than reliance upon the indirect use of incentives. This principle may apply to some pesticides, other organic chemicals, heavy metals, or land use practices.

Neutralization of residuals prior to discharge is another area where technology may make valuable contributions. The effect is little different from a reduction in volume but it is often appropriate where such reduction is infeasible. It seems especially applicable to the further treatment of wastes from sewage systems, to waste heat discharged to water, and to some residuals from dispersed sources and industry. Instead of discharging raw, harmful substances, various techniques of treatment may change them chemically, biologically, or physically to eliminate objectionable qualities. Again, the possibilities of recycling and by-product recovery may be important. Neutralization after discharge will be required in some cases, especially in the event of accidents (e.g., oil and chemical spills) and may be required in other cases to compensate for poor practice upstream in a technical process.

Containment of harmful residuals also can be effective. It may take the form of temporary storage while some process of degradation occurs or until dilution is feasible, or it may entail permanent containment, as with certain radioactive materials and many solid wastes. Generally, biological materials need only temporary containment, while for certain chemicals this will not suffice. Our normal expectation is that the pollutant is to be contained and the environment left free. Under some local circumstances in which pollutants are very difficult to control, it may prove easier to create a contained, sanitized environment. This is the practice in some industrial plants. The use of earplugs to exclude noise is another example. The specter of the domed city or the gas mask-equipped urban dweller suggests how far the sanitized environment idea could lead us.

Measures to improve the assimilative capacity of the environment are easiest to envisage with respect to water. Flow regulation and artificial aeration permit dilution or degradation of larger amounts of waste. Possibly techniques of weather modification could allow us to manipulate the atmosphere for similar purposes, but technically this is a far more formidable problem. Noise-absorbing materials and plantings can be employed to dampen sound. Earth and sea are effectively beyond our power to modify, although we may be able to use the deeper reaches of each to dispose of some categories of waste.

We have noted some of the technical possibilities of combatting pollution; the choice of means will be conditioned in all cases by the institutional setting. For example, a completely unregulated automobile industry would compel local air quality authorities to restrict auto use during critical periods—a primitive means of reducing the amount of residuals. Or an alarmed public may demand relief in the form of designed limits on discharges, placing the onus on the manufacturer. Should he be unable to meet the technical requirements and should no alternatives be forthcoming from industry, then we would be forced to consider a different transportation system—an undertaking certain to require a major government role. Such a progression toward more comprehensive and fundamental technical solutions is compelled at each stage by broadened public interest in the result and by the institutional responses to this interest.

Institutional Responses. Institutional responses can take the form of modifying economic incentives, direct regulation, actions at law, enlarged systems management, and the various instruments for education and suasion. All have their uses, but economic incentives, whose employment is most consistent both with efficiency and with individual latitude, probably have received least adequate attention.

The aim of economic incentives is to stack the deck so that the pursuit of private interest will promote the common interest in preserving environmental quality. It can be argued that in competitive markets, with a given income distribution, this mechanism leads to maximization of social welfare as interpreted by the participants in the game. It is widely recognized, however, that in circumstances where competition cannot operate, the goal of maximizing welfare must be approached by attempting to approximate the market result by other means—usually with guidance from some variant of benefit-cost analysis. Ideally, those who gain are expected to pay the cost and those who lose to be compensated.

In most situations that affect environmental quality we are making use of open-access resources not ordinarily traded on competitive markets. If we can more accurately measure and allocate costs and benefits from the use of such resources, including compensation to those damaged, we may at the same time increase the efficiency of their use, limit congestion, and add to welfare. The open-access resource (or commons) can be closed, managed to provide services to the maximum of its capacity, and its use auctioned off to those who most value it. This would appear to provide an optimum solution.

However, the closure of the commons does present a problem, for it deprives some—perhaps many—former users who may not only be uncompensated but opposed to the new use. Some may argue on efficiency grounds that the new use is the higher one in the sense that no one will bid more for the resource, but the welfare result is clouded if a former user must be deprived and not compensated at the level he feels necessary.

Moreover, there is no assurance that such a quasi-market result will conform at all to ecological standards or to the long-term needs of the race. Private holders of an asset normally try to realize their returns quickly, and under certain circumstances there is nothing to prevent them from using acquired rights to some parts of the environment in like fashion. We could hardly assume that either the long-term or nonpecuniary ecological values would automatically be served by closing the commons, and, as we have seen, equity may not be served either. What we gain is short-term efficiency in management.

This conclusion does not rule out the use of economic incentives, however. It merely suggests that the determination of social objectives must be made by other than purely economic criteria and cannot be expected to grow exclusively out of the market or its surrogates. Social objectives may have to be imposed—e.g., in the form of air and water standards. If this is done, the use of benefit-cost analysis and economic incentives within the socially imposed constraints can be a very powerful means of approaching the social objectives. Efficiency is possible within the framework of the constrained system, while questions of equity and long-term needs are resolved by other means.

Subject to these principles, there is everything to be said for making the polluter pay so long as he does not thereby purchase an unbounded right to pollute. Many variants of taxes and fees can be used. The idea of effluent charges is a useful one (where discharges can be identified and measured), provided standards are established for the quality of the receiving media and the charge is used as a method of allocating the use to be made of them. Determination of the quality standards to be maintained is only partially an economic question.

The superiority of effluent charges over subsidies has been cogently argued. If one faces an effluent charge he will be motivated to economize on costs by choosing among the technical possibilities suggested earlier. The initiative will be dispersed. Those to whom use of the environment's assimilative capacity is most valuable will be prepared to pay the most for it. The charge can be established at a level that will preclude excessive discharge being made into the medium, standards for the latter being determined by the social purpose to which it is dedicated.

Subsidies do not provide the same positive incentive to consideration of all of the myriad possible ways of reducing discharges. Suppose, for example, that a treatment plant of approved design is offered a subsidy. Even if the subsidy is 100 percent of the cost of the facility, the firm gains nothing by installing it. At a smaller percentage the firm is out of pocket for the difference. Cheaper process changes that might achieve the same environmental effect will be ignored, and there is no reward for operational efficiency in use of treatment plants. However, when combined with regulation, subsidy can speed changes in technique. Ordinarily this would be a transitional device to ease the expense of conversion. It retains the undesired effect of suppressing possible alternative technical solutions.

The use of economic incentives—whether the subsidy carrot or the effluent-charge stick—can guarantee results only when combined with regulations or standards that represent social decisions on the quality results demanded. These incentives can be used to deal both with industry and with household discharges to the environment. The effluent charge is far easier to administer, however, when dealing with industrial or municipal discharges of waste than when dealing with individual discharges. Monitoring is possible where few sites are involved but becomes burdensome when there are many or the source is mobile. At the consumer level the effluent charge is rarely practical. It might be possible to impose a charge on household heating emissions but to do so would lead to an administrative morass. A charge on auto exhausts would be even more difficult. Alternative devices would be preferable in such cases—manipulating the supply and cost of fuels or regulating the characteristics of products at the manufacturer's level. A less offensive fuel could be promoted by a tax on its competitor or by a subsidy to the preferred alternative. Engineering changes at the manufacturer's level could be promoted by regulation and (in selected cases) by technical help or subsidy.

The kind of response with which we are most familiar is government regulation. This can take the form of banning certain products, discharges, or practices or of requiring adherence to standards, with sanctions against violators imposed by the appropriate agency and level of government. Many problems that would be amenable to the use of incentives are in fact dealt with by regulation. However, where a threat is independent of the degree of congestion, regulation becomes necessary as a means of excluding an environmental insult rather than of rationing it. We restrict the use of drugs, insecticides, and the like if we deem them directly harmful, whether or not they overload the environment. Regulation may usefully reinforce a subsidy, forbidding that which the subsidy aims to correct and thereby providing necessary incentive to use the subsidy. Where dispersion of sources makes it difficult to impose charges, regulation of classes of use may provide a simpler means of rationing. Finally, it is also useful to abate common nuisances and totally irresponsible behavior. A law is the simplest recourse where the behavior of some interferes with the rights of others.

The courts have a role in adjudicating laws and administrative actions designed to preserve environmental quality. However, they also may evolve law of a more positive nature relating to common property resources. Possible extensions of law include receptivity to private class actions in defense of environmental values or more vigorous government suits for the same purpose. The appeal is to the principles of property law in asserting the general right to unimpeded enjoyment of the common property resource as a public trust. Where others' use damages this enjoyment, a "property right" has been abridged. This approach promises to be a tortuous path indeed, since any deviation from past practice will encounter the claim that someone's rights are damaged. Defense of the status quo is inconsistent with the changes required for efficient use of the resource and may impair rational management even under government auspices. However, it could become a powerful preservationist tool, exchanging for possible economic values the values (often nonmarket) of those who make the claim.

Government can play another role in preserving quality. On a number of occasions we have seen how a concerted attack on a problem under government sponsorship can yield success that probably could not have been obtained otherwise (TVA, Manhattan Project, Apollo). In these instances the size, scope, and purpose of the undertaking excluded private organizations, none of which could assemble the expertise or assert the authority to manage the project alone. Likewise, industry and private research groups are not organized (and lack authority) to consider matters on the scale of, say, national energy policy (environmental and climatic effects included) or transportation policy with the same considerations. Where common property media that receive residuals—a watershed or airshed—can be managed, only government can undertake the combination of asserting authority, providing incentives and sanctions, and assuming responsibility for the result. Thus, in mounting studies of the largest scope and in outlining policies and engaging in systems management of like magnitude, the government is the only game in town.

Some Major Problem Areas

Now let us seek to relate these general comments on technological and institutional responses to some of the major problem complexes that we face: energy, food and fiber, household and industrial wastes, and our occupation of space.

Energy. Man's ability to harness and use energy is fundamental to his mastery of the environment. When we take for granted higher income and increased population we assume both the availability of sufficient low-cost energy and our ability to manage its environmental consequences. Indeed, our ability to deal with numerous other environmental problems hinges on the use of energy.

The industrial revolution was accomplished with the use of fossil fuels and for many decades we shall still be largely dependent on them, but the longer run requires that we use nuclear fuel. The environmental consequences of this are that we shall be exchanging some of our current problems, particularly in air pollution, for the problems of managing radioactive wastes. The former are mostly health and aesthetic threats while the latter are hazards to human health and genetics. Whatever our sources of energy, we face the problem of disposing of heat.

For a long while (a century or two) we will have no problem of disposing of excess heat on a global scale. Insofar as this problem calls for action now, it is mostly along the lines of policy for holding population to an eventual figure that will permit us to maintain a high standard of consumption by employing the energy needed to recycle materials or to acquire and process low-grade ores. If we face some limit on the amount of energy that global heat considerations allow us to convert in the future, the usefulness of that energy will depend on the efficiency with which we harness and consume it.

Greater efficiency is of current interest on general grounds of economy, but often this interest is not compelling because of the low price of fuels. Energy is cheaper than it would be if its price reflected all of the environmental effects of combustion, not to mention danger to miners, unsightly mine wastes, despoliation of landscape by strip mining, acid mine drainage, and so on. Public policy appears to be headed toward making fuel prices include these costs more completely, which would encourage more efficient use of fuel.

On a local scale there may be a stronger interest in the efficiency of electric generating stations in order to minimize problems of thermal pollution. It is theoretically possible to get more usable energy out of fuel burned to generate electricity by using the magnetohydrodynamics (MHD) process. However, the research needed to perfect MHD is not likely to be forthcoming solely in order to reduce waste heat, since by various means, such as ponds or cooling towers, we can diminish heat discharges to natural waters at tolerable costs ($4-$13 per kw instead of the $2-$5 for once-through cooling).[2] Thermal pollution damages aquatic life and recreational use of water and reduces its waste assimilative capacity. There are possibilities for utilizing waste heat in space heating, sewage treatment, or in agriculture, but research will be required to establish them. Thermal pollution is entirely manageable by the effluent charge and stream standard techniques noted earlier.

Reliance upon fossil fuels inevitably results in more CO_2 in the atmosphere. We should learn more about this problem since we may wish to

[2] U.S. Congress. *The Economy, Energy, and the Environment*, p. 100.

continue using fossil fuels for a long while. Given the finite limits of fossil fuels, their value in nonenergy uses, the special adaptability of petroleum in mobile uses, and the still difficult problem of containing air pollution generated in combustion, along with the uncertain effects of CO_2 on climate, and even national security considerations, energy strategy should face up to the basic question of choice of energy sources for each use. Policy at the governmental level affecting research, pricing, and regulation of pollutants could easily shape the result. The more difficult problem is that of deciding on a strategy. In an industry where regulation, subsidy, and trade controls set the conditions of the market, human and environmental costs are poorly reflected in price, and the commodities themselves are gifts of nature for which we pay only the cost of exploitation, it is an extreme oversimplification to invoke the market as the arbiter. The market can assume a large role, but the results depend on the framework in which it operates and this is the substance of strategy.

Our best long-term bet appears to be the development of efficient controlled fusion reactors. Their use would ensure adequate fuel, reduce atmospheric pollution, and limit the production of radioactive material, and might increase the proportion of useful energy extracted from the heat generated. Pursuit of this aim requires government-supported research. At present the risks of ill effects from fission reactors seem small, although those that could occur are of the most disquieting sort. Given what we know about the consequences of fission, from an environmental standpoint there appears to be little immediate urgency about the fusion reactor so long as fission reactor technology (including fast breeders) develops satisfactorily. However, the superiority of the fusion reactor is so great from the environmental standpoint that research on its development should be allowed to proceed as rapidly as good ideas and competent scientific manpower permit.

There is much to be said in favor of reducing our reliance upon combustion. It is the principal source of air pollution—sulfur, NO_x, hydrocarbons, and particulates. We do have an alternative in the case of electric generating stations. In switching to nuclear reactors of the current type we lose some thermal efficiency (about one-third) and, therefore, may impose greater thermal burden on local waters, but this can be dealt with by other means. We release some radioactivity to the environment, but perhaps no more than now comes out the stack in fossil-fueled plants. The potential effects of accident are greater but could be much reduced if we chose. And we could avoid all of those troublesome combustion products. Any such comparison also should consider the industrial hazards of fuel acquisition, refining, and transport. Mining of any kind is a dangerous occupation and it clutters the landscape. The number of people involved and the volume of material handled with consequent hazard to the environment are far greater for fossil fuels than for nuclear, although the greater longevity of nuclear residues makes the choice less certain. So far, virtually no energy source has been charged with the full social cost of its use. An attempt to do so might well force technical developments that would alter relative competitive positions.

A case can be made for more intensified research to reduce the adverse environmental consequences of burning fossil fuel, especially coal. There are possible improvements in combustion techniques that could greatly reduce particulate discharges from coal-fired generating plants. Sulfur removal also could be incorporated more effectively at an earlier stage of the process. Further, there are possibilities of gasifying coal to produce cleaner fuel. Research might yield acceptable environmental consequences and leave coal economically competitive with nuclear power. U.S. coal reserves are vast and could be used for a long while. However, all of the environmental damage from mining would still have to be faced.

Our commitment to combustion is stronger in the case of mobile energy consumption. We could electrify the rails more completely and provide reactors for ships. No ready alternative is in sight for aircraft—a growing consumer of fuel. But the real problem lies with the automobile—our number one polluter. Here, there are alternative energy sources—gas turbines, steam, battery fuel cells, hybrids, and so on. For local traffic we could use electric cars or channel more traffic into electric-powered public transportation. Many other possibilities could be imagined for a longer time horizon. The general aim would be to procure transportation with a smaller or less noxious throughput of fuels, perhaps by concentrating combustion in generating plants where the process would be more efficient and the residuals could be controlled more easily.

As an example of what can be achieved by switching from cars to electrified rail transit, one calculation showed that for 100 million passenger miles the saving would amount to 16,000 tons of gasoline, a net decrease of 6,000 tons of CO, 1,300 tons of vaporized HC, and 200 tons of NO_x. If the power is derived from conventional thermal plants, there would be an offsetting increase in the production of SO_2.[3]

[3] Allen V. Kneese, Robert U. Ayres, and Ralph C. d'Arge, *Economics and the Environment: A Materials Balance Approach* (Washington, D.C.: Resources for the Future, 1970), p. 27.

Taxes, licensing fees, parking charges or restricting the availability of parking places, and subsidies to public transportation could all be used to shape such a change. It could be argued on good economic grounds that in some of these cases we would be doing no more than making the auto user bear the costs he imposes on the community. In fact, the automobile has shaped our whole style of life and structure of cities. It is impossible to calculate its total cost to society—or the value of the flexibility and convenience it also brings.

We can, if we wish, cut down on size and horsepower of gasoline-fueled cars, with proportionally beneficial effects. Even if we stay with big-muscled cars we could alter engines or fuel so as to reduce pollution. The steam car might be an improvement. But Detroit knows best how to produce internal combustion engines, mechanics sometimes know how to repair them, and oil companies delight in fueling them. For the time being the easiest path is to try to fix up what we have. In this case the most promising course is to set emission standards by law. A tax has been proposed on leaded fuel to curtail its use and to assist in meeting the standards. It remains to be seen whether the emission standards can be met. Moreover, past experience has shown that, while the factory product may meet them, inadequate maintenance can dilute the effect. Finally, growth in use of automobiles eventually swamps any percentage reduction in emissions. It is clear that the reign of the internal-combustion-powered private car cannot extend beyond a few decades.

Meanwhile, it is possible that the measures just described will meet our immediate needs. Air pollution from cars is principally a threat to health and amenity. In acute form it is local and sporadic. For several decades we can keep it below the limits accepted heretofore if anticipated technical changes are successful. Are such limits adequate? We do not have to answer to posterity on this question since most of the effects are those we suffer ourselves. (The effect on global climate is a question for all energy use—not just automobiles.) We should seek more sensitive ways of determining collective public preferences with respect to the aesthetic aspects of clean air, whenever possible posing the problem in terms of real alternatives with prices attached.

We do not really know the full effects upon health of long-term exposure to various levels of auto-related pollutants. How would we react if it could be shown that deaths and incapacity from this source were comparable to those from auto accidents? Only lately have we done much about the latter. Since exposure to fumes is even more unrelated to personal behavior than is accident, the need for establishing strict controls perhaps is greater.

Any longer-term solution to the problem of auto emissions will have to be found in a broader context. If we gave thought to the shape of our cities, the style of life we favor, and the transportation requirements this would impose, we could take a systems approach that would permit us a more fundamental solution. Meanwhile, at some cost in health, comfort, and convenience, we should be able to cope.

Space heating is not generally a major source of air pollution at present, in part because relatively clean fuel is burned in many areas. If resource availability compels more general resort to high-sulfur oil or coal, either directly or via thermal electricity, space heating could become a problem. Because of the difficulty in controlling emissions from dispersed sources, policy could act either to influence the type of fuel or to concentrate the source of energy. In fact, policy has favored the use of natural gas, a rather clean fuel. Gas is in limited supply and, though advances in transportation will extend its availability, eventually it will have to be replaced. A research effort aimed at gasification of coal would be justified to ease environmental burden and also to protect investment in gas-fired heating systems. Municipal central heating systems are used in some European cities and can be adopted where population density is great enough. It might be possible to employ waste heat from generating stations or industrial plants in such systems. Because of the cost of the distribution system and the requirement that it have right-of-way under streets, government franchises would be necessary and steps to ensure general use would be desirable.

The most flexible central heating source is electricity, for which the distribution system exists. The loss of heat in generation and transmission makes electric heating thermally inefficient, though we do gain efficiency in use. But in areas of severe atmospheric congestion where the choice is between clean electricity and dirty space-heating fuel, the equation changes in favor of electric heating. Private households also may have the opportunity to make use of solar heating—a still undeveloped technology but one that probably could be brought within the range of technical and economic feasibility in some areas if other energy sources become environmentally burdensome.

Industry uses electric energy for mechanical purposes and in electrolytic processing. Metallurgy is a direct user of fuel, while process heat and steam are needed in many branches. Industrial use of electricity has the same implications as other electricity uses. In metallurgical industries the special problem is the production of particulates—generally controllable—while other combustion products resemble those from fossil-fuel generating stations.

Since the remelting and refining of metal require only a fraction of the energy required to smelt it, our stock of metal may be viewed as a store of energy to be conserved if energy use limits us. We are not at that stage now. If we arrive there, it would be possible to encourage recovery of scrap metal by imposing an extraction tax on new ore.

The time when we must economize on total energy use for environmental reasons is far away. Aside from some local situations, the main reason for economizing now is to conserve the resources used. Our more general problem is to convert to less noxious sources of energy and, where that is unfeasible, to refine the fuel or retain and neutralize the emissions.

We have special aesthetic problems with regard to the siting of generating stations and transmission lines. Even if these are made entirely free of air or water pollutants and attain the highest degree of safety, few will be happy to have them as neighbors. This unavoidable difficulty can be minimized by long advance planning, public participation in decisions, and perhaps by innovations in design and landscaping. For example, it has been suggested that stations may be located offshore on man-made islands in coastal locations or underground in some cases. Transmission line rights-of-way could be shared with pipelines or other carriers and landscaped or used for recreation. It may prove possible with advances in technology to put lines underground, although with present technology the cost is prohibitive for long-distance, high-voltage lines. Because of the varying governmental agencies and jurisdictions involved in siting, it has been suggested that the companies need a single public authority that can give a positive response to a siting proposal instead of being left to deal with the many who can veto it.

Food and Fiber. Another set of environmental problems centers around the production of food and fiber. Intensified use of the land as a consequence of population growth and higher protein consumption compels the abandonment of natural cultivation in favor of new technologies with the potential for serious damage. Moreover, bringing marginal land into use and the sheer volume of farm wastes create added problems.

On a world basis there already are signs of a potential food problem. Rapid technical advance races against equally rapid population growth and against ignorance, social rigidity, and lack of capital. So far those who argue that the green revolution is no answer have yet to establish their case. Should their fears prove warranted—the pace too slow, the investment too great, the new cultivation vulnerable to disease and pest—the consequences will be visited in the first instance on hungry populations. The environment will then inevitably suffer as desperate people turn to marginal lands and perhaps injudicious use of pesticides in search of quick results. U.S. capacity and willingness to help will be limited, and serious questions may be raised about the viability of an international system for limiting environmental damage in these circumstances.

In the United States, high-productivity agriculture is a reality. Output has more than kept pace with population growth, allowing improved diet while reducing both cropland and agricultural labor force. Further population growth presumably will at some level force reversal of the trend to reduced acreage, and one can conceive of circumstances where our capacity to produce food would fall short. However, by limiting our protein intake nearer to biological requirements and by substituting among protein sources we could greatly extend the capacity to feed ourselves. The main effort in the event of food shortage, however, would be toward more intensive use of the land.

We could, if sufficiently pressed, move to a completely controlled environment for food production. Perhaps we should invest in a modest research effort on the techniques and costs of a space-age food industry. Contemplate the possibility of a glass- or plastic-enclosed photosynthetic factory. It would require a root medium, inputs of nutrients, and application of water. Naturally occurring pests would be eliminated and thereafter scant control required. Erosion would be eliminated. Production could occur throughout the year, benefiting from specially bred varieties. Organic wastes could be reprocessed and returned to the system. Contact with the outside environment would be minimal—sunlight entering, some input of water, produce emerging. Output could be controlled, certain, concentrated in space. If conventional agriculture meanwhile had been forced to bear the full costs of disposing of farm residuals, the shift could even become economic. Of course, the natural cycle accomplished all of these things—nourishing, watering, decomposing—without intervention. It is because we stand in between, intervening massively without good control of our materials, that we face environmental consequences from agriculture.

So far as these concern use of fertilizers, the most obvious policy response appears to be research and monitoring. Diminished soil tilth, if it occurs, will be progressive and discernible. We will have the opportunity to back off or move to still another technology. Likewise, the buildup of nitrogen in drinking water will not become a sudden health problem, although it warrants monitoring and periodic review. Loss of tilth can be combatted by restoring humus, which farmers presumably will do if convinced that it improves the profitability of farming. The standard of profitability would not help us,

however, where excessive fertilization might contaminate drinking water supplies or contribute to eutrophication of natural waters. So long as the
farmer's net yield improves with additional application, he is tempted to
pursue this course irrespective of its effects on water. If we conclude that
fertilizer use must be curbed to restrict its movement into water supplies, we
could reduce profligate use by a sufficiently high tax. Quite evidently there is
no need to ban the use of fertilizer if we can make it economical to limit
application to that amount taken up by plants.

The technical possibilities for controlling pesticide use, including such
alternatives as biological controls and substitution of land for pesticides, were
discussed in Chapter 4. Perhaps all of the possibilities suffer from the disadvantage that they may be more costly under present circumstances. The
broad-spectrum, mass-produced, persistent chemical can save the farmer
much time and effort.

There is room for debate on whether we deal here with an environmental
insult that is cumulative and irreversible or one where renewable assimilative
capacity must be rationed to prevent current overloading. The heavy-metal
compounds seem to fall in the first category. Despite their high physical
immobility, the fact that they can be taken up by life forms and biologically
concentrated argues for great caution in their use. Persistent pesticides degrade, but at excessive rates of application they can accumulate and cause
severe ecological damage. If species are extinguished the damage is permanent
and its implications hard to predict. Moreover, the full effects of pesticide
burden on human health are not yet known. Under the circumstances it
seems best not to treat the pesticide problem as simply a question of allocation. The farmer must surrender his right to apply persistent pesticides in the
kinds and amounts that would be most profitable to him. The simple and
obvious expedient is to limit the manufacture and sale of those pesticides
determined to constitute possible long-term threats. Or we may control their
application by allowing only licensed operators to use them under prescribed
conditions.

An energetic research effort on substitutes for hazardous pesticides would
be in the public interest. Industry can be relied upon to propose chemical
alternatives that will need to be evaluated. The proper mix will certainly vary,
depending on area, crop, and pest. Placing manufacturers on notice that their
products will be reviewed in terms of broader environmental consequences
should stimulate greater responsibility in the development and marketing of
new chemicals.

Farming areas productive under the pesticide regime may not prove so in
its absence. Relocation of production will occur. It is common practice in

U.S. agriculture to ease such shifts with government aid. And what about competitiveness? Should the American farmer be outsold by others not subject to the same restrictions? Clearly we should not allow this if pesticide use abroad is threatening global systems we value. If the damage is restricted to the country concerned, we might argue that it is their own affair and trade should proceed, but in practice U.S. farmers would oppose granting unrestrained access to domestic markets to output produced abroad under this competitive advantage.

Erosion is not now a major threat in the United States. Furthermore, at present output levels we could control it still further at reasonable cost if we wanted to give priority to this objective. If population growth, curtailment of pesticide or fertilizer use, or other developments forced us to crop more marginal land our problem would become less manageable. Moreover, loss of topsoil is permanent by the human time scale, and soil is still essential to the modified production system that we rely on as well as to the natural ecological systems (or current approximations to them).

We have combatted erosion in this country by a combination of education and subsidy, and have been assisted by the increased productivity of good-quality land. Yet past history shows that the farmer's self-interest (as he perceives it) is not necessarily strong enough to ensure care of the soil, and even today in many parts of the world rational private economic responses produce destructive uses of the land.

In this case, as with persistent pesticides, it may be necessary for policy to override the market. No market calculus can be used to justify permanent damage to the earth's life support system. Where the damage results from improper (though perhaps economic) practices of land management, the response is difficult. Education and a graded series of sanctions could be considered. We have had success with subsidy but have been favored by the economic trend. Under some circumstances it might be necessary to assert a kind of eminent domain to protect society's interest in cases where private management operating under market signals fails to do so.

Another set of problems with implications for health and aesthetics concerns the disposition of farm wastes, such as dusts, mineral salts, plant residues, smoke from burning and forest fires, and allergens. Disposition is especially troublesome in the case of farm animals.

The problem of animal wastes is entirely a matter of relative costs; the damage is mostly to amenities and to a lesser extent to health, and the technology for dealing with it is accessible. We concentrate cattle in feedlots for good economic reasons and we do not return wastes to the land because chemical fertilizers are cheaper. The inconvenience is visited on those within nose range, and on users of affected watercourses. Proper siting under guidance of zoning provisions and the principle of nuisance abatement can reduce these problems. Where operations encroach on populated areas or threaten to contaminate water, they could be held to more stringent requirements. Ponding with anaerobic degradation can protect watercourses, and chemical treatment will reduce odor. However, since the problem is likely to grow and at some scale become more objectionable, it merits research on economical and inoffensive ways of reducing and transporting wastes. If sufficient area is provided, the soil can absorb and use the effluent, and efforts should be made to distribute it to the land more economically.

Household and Industrial Wastes. Household and industrial wastes present another complex of problems. While some industrial processes burden the atmosphere, their more common route is to water and land. Likewise, human consumption of food and goods casts ultimate burdens upon these two media.

To a certain extent the receiving media are interchangeable. For example, some solid wastes that impose a burden on the air if burned could either be ground up and delivered to sewers or be disposed of as landfill. In general, human sewage in advanced countries is a burden on water, as also are many industrial process liquors. Wet garbage can go either to water or to landfill. In all cases, but especially with metal from discarded durable goods and with metallic and nonmetallic packaging materials, there are good possibilities for recycling as well as for control of volume generated.

Discharges to water threaten its quality for recreational and other uses and also threaten its ecological viability. Since water is constantly renewed by new flow and self-purification, the damage for the most part is not permanent and cumulative in any absolute sense. The problem is permanent, however, in the sense that we must always be prepared to cope with congestion and with growing pressure on the assimilative capacity of natural waters. Because sewage and liquid industrial wastes (1) are discharged at comparatively few outfalls, (2) can be diminished or neutralized with diverse technologies, (3) have few irreversible consequences, and (4) go into a medium subject to congestion, they are well-suited to the use of charges to allocate the use of assimilative capacity. Moreover, systems management, including increasing assimilative capacity, timing discharges, specialized uses of some waters, and the like, can greatly increase the efficiency of this use of water.

It is imperative, however, that objectives and water standards be set independently of pricing or efficiency considerations. Some categories of discharge may prove incompatible with other intended uses of the water and have to be forbidden. In every case the standards and objectives will be unique to each situation and the means of attaining them highly varied.

A few discharges to water do not respond well to the approach just outlined. Such compounds as mercury, other heavy metals, and polychlorinated biphenyls (PCB) are quite immobile and not readily degradable. Moreover, they are known, or suspected, to be very harmful to many forms of life, including man. In this case we face the possibility of doing permanent damage even at low concentrations. In such cases allocating assimilative capacity is no answer. Close control and regulation of the materials must be undertaken to ensure that they do not enter water until and unless we can establish some maximum level of concentration that is considered safe.

Present policy for water pollution control relies upon subsidies to municipal waste-treatment plants and on state-established standards of quality. Poor funding and weak enforcement have made the policy ineffective. A system of effluent charges would be easier to monitor and would generate funds to support regional management authorities.

Our present tendency is to concern ourselves with streams, lakes, and estuaries while still treating the ocean as a sink. We congratulate ourselves on our cleverness in diluting and flushing pollutants to the sea without too much destruction en route. Once there, we rely on the vastness of the sea to accommodate our effluent. This assumption is too lightly made. Ocean circulation periods are very slow and even slight changes of concentration can make a difference. Some inland seas (e.g., the Baltic) are not vast in comparison to the burden placed upon them. Moreover, the processes of degradation or precipitation to the bottom tend to occur in limited zones of the sea, so the ocean may not be so effectively large as we suppose. Far more should be known about these processes before we increase discharges to the sea by orders of magnitude.

Many contaminants reach the sea by drainage from land, others through interaction with the atmosphere. In restricted waters where both offenders and offended can be identified there is hope for international agreements to control such pollution. More generalized pollution of the open sea through drainage and precipitation presents greater difficulties. So far, one cannot establish serious or permanent damage through these channels; perhaps if we do, we will be more ready to act. Meanwhile there is opportunity to agree on contaminants accidentally or deliberately dumped at sea. This category would include war gases, radioactive wastes, wastes from shipping, and petroleum. Of these, petroleum is the most pervasive by reason of its ubiquity on the sea and the large volume discharged both through deliberate dumping and tank cleaning and through loss via poor practices. Also, given the scale of petroleum transportation by sea, it will be very difficult to prevent some from escaping in accidents. In all of these cases, however, we can minimize loss through regulation and design of equipment.

Beyond this, do we wish to treat the ocean as just another common property resource whose assimilative capacity is to be allocated like any other? In principle, there is no reason why we should not, assuming suitable international agreement. Yet its position as an ultimate sink places the sea in a different category from that of a stream or the atmosphere, which can be cleansed by time or by the arrest of the insult. Moreover, we know so much less about the sea than about fresh water and air that we would be hard put to figure its assimilative capacity for various burdens. In the face of this uncertainty, and until it is resolved in favor of relaxation, we would do well to require exacting standards for deliberate dumping. The same considerations should prompt us to learn more of the effects of unintentional man-made pollution of the ocean deriving from land and air.

The problems of solid waste (mentioned in Chapter 5) come chiefly from the cost of collection and the ease of littering. Public cooperation, both in reducing the demand for packaging and in refraining from litter, will be needed. Innovations in collection technology, perhaps reducing much of the waste to liquid for delivery to sewers, are one possibility. Because there are readily available substitutes for aluminum cans and nonreturnable bottles, their use could be reduced or precluded by taxing them. A tax level sufficient to subsidize the return of these containers for reprocessing might give them a chance to compete. Perhaps a simple solution of the growing problem of discarded automobiles would be a tax on new car sales to finance a bounty on junked cars delivered up for salvage. In this way the difficulties of collection and of scrap-market fluctuations could be finessed. It is hard to meter refuse. We shall have to live with the costs, and we must seek to improve both collection and recycling technology while reducing volume by changes in packaging standards and the like.

The Use of Space. Many of our problems are aggravated by the way in which we occupy space. Our dilemma is that this pattern, while shaped by inertia and perhaps by unwise incentives, nonetheless appears to respond to public preferences and economic realities. It may be, however, that this appearance is the result of the way we have structured things and of our failure to provide attractive and viable alternatives.

Some of the paradoxes were touched upon in Chapter 2. With farming in retreat and parts of the countryside becoming depopulated, we nonetheless place growing burden on wilderness areas, threatening their very use as wilderness. Urban growth has a perverse tendency to occupy flood plains and spread out over the best adjacent farmland, forcing agriculture to decamp to less favorable sites while the city contends with flood and fumes in the low valley. Land developers pay little attention to the integrity of the landscape or the best uses of its physical features. Urban growth concentrates in a few giant cities of dubious efficiency, whereupon those who are able hasten to escape to the suburbs. Many who remain closest to the commercial and cultural attractions of the city are least likely to enjoy them.

Meanwhile, almost all rational land planning is defeated by dispersed owners with speculative objectives. Private calculations of costs and gains by anonymous corporations guarantee that most new urban building will have no architectural distinction and as cities expand beyond the control of those who once assumed responsibility for them, no one cares anymore. They are left to decay. In this morass most of us seek occasional escape according to our means, and we frustrate each other in the process.

We all have a stake in the countryside not measured by the market or compensated in any way. The countryside is landscape. A functional, well-tended farming area is a source of as real aesthetic pleasure as any natural area—it was even more beautiful to our ancestors locked in combat with the wilderness. Policy has only the weakest leverage here. An attractive countryside requires a vital and prosperous farm economy. But it also requires operators who know and love the land and conform to its harmonies. These traits are not likely to grow out of exclusively commercial considerations. While zoning and related land use regulations can retard degradation of the landscape, policy cannot produce lovers and artists.

Most city problems are not environmental quality problems in the strictest sense—they are quality-of-life problems. But we aggravate environmental problems by this pattern. Urban sprawl made possible by the automobile in turn makes mass transit difficult and guarantees that we will have all of the attendant discomforts and hazards of the auto age, the worst of which at present are air pollution and exposure to accident. The efficiency of cities, which depends on quick and easy interchange of people and of goods, is sabotaged as more and more energy is lost in commotion. Well-publicized transportation and utility planning pursued with determination could be a powerful instrument for channeling growth in more rational directions.

The difficulty is in staying with the plan when pressures grow for departing from it. For example, Ian McHarg's "plan for the valleys" northeast of

Baltimore is premised on the idea that orderly, controlled growth could be more profitable than unrestrained speculation and that those whose land remains undeveloped as required by the plan will be compensated by profits made elsewhere. It remains to be seen whether necessary private and government structures can be devised to ensure this result. If they cannot, then we may be compelled to seek other measures restricting property rights.

The opportunity to make a speculative killing is cherished in our society. Viewed as a device for converting rural to urban land, it is difficult to see that it serves any great social purpose. The opportunity for gain arises from the process of growth itself, and it cannot be argued that its direction by speculative motives gives the best result. More often than not it simply provides added incentives to manipulate policy in quest of private gain. The aim of control and planning would be better served if the gains in value resulting from the social process of urban expansion were retained by the public. This principle has been employed in England with some success and it could be adopted in the United States by means of any of a number of devices such as taxes or public acquisition.

Restructuring the center of the city is a more formidable task than controlling the growth fringe. In the center, established values are at stake and ownership is highly dispersed. Assembly of parcels large enough for major reshaping requires use of the power of eminent domain. Policy on transportation and zoning can influence the result, but in addition a clear concept of function is needed. It is impossible to think of housing for low-income people in the city without subsidy, and such people cannot move out unless the fringe is willing to accept them. Social policy becomes indistinguishable from environmental policy.

Cities impose heavy burden on the environment—creating air pollution, heat islands, sewage disposal problems, and difficulties for solid waste management. Yet at the same time concentration has environmental advantages. It permits the use of mass transit, eliminating a major insult to air; sewers and utilities allow us to control effluents either at the outfall or by way of shifting the types of fuel used; and there are marked advantages of scale in disposing of both liquid and solid wastes. As society moves away from dependence on the assimilative capacity of the natural environment toward more complete recycling, the environmental disadvantages of concentration are reversed in favor of the technical advantages of concentrated collection and processing of residuals. Also, we leave more of the landscape open for use by other species and for our own enjoyment of a pastoral experience. If people were offered a safe, convenient, and agreeable cityscape with ready access to a distinct and uncluttered countryside, would they be less insistent on their own half acre? We cannot know, for the offer is not made, but if the answer should be yes, then a great many environmental problems would become easier to handle.

If city sprawl could be contained with results favorable to the efficiency and livability of the city and also to the appearance and accessibility of the countryside, we would have taken an important step toward preserving our essential option of contact with nature.

People seek a wide range of satisfactions from outdoor recreation. Some want strenuous activity, novelty, or privacy while others seek the reverse. Therefore recreational uses may be incompatible with each other—water skiing and swimming, bird watching and hunting. It is impossible to provide a full range of outdoor experiences at the same site. Most people would be better served if the facilities were specialized. Rather ordinary but conveniently located areas can be adapted for outdoor recreation of the intensive-use kind or for many specialized purposes. It should not be necessary to visit a unique national park simply to go camping.

Facilities for the mass market can be provided fairly easily and probably could be financed in large part by user fees if demand is strong enough. Separation of different types of use also can be helpful in reconciling conflicts with other uses like mining, lumbering, or power production. The less exacting kinds of recreational demand can often be made compatible with these other activities. Seashore, especially in convenient locations, is not easily provided, and we will need to take steps to ensure public access. Moreover, as time passes, increasingly we will find that much land has greater value in recreational use than as a source of materials or energy, which we can derive from less attractive areas. In sum, with sufficient investment and planning we should be able to meet most of our outdoor recreational needs far into the future.

Off in the back country, however, lie areas of wilderness of unique scenic value, especially inspiring to some and valuable to all of us as biological preserves. Can they be protected from the miner and the dam builder, or even from the press of the leisured, monied multitude hungry for wilderness experience, which demographic and economic growth will loose upon them? Even on strictly economic grounds the demand for wilderness, as wilderness rather than as a supplier of goods and materials, will increase. Its qualities are unique and irreplaceable, and their value grows. At the same time we have other sources of materials and energy, often available at falling cost. Thus, in many circumstances preservation can even make economic sense.

Whatever the outcome of the economic calculations, many, perhaps most, of us will want to retain our option to use the wilderness in its natural state and to pass it along in that condition to our heirs. If wilderness is preserved and its use rationed, the market—through entrance fees geared to turn back all but the desired number—would provide one way of rationing. Since there is no cost of production, supply is not expandable, and all is part of a common heritage, one may ask why market allocation is the equitable solution. Perhaps some more egalitarian sharing combined with the requirement of a demonstrated capacity to respect the wilderness would be a preferable approach.

How Much Might the Job Cost?

The environmental problem is often posed in terms of "the cost of cleaning up the environment" and figures are offered purporting to estimate this. They must be viewed with great skepticism. Even conceptually the meaning of cure and cost is ambiguous. Are we to restore the environment to some pristine state? (An impossible hope.) To some previous level? To some tolerable level? We would need to specify in detail by pollutant and receiving medium what conditions we seek. With respect to cost, what time span is allowed for making remedial investments? What are operating costs? What rate of investment will be required thereafter to maintain desired conditions? If we speak of net cost, our computations will have to distinguish supplemental outlays from those we would be making just to maintain present conditions. If we succeed in reducing the environmental damage that society already incurs, perhaps in amounts greater than the cost of the cure, is it appropriate to speak of new environmental investments as net costs?

Even if we are able to resolve the above questions satisfactorily, there still will be enormous difficulties of estimation. We do not know the source or volume of pollutants discharged at present, or the extent of damage. While in some cases we could determine investment and operating costs required to meet standards by using known technology, we can be sure that readiness to invest on a large scale would invite unpredictable technical changes of a cost-reducing nature. This tendency would be reinforced if the scope of analysis, planning, and management were greatly expanded, as we might expect in case of serious dedication to action. And this makes no allowance for the possible changes in consumption patterns that would occur if product price were to reflect the cost of environmental damage.

Allen Kneese, in a paper for an Atlantic Council-Battelle Institute conference, attempted a rough calculation of the cost of achieving "substantial" reductions in environmental pollution over the years 1970-75. His figures, arrived at by what he describes as "drastic rounding and heroic judgments," are shown in Table 5. About three-fourths of the total is investment, much of it for catching up with neglected problems. There is no allowance for savings through sophisticated management approaches or major technical advance. Further, these figures do not represent the cost of doing a complete job, particularly for advanced sewage treatment.

Table 5. Rough Estimates of Increase in Costs During Period 1970-75 to Achieve "Substantial" Reductions in Environmental Pollution, Including Investment and Operation Cost

($ billion)

Water	
Treatment of municipal sewage	12
Reducing nonthermal industrial wastes	6
Reducing thermal discharges	3
Sediment and acid mine drainage control	3
Reducing oil spills, watercraft discharges, and other miscellaneous items	1
Added reservoir storage for low flow regulations	1
Separating storm and sanitary sewers	40
Total	66
Total without last item (industry share of this may be 50%)	26
Air	
Controls on stationary sources (1/2 industrial)	5
Mobile sources:	
To modify refining and distribution of gasoline	2
Engine modifications	2
Added fuel costs	1
Total (industry share of this may be 2/3)	10
Solids	
Increased coverage of collection	1
Increased operating cost, including environmental protection costs	3
Total (industry share? Nothing included for increased recycling of autos and other things)	4
Other	
Control of heavy metals (mercury, cadmium, etc.), stopping use of persistent pesticides, improving water treatment, control of pollutant-bearing soil runoff, control of feedlot operations, etc. (a sheer guess)	15
Total	95
Total without storm sewer separators	55

Source: Allen V. Kneese, "The Economics of Environmental Pollution in the United States," in Allen V. Kneese, Sidney E. Rolfe, and Joseph W. Harned, eds., *Managing the Environment: International Economic Cooperation for Pollution Control*, Praeger Special Studies (New York: Praeger Publishers, Inc., for the Atlantic Council of the United States and the Battelle Memorial Institute, December 1971).

The entire cost of the computed items, even including the expensive separation of storm and sanitary sewers, would require less than 40 percent of the expected increase in GNP over this period. Over a longer period the fraction probably would be lower. Again, it must be stressed that the figures are intended only to illustrate the roughest order of magnitude of required spending and should not be interpreted as accurate estimates. The important conclusion is that much can be done at tolerable cost, although it should not be pretended that spending at this rate would be painless.[4]

The assertion that pollution control can be had at tolerable costs assumes that we will not be dogmatic or hysterical about the requirements that we place on industries or public agencies. Crash programs of doubtful necessity can be very costly. On the other hand, if we press ahead with a clear sense of direction and urgency while still allowing reasonable time to gestate necessary technical measures and to plan investments on an orderly basis, the costs can be far lower.

The Overall Prospects

We should by no means underestimate our capacity to cope with environmental problems. The technical and institutional possibilities, if properly used, offer the promise that we can deal with most of them as they arise. The most annoying sorts of degradation are those involving amenities. But these also are the most curable if we wish to pay the cost and devise the necessary policies, and the least disastrous if we do not. As with most social issues, however, there has been an ad hoc quality to our response, which has not made maximum use of our capacity to anticipate and shape events. It favors adaptations and marginal adjustments rather than fundamental cures and it carries always the risk that we shall overstay our time with these measures.

On the level of simple feasibility the major issue in defending environmental quality concerns the energy requirements. If we recycle more exten-

---

[4]After this study was completed the Second Annual Report of the Council on Environmental Quality appeared, containing an extensive and heavily qualified discussion of the cost of correcting environmental pollution. Its figures are considerably more refined than those shown here. In general, the Council indicates that costs will be higher than we have shown, but, at the CEQ figure of 1.6 percent of GNP over the period 1970-75, costs would not be so high as to invalidate our conclusion that costs in relation to income will be tolerable (*Environmental Quality, The Second Annual Report of the Council on Environmental Quality, Transmitted to the Congress August 1971* [Washington, D.C.: Government Printing Office, 1971], pp. 108-31).

sively while still seeking more goods for ever more people, we shall find both the social and the environmental cost of energy becoming burdensome. Technology will be hard put to find escape from this dilemma, for the record shows that our technical advances have been voracious power users rather than power savers.

In numerous circumstances our traditions of sovereignty and property restrict what can be done. At the international level this is apparent enough. We have no real way as yet of dealing with global threats to air and water—no way of appraising danger, agreeing upon the seriousness of threats and measures required, or of enforcing responsible behavior. Within the United States many environmental problems have broken the bounds of traditional government units and we are slow to devise new ones of proper jurisdiction or with validity in the eyes of the public. The concept of property, generally a constructive force in our society, becomes very troublesome in dealing with land use and planning. There is grave doubt that the farmer, possessed of the results of a geological and ecological process, and controlling the fate of other species and future generations in the way he manages the land, should operate exclusively under the guidance of short-term economic calculus. Likewise, speculation in urban land, which is the most serious obstacle to the restructuring of cities, has consequences so enormous and a social value so small that it is hard to justify. Coping with environmental threats would be far more effective if we could give a bit on these matters.

Over the longer term there is no promise that ad hoc measures, however clever and well-managed, can cope with the problems of exponential growth. The decisions that we face in that connection are the subject of the next chapter.

Selected References

Haefele, Edwin T. "A Utility Theory of Representative Government." *American Economic Review*, June 1971.
Kneese, Allen V. "The Economics of Environmental Pollution in the United States." In A. V. Kneese, Sidney E. Rolfe, and Joseph W. Harned, eds., *Managing the Environment: International Economic Cooperation for Pollution Control.* Praeger Special Studies. New York: Praeger Publishers, Inc., for the Atlantic Council of the United States and the Battelle Memorial Institute, December 1971.

Krutilla, John V. "Conservation Reconsidered." *American Economic Review*, September 1967.

Sax, Joseph L. *Defending the Environment: A Strategy for Citizen Action.* Introduction by Sen. George McGovern. New York: Alfred A. Knopf, 1970.

Squires, Arthur M. "Clean Power from Coal." *Science*, vol. 169, no. 3948 (August 28, 1970), pp. 821–28.

Tybout, Richard A., and George O. G. Löf. "Solar House Heating." *Natural Resources Journal,* vol. 10, no. 2 (April 1970), pp. 268–326.

SEVEN

SOME
LARGER CONSIDERATIONS

Up to this point we have seen how human demographic and economic activity adds to the environmental burden, have examined the nature and extent of some of the environmental threats arising from it, and have looked at means for coping with certain of the threats. Our perspective has been limited to current and foreseeable threats and to existing or prospective technology. The long sweep of human history is of limited value in the assessment of our new problems. The exponential nature of growth in population, economy, and technology now gives us a situation without precedent.

However reassuring our ability to deal with this situation in the intermediate future, a longer-range view offers less assurance. Many of the environmental insults that now are tolerable will become intolerable in the future, and mankind will face basic decisions that so far it has been able to postpone. Moreover, the response to these questions, even within the lifetime of many of us, will condition the future options of the race. Although we cannot hope to resolve many of these issues, it is appropriate to call them into discussion.

Areas of Ignorance. Time and again our examination of certain threats (such as radioactivity, pesticides and some types of chemicals, and global climate and heat) has brought out the extent of our ignorance about long-term conse-

159

quences. Ignorance is an intrinsic part of our problem. We need both a strategy to diminish it and tactics for proceeding in the face of it.

Apprehensions for the long future arise principally from the exposure of living things, men included, to low concentrations of environmental hazards over extended periods. We are more likely to be alert to acute concentrations whose effects, if harmful, will be detected more quickly and to undertake remedial measures promptly. Longer-term consequences of low concentrations are harder to establish and to relate to causative agents. In some cases the effects may not become evident until certain thresholds of time and concentration are reached. To require that new substances be tested long enough at low enough rates to establish their harmlessness (guilty until proven innocent) would be to preclude their development and use in many cases. The testing period might span the entire life of the exposed population. When could we be sure? What firm could wait so long before beginning to realize a return on its investment? We have a situation where the pace of technological advance far outraces that of human response. Moreover, we introduce new substances into the environment with a frequency that greatly complicates our problem.

One response might be to accept a slower pace of change. This would mean deferring the use of technologies that introduce new residuals until they had undergone long periods of testing. If such advances could not be rather promptly employed the incentive to develop them, at least in the private sector, would be lost. Government research still could move along, but its élan also would diminish with delayed application, and public support could be expected to shrivel. In this event the assumption of rapid technical progress, which buttresses most of the optimistic hopes for our society, would need to be modified.

It is far more likely that we will continue to experiment on ourselves. If so, our aim should be to do it more intelligently and perhaps more cautiously. We could increase the monitoring of low-level residuals as they move in the environment and affect living things. In many cases this would call for developing more refined measurement of trace amounts, making more detailed studies of the dynamics of the oceans and atmosphere, and tracing the biological record of residuals as they move in and out of living organisms.

Although we can monitor, we still are often unable to test the effects of long exposures at low levels with much confidence; we need a better basis for predicting the likely results. This points toward great effort at understanding what goes on within the living cell—how the controls over the basic organic chemicals are exercised and what is likely to disturb them. While our predictive success will never be perfect, it should be possible to reduce the degree of uncertainty that now attends much of our residuals-producing activity. Until better prediction of consequences is possible, it will prove very difficult to accomplish the public purpose of reducing damage from low concentrations of residuals.

Although we must rely on science, it is not well structured to provide the answers we need; in fact it adds to the problem as fast as it provides solutions. The intense specialization within science leaves very few persons of scientific bent with the necessary breadth of interest to perceive the many facets of environmental problems. The very analytical technique of science does not favor unifying views that reach beyond the specialties. Who, then, is to advise the policy maker or the larger public? Perhaps the inherently interdisciplinary nature of environmental studies will encourage the growth of a less-specialized group of scientists whose broader interests will bring them into easier communication with their brethren in the humanities. Society can stimulate this development, if it chooses, by providing institutional and financial support. Yet science, and its offspring, technology, have a dynamic of their own. They will continue to throw up discoveries that enhance man's power to manipulate the environment; our capacity to understand their implications will always lag.

Man's View of His Place in Nature. Can we accompany our increased power to manhandle nature with sufficient wisdom to do it in our own interest? Throughout our biological history we have learned slowly, incorporating our wisdom into custom, taboo, and institutions. If we erred, we did so at considerable penalty to ourselves and to other species, but for most of that time we lacked the numbers and instruments to wreak catastrophic damage to God's creation. This is no longer true, but the change came so recently and so fast that our inherited wisdom no longer appears to serve as a useful guide. If man is to find his place amidst rapid change that he seems unable to arrest, perhaps he needs a new concept of his role.

It has often been observed that Western religious tradition grants man dominance over nature, thereby setting him apart from it. For most of our history we have had to wrestle to assert our dominance and never have had to face the consequences of achieving it. Eastern tradition has not made the distinction between man and nature, seeing man rather as part of the web. It also has had a strong element of fatalism and passivity—hardly appropriate to our situation—in which man is not seen as an active agent of change. Neither Eastern nor Western view seems well suited to our present needs.

Man is still an animal, a living thing, entirely interdependent with the web of life. Awareness of this seems essential not only to our survival but also to our happiness. Science now permits us to become the manager of the ecosystem. While we have great power over how it shall be run, including the power to destroy, we have no power to change its inner rules. We are not gods, but merely stewards of the gods. To be a good steward, to grow in wisdom as well as strength, is challenge enough for us.

If man sees himself fated to be manager of a system of which he is part, then many other things fall into place. First of all, other life assumes an intrinsic value. It cannot be measured solely in terms of its usefulness to a separate set of human purposes. Man is entitled to defend his niche, but he must restrict his numbers and occupancy if he is to allow space for others. The steward's role allows full play to human curiosity in understanding the system, its requirements for viability, and the significance of human activity within it. Science becomes not a weapon of war on nature but a form of worship—an attempt to comprehend the interrelatedness of things. Through such comprehension man arrives at a more confident understanding of his own role in the grand harmony where he becomes a restrained and benevolent leader. Rather than being the measure of all things man is knowingly and willingly fitted to the measure of things and thereby gains bounds and limits within which he can live.

The kind of short-term calculus by which we make decisions now will not serve us well as manager of a timeless system. We are very conscious of history, but for the most part we live by ad hoc and short-term arrangements. Like most animals, we gratify current wants. True, we go beyond the animal in giving thought to the morrow, and in our individual behavior we may even pretend to plan for a lifetime, yet we have no institutions and no methodology for planning beyond such a span. Our range of vision no longer is adequate to match our power. We drive beyond the beam of our headlights. We cannot rely upon the body of custom and taboo which long ago supplanted so many of our instincts. Instead we are compelled to press on and we need principles to guide us.

When dealing with immediate amenity and health considerations, our limitations of vision may be inconvenient and perhaps even disastrous, but most of the consequences are visited on the current generation of offenders and do not threaten the race or other life. We can use familiar methods to estimate benefits and costs and evaluate current as against deferred consequences. This is no mean accomplishment, and properly handled it can alleviate many of the most annoying environmental problems.

What we lack is any device for evaluating long-term cumulative or irreversible consequences of our actions. We have no way of mediating between generations or between man and other life. Economics, which has proved so valuable a tool in making short-term decisions where human wants are the supreme counter, is a weak reed when we extend our horizon. The economist can provide no rationale for decisions for the very long term. While the concept of option demand may be further developed along with evaluation of the desire to leave a legacy, at best these refer to the next generation or so. The true perspective of the economist is that in the long run we are all dead. The economist, happiest with a simultaneous market, exhausts his boldness when he looks out twenty years and approaches it a year at a time. We have no economics for the next thousand years.

By contrast, the ecologist looks far out—and trembles. The ecologist who often appears impractical when dealing with current problems and a stubborn preservationist when addressing the remote future, nonetheless has an appreciation for the integrity of the system. He uses a time frame appropriate for dealing with intergenerational problems. If we think of the welfare of the race and of other life rather than that of individuals in a current generation, then we are hard put to justify actions that might do permanent damage to gene or the life support system. Acceptance of this restraint would be consistent with the idea of man as the ecosystem manager who sees his own future as part of it and it would provide a guideline for use in facing many other problems without eliminating flexibility. It does not make us mere preservationists, but it does favor restraint.

What is involved here is somewhat different from the problem of the consumption of nonrenewable resources. Past generations have mined our richest veins, cut the virgin forest, and extended outward from the best lands. In our time this process accelerates. In a finite world do we not thereby deprive future generations of the earth's usufruct? We have sought justification for our behavior in the argument that we have appropriated the earth's natural capital and transformed it into physical, intellectual, and scientific capital at a rate that has made resources ever more accessible. We bask in the comforting glow of progress and see future generations as undeprived by our consumption. By contrast, if we see human life as dependent on other life and human value as part of a life system, we can take no such comfort from actions that damage the life system, whatever the effect on current living standards.

The Population Problem. "Be fruitful and multiply," we are commanded. If we allowed ourselves to impute purpose to nature, reproduction would certainly rank high. In any case, it is the first requirement for success of any species, and the enormous profligacy of nature in this regard is cause for awe. What irony that just as man escapes predator and pathogen and achieves great reproductive success he must deliberately limit his numbers! Yet there is no doubt that he must do so lest he destroy not merely himself but other life besides. The arithmetic of exponential growth rates is sufficient evidence of the need for restraint. The old objectives of high birth rates—family survival and security, and national or social extension—are no longer compelling. They survive in some cases as relics. The religious sanction still has some grip, but it too is fast assuming the character of a relic.

It is hard to make a positive case for increased population. In modern societies security derives from the social system rather than the family, and national power is a function of income and social structure rather than number of soldiery. Moreover, progress to modernity is impeded by rapid increase in numbers. In terms of occupancy of space, draft on resources, insult to environment, and threat to other species, increased population aggravates our problem. Whatever the income level of the population, this proposition holds. It would be scant comfort to anyone to argue that by reducing or equalizing incomes we could accommodate more people. Why more?

Demographers point to the transitional problems incurred in moving from a rapid growth rate to a stationary (or declining) population. But if we must reach that stage at some point—and no one denies that proposition—then the transitional problems must always be faced. If we consider the problems of moving to a net reproduction rate of 1, would it not be more sensible to face them sooner while the stationary level is a tolerable one than to delay until it is not? What is gained by delay other than further indulgence (presumably) of a present generation?

Some observers are ready to concede the necessity for limitation but are hung up on the question of what is an optimum population. They may be reluctant to restrain population growth until that level is reached. Others may believe that it already has been passed, for so far there is no agreement on what is meant by optimum population. There is unlikely to be agreement, for the concept can be defined from many points of view. A conservationist might favor a greatly restricted population which would permit the preservation or enlargement of natural areas. (Of course, approach to that objective is also a function of our style of occupancy and behavior in nature as well as numbers.) An economist might stress the importance of scale and specialization, and balance this against resource scarcity in seeking a level—perhaps a shifting one—at which per capita income would be maximized. Scale and opportunities for interaction might be important to a sociologist, but again population is only one of the variables at work. The concept is a chimera unlikely ever to be apprehended.

If we delay achievement of a stationary population, what is it that we indulge? One answer might be the pleasure derived from producing and rearing children. In an optimistic and expanding society characterized by nuclear families this is an understandable proposition. Many disillusioned American parents would be inclined to question it today, however, and if the nuclear family disintegrates further, this rationale will lose much appeal. Moreover, if social approbation no longer accompanies childbearing, its appeal could be further diminished.

During the post-industrial period birth rates in northern and western Europe have declined. In that constricted space the relationship between prosperity and fecundity was too close to be ignored, and people chose the former. European growth rates no longer are explosive, although expansion has not ceased entirely. The more alarming event was the postwar surge in the United States where our more prosperous citizens chose to forgo some potential increase in family living standards in favor of more children. We have settled back from the earlier trend, and demographers believe that the prevention of unwanted births would bring us near the rate for a stationary population. Again social trends can be important; if women see opportunities opening for them in society apart from the role of motherhood, they may be less intent on playing the latter.

Yet it would be a surprising coincidence if human psychology in regard to reproduction exactly matched the need for man to restrict his numbers. The entire history of the race and the thrust of nature is different. If we must restrict, how will we do it? And if we restrict, do we also select? Indeed, can any method for restricting be neutral with respect to selection?

Our society has always stressed maximum individual freedom and has shunned compulsion, especially in such "personal" matters as family size. There was the implicit assumption that individual decisions would be compatible with social requirements. To the extent that we in the United States have had a population policy, it has been one of encouraging growth. Immigration was a principal instrument here and in other lightly occupied areas, and we never had to intervene with a policy of encouraging births. In Europe, where the stress was on military capability, financial incentives and exhortation were used to promote growth. Little serious effort at limitation as a matter of policy has been made in Western countries where the voluntary tradition prevails. Primitive societies have gone as far as infanticide and gerontocide, but no modern country would tolerate that. It is comforting to argue that eliminating financial incentives and establishing penalties for childbearing will prove effective in bringing the birth rate to a desired level. However, in the welfare state such penalties have only limited meaning; a determination to impose them might simply result in a group of ill-cared-for children who would become a social problem in their own right.

If, contrary to all nature, reproduction is rationed, is it to be done on an egalitarian basis? This would be the presumption of our society. It would be an interesting abdication by man from control of his own genetic makeup at the same time he intervenes so confidently in that of other species and indeed has unwittingly, through health and welfare measures (as well as wars), had unmeasured effects on his own gene pool. If we come to the point where a policy to restrict population becomes a social necessity, then a voluntary system or one based on financial incentives, even if statistically a success, is likely to be of very dubious value from the standpoint of the race, and the implications for another human freedom must be faced quite seriously.

Getting and Spending. In part, population policy is also income policy. If we want to prolong our period of increase in numbers, we can do so at sacrifice in per capita income. Whatever our decision about population, however, we should examine our assumptions about future income growth.

Throughout most of human history the idea of economic progress held no grip. The masses toiled. If nature was generous it yielded the rulers surplus that could be devoted to wars or conspicuous consumption (including the indulgence of a few thinkers) but for most there was no escape. Now we have learned how to learn more, and above all how to organize ourselves, and we offer rising income to growing numbers of people. Population growth conceivably can defeat this trend; some pessimists, fearful that we have depended too heavily on mining nonrenewable resources, see an end to this in any case. But the common expectation is for rising income. The expectation indeed is an important motive force at work, for in its absence we would be more patient with traditional or customary ways of doing things.

It is proper to question the assumption of infinite growth in per capita income—its environmental feasibility, uses, and meaning. It is possible to continue to raise per capita income provided we control the number of heads and maintain the necessary rate of technical progress. One may postulate some level of environmental burden which establishes a fixed limit within which we must operate if we are to maintain the life-supportive capacity of the earth. At each higher level of technical sophistication the possibilities of trade-offs between per capita income and population are increased. As we have seen earlier, at a given technical level the environmental burden is more a function of income than of population. The consumption-production pattern also will affect the trade-offs; there may be more leeway if increased income takes the form of services rather than material goods. Finally, one could not expect some technical levels to be sustainable except at relatively high levels of income because the human requirements of the highly skilled personnel, if they are to be productive, simply would not be compatible with a depressed living standard.

There are several factors other than environment that may limit per capita income growth. Resource scarcity is one possibility. Another is social deterioration; complex and highly specialized societies are especially vulnerable to this. A loss of motivation also may occur at some point. However, to the extent that we are constrained by an environmental limit it need not be a fixed limit; our assumption of technical progress permits us to expect higher curves of trade-off between population and per capita income.

The desirability of further per capita income growth is challenged by many environmentalists. This view is almost entirely limited to rich countries and usually to the favored classes within them. The rest of the world is composed of strivers. Even within rich countries, the private actions of most of the population belie any lack of interest in income growth.

Most people see income growth as widening their range of choice. It can be argued that our wants are manipulated and many of the available choices trivial, yet very few of us have a feeling of satiety. However foolish our spending in fact, we usually have an unexceptionable list of unfilled wants. This is not to contend that such wants deserve great priority or that they could not be forgone with a minimum of pain, but only that they cannot be termed valueless. Most of us prefer to exchange leisure for income-producing work. Moonlighting, working wives, ulcer-bearing executives are still well within the pattern of our society.

The social area of choice also is widened by income growth. Poverty is more easily dealt with out of a social dividend than through repartition. If we choose to engage in charity abroad, the same principle applies. And in a world where national sovereignty still is valuable, the capacity to defend it is a function of income, among other things.

The disillusionment with income growth is associated with a growing disparity between income and contentment and with doubts about the meaning of our measure of income. Folklore is full of tales of how money does not buy happiness, but the message has always related to moral imperfections which we innocents were certain to avoid. Now we find the imperfections are in society and the goal as remote as ever. Undoubtedly our single-minded pursuit of income has contributed to this mood. The rat race, the mobility and rootlessness of our communities, the consequent poverty of human relations, the voracious appetite for goods and amusements to fill the void—all are related to the needs of a high-income, technically oriented society. Some of these reactions may be related to the recency and speed of change. To arrest the growth of income might aid in the reestablishment of psychic equilibrium, but for some time the dynamics of society will militate against this, and technical progress in any case remains important to us in coping with the environmental crises.

Perhaps our sense of frustration would be less acute if our misgivings were not accompanied by constant assertions that we are ever better off. Our GNP statistics not only fail to measure important dimensions of welfare, but are becoming ambiguous measures of output itself. In contrast to an earlier period when discharges to the environment did not enter national accounts, in the future we can expect to devote a growing share of measured output to cleaning up the consequences of our activities. Even so we are likely either to suffer a loss of amenity not currently recorded in national accounts or to see it preserved at a cost that inflates the figures but not our welfare. Thus in various ways our income figures fail to reflect changes in the flow of real goods and services. The concept of income in circumstances where we deplete a stock and must undertake to cure damages needs refinement. If we move toward a recycling economy where a (perhaps) restricted flow of services is provided at higher cost, the meaning of the traditional income concepts becomes obscure.

The environmental movement shares with the consumer protection movement a concern about the quality of goods. We live in a disposable society. Not only do nondurable goods generate much of our solid waste problem; we find also that many of our durable goods are all too disposable. Our worship of fashion and change is one root of the problem. Products are not built to last, minimal attention is given to repairability, and repair may be neglected, all on the assumption that we will want something new. In consequence we have the added environmental burden of needless production and the problem of disposing of discarded merchandise. Our classic example is the automobile industry where at great cost we retool for frequent model changes that rarely incorporate new engineering. Even those consumers who resist the blandishments of Madison Avenue and seek to buy quality find the market ill-equipped to serve them and cannot shop knowledgeably among the welter of products where technical information would be necessary to a rational judgment.

Exuberant and ill-informed spending is a characteristic of our society. It is propelled by advertising, by the needs of commerce built on mass production, and by the level of income. Our wants could be equally well satisfied with less throughput of goods if our information were better and we could choose among real alternatives. Government or voluntary consumer organizations could play a more active role in making such information available. One consequence would be to diminish the power of advertising which stimulates wants and the proliferation of goods that are essentially alike. It would permit a manufacturer to benefit from making quality goods.

Consumption makes the engine go. If we reduce our purchases of some goods, does this slow the growth of income, or do we simply divert demand to new products with perhaps equally deleterious environmental effects? Many environmentalists would be happy to see income retarded and would see no loss of human satisfaction in the process. Yet there are uses for income that are not environmentally damaging. If we slow the expansion of goods consumption by insisting on improved quality and durability, we can expand our consumption in other areas—some kinds of leisure, cultural, and intellectual pursuits. Aesthetic improvements in the urban environment could absorb endless resources with minimal environmental insult; opera can be terribly expensive, as can basic research. An alteration of consumption patterns toward environmentally innocuous forms is entirely compatible with rising income and increased satisfaction. It must be admitted, however, that such a shift would be resisted. A change in values of major dimensions is implied and this is likely to occur only if the public is convinced of the failure of present sets of values. In the interim we might at least insist that the consumers of goods should pay the full social cost of their production and use.

The entire race shares interest in certain aspects of environmental quality. Only the mad or the most heedless hedonist could knowingly condone destruction of the life-supportive capacity of the earth. Few would tolerate significant damage to the human gene pool. But when we deal with human health, all sorts of amenities, and the preservation of natural areas, and juxtapose these concerns and other social demands, we encounter quite divergent interests. In consequence the willingness to undertake meliorative measures will vary greatly. Unhappily the divergencies are real in some cases and cannot simply be ascribed to a lack of understanding for which education is the cure.

The Rich and the Poor. The environmental movement is chiefly a middle-class movement confined to rich countries. The split between rich and poor over this issue prevails both within and between countries. The ability to make free use of the earth's assimilative capacity has been a factor in our per

capita income growth. The expiration of this privilege compels costly measures that will impair or retard growth. The rich can afford such measures
while the poor will be reluctant to undertake them. Again, if, at some point,
environmental burden becomes a limiting factor on income growth, then the
poor will not accept the assumption that the rich should preempt a greater
share of the earth's assimilative capacity. Are the poor to be penalized for
their late entry and denied the opportunity to catch up? If they do not
accept an inferior position, and if we are to remain faithful to ecological
principles, then sacrifice of income by the rich appears to be one implication
of our situation.

On an international scale the problem relates to the threats that cross
national boundaries—especially those that affect the sea, international lakes
and rivers, the atmosphere, and climate. In some cases international agreement is needed on the acceptable level of environmental insult. It will be hard
to come by, not merely because of scientific or philosophical disagreements,
but also because some countries are better able to bear the cost of environmental protection than others or because some place a lower value on it.
Presumably a minimal level on which all would concur can be attained. Beyond this there may be an area of bargaining, with those least able to undertake abatement, or least interested in it, demanding subsidy or indemnity in
return for such efforts. Fortunately, the problem at the international level is
not yet acute, but it will grow.

At present, rich countries use a disproportionately large share of the
earth's assimilative capacity. If we think in terms of equity rather than precedent or power, how should the global aspects of this capacity be divided
between nations? That the rich have no right to deny the poor equal access
seems a fair proposition. That such access includes different evaluation of its
importance and the right to compensation for accommodating more stringent
standards also seems defensible. But should the division then be on a per
capita basis? This would make environmental use (and therefore per capita
income) in one country dependent on the population growth of another and
would provide only the most diluted penalty for irresponsible national population policy. If the environmental constraint becomes operative after a
period of rapid population growth in less-developed countries and in the face
of widespread income inequality, it may defy any attempt at agreement
consistent with national sovereignty.

Moreover, tolerance of income inequality itself could be called into question. We have accepted it at a philosophical level (questions of power apart)
as a rough reward for effort or for differences in talent. However strained this

interpretation, it could be defended in open and progressive societies on the grounds that the poor had opportunity to improve their situation without damage to others. While we recognize that such factors as resources, history, religion, and social organization help to account for income differences between nations, we again assume that, given sovereignty, nations also have the opportunity for improvement. If we operate within an environmental constraint, this assumption may no longer be true as between nations or for individuals within them.

An environmental constraint on income growth therefore seems to point in the direction of greater income equality. At the same time, if the less-developed countries (or domestic social groups) pursue the objective of economic growth but forswear population control, others are not likely to accept an equalization that would mean continual erosion of their own income. If we must equalize at some level, at least we should try to do it without submerging.

If we return to the domestic level, the principal divergence remains between rich and poor, but the range of issues now is broadened from global systems to include all of the amenity and health concerns that are of a local nature. There is little consensus among Americans on a wide range of environmental questions. Even within the middle class, people demand more protection in their public role as citizens and voters, while in their private decisions in the market they aggravate the problem. A radicalized group of middle-class youth seems prepared to alter their personal life styles so as to relieve the environmental burden, but most of the rest remain ambivalent, sacrificing little in the way of direct personal wants while demanding impersonal action at the level of government or business. Most black Americans stand conspicuously aside from the movement, considering it a diversion from more urgent priorities. Blue-collar America wants its favorite fishing and hunting grounds preserved but is far more intent on jobs, cars, and a step up the ladder for its children than on environmental quality. The traditional handful of conservationists is augmented and their voice magnified, but they remain few. They can dramatize an issue and gain support, but their point of view has not penetrated the society in a fundamental way.

Collective Choices. Few dimensions of the quality problem are sufficiently immediate and obvious to elicit direct reaction from the public. Air pollution and water perhaps come closest. If there were an explicit disaster in a major metropolitan area, a public outcry for action could be expected. Short of that we accept what is; many have forgotten the taste of sweet air and have never known the joys of swimming in an open river. While we lament smog, we see no reason why we personally should keep the car at home more or pay more to install antipollution devices. Most quality considerations are subtle, operating insidiously over long time spans, or they involve refinements of taste and a concern for values, all of which imply a degree of sophistication.

A persistent dilemma in a free society is whether public officials should give people what the public wants or what they believe is good for it. In the matter of global threats to life support systems and genetic damage there can be no compromise. Of course, it is the responsibility of leaders to lead, and in the final analysis a society that does not accept the necessary conditions for survival will fail. Widespread awareness of the consequences of irresponsibility is abolutely essential. One must remain an optimist and believe that the public can be convinced to accept the medicine. The chances of this taking place will be greatly increased if the more emotional environmentalists will refrain from overstating their case, for the reaction to their unrelieved forebodings may anesthetize the public to the true cry. It is particularly important for scientists who accept responsibility for educating the public to state the situation carefully.

Where we deal with amenity, and even with health problems, we have more freedom of action. These must be paid for and can be bought in such quantity as we desire (always at the expense of other consumption). To the extent that they can be purchased individually we can make our own choices. Each of us plans his work-living arrangement with an eye to amenity and health. But because we circulate in society, use common arteries, rely upon public utilities, are surrounded by the noise, smoke fumes, and trash of others and in turn contribute our share to these, many aspects of amenity and health can only be decided within a framework of law and public decisions.

One possible approach—to make the polluter pay—is especially suitable for industrial discharges to water and air, but it is harder to manage in the case of more dispersed discharges such as those from farms, homes, and autos. A combination of prohibition, incentive, regulation, suasion, and public planning is required. Since the cost must be paid, there will be important distributional effects depending on whether cost becomes reflected in the price of products, in the exclusion of some products, or in remedial measures undertaken through public agencies.

Equally difficult is the fact that common decisions must be taken in areas where individual evaluations differ sharply. Noise, for example, offends some but not others. Attitudes toward nature cover a wide range. Even health, which in common rhetoric is treated as an absolute right, poses difficult problems of choice when we treat the old, the hopeless, and the chronically ill at great cost and perhaps to the neglect of other vital human needs. Within the context of collective decision we can accommodate varying tastes, in some instances by providing separate facilities, special zones, and the like. In other cases, the collective decision means that some must surrender what they value. There is no escaping this, but it could be established as a principle that no one can foreclose another's right to enjoyment of the amenity or health aspects of the environment to his private benefit, and that the community can do so only under restricted conditions. In the United States and in other Western countries we have reconciled a constitutional respect for private property with the practice of democracy. Property is to some extent held out of reach of the public, ever subject to due process when limitations are placed on it. This concept can be turned to account.

For example, one could challenge the assumption that a community may opt for higher income at the expense of the common amenity, overriding the opposition of those who disagree. In effect this would involve depriving some of existing property without compensation. If we can deny the polluter the right to make unlimited use of an open access resource because he thereby reduces its value to others, can we not on similar grounds question the community's right to deprive some members of their amenity rights in it? Evidently there will be situations such as those involving transport routes and plant sitings where the public purpose must prevail over individual enjoyment of amenity, and in many cases compensation is possible. In other situations the public purpose may be questionable, and may be designed to serve a narrow segment of the population and be unrelated to widely shared values. Somehow we must walk a fine line between public paralysis and democratic tyranny. No decision machinery is available to define that line, but greater sensitivity to individuals' claims to rights in existing amenities will be useful in establishing a policy climate. There will remain considerable differences in values with respect to some amenities and the preservation of nature. The only solution appears to be to maintain a range of options.

Some assert that "the system" is at the root of our environmental quality problems. Broadly enough defined, this is undoubtedly true—the system has yielded large populations with high income aspirations and too little understanding of man's role in the life system or attention to minimizing the damage he does. In context, however, such attacks are usually meant as indictments of the capitalist system. Revolution is sought but a vision of utopia is lacking. In truth, no one has given serious consideration to a new set of economic and political institutions for the spaceship earth. To do so in detail here is beyond our reach. In any case, the shape of future institutions depends very much on the population and income levels we must cope with and on the consequent degree to which we must aspire to recycling of materials. However, the indictment should not be accepted in blanket form. Examination of some features of the system will indicate a need for modification but probably not wholesale destruction.

Our economic system is characterized by private property, the profit motive and a market, all historically intertwined and jointly comprising the capitalist system. As an engine of production it has been successful and has yielded the high-level economy that now confounds us. Historically it has prevailed during a period of extensive development in which Western man appropriated great areas of land and resources and submitted them to exploitation. It was shaped during a period when man could do only localized damage to his environment, however much violence he did to his fellows.

In a popular formulation, private greed, unmindful of the public welfare, is seen as wasting resources and polluting the environment to the detriment of most citizens and future generations. According to one variant, such private interests must be subjected to regulation and penalty to ensure proper behavior. In another it is argued that private interests will always defeat public purposes and that the elimination of private property and the profit motive is the cure. The role left to the market is usually not made explicit.

Unhappily the record in socialist countries does not offer much comfort, for they have not evidenced great sensitivity to environmental quality. Reports of pollution in the Volga River and Lake Baikal (and of belated attempts to alleviate it) have a familiar ring; if we allow for the much lower level of economic activity, the problem does not seem so different. Socialist countries are perhaps even more obsessed by economic growth than we, and as long as rewards go to those who exceed output quotas, the temptation is strong to achieve by environmental shortcuts.

To the market economist, pollution is largely the result of externalities (costs not borne by the polluter) with the result that those who make decisions optimize only their private costs and benefits while the social optimum may be neglected. The inclination of economists is to internalize costs to the extent possible, thereby encouraging efficiency and allowing maximum use of the market. Where the market cannot operate, they seek substitutes for it, generally through benefit-cost analysis and the use of shadow prices.

The essence of property is the power to exclude. Even in a system of generally private property, some resources—the open-access resources—do not fall under exclusive control, either public or private, yet they are freely used to receive wastes. If this use is within the assimilative capacity of the resource, one person's use need not impair another's. Now, however, we have reached a stage of congestion where use by one often damages the interests of others.

Among private owners each is accountable for damage to others and each will manage his property not only to avoid such damage to others but to preserve its long-term value. Those who use open-access resources, being unable to exclude others, gain nothing by restraint in use, since this simply means the resource will be appropriated by others. It is this situation that leads to overloading, failure to attain maximum return from the resource, and in some cases its damage or destruction. The same resource, if privately owned, presumably would be managed in a way to avoid these results. However, there is no need to place the resource in private hands. Public ownership also carries the power to exclude and thereby to manage rationally.

The profit-market system unquestionably provides incentives to use open-access resources inefficiently at the same time that the heavy throughput of goods implied by economic and demographic growth threatens to overload them. Some form of exclusion analogous to that practiced by private owners is necessary, although complete exclusion would deny us the use of a valuable resource. When dealing with waste-assimilative capacity of air or water, the level of use depends on our objective. Whatever level of waste load we find acceptable the market can be used to allocate.

There is much question, however, whether economic criteria alone should determine the level of use. The tendency of welfare economics is to hold that they should. By this view, individuals are the best judges of their own welfare and, within a given income distribution and assuming free competition, they will be able to command the output that best suits their wants. If a higher price is offered for the use of a stream as a sewer than for recreation or to preserve its ecological integrity, then the presumption would be in favor of that use. Efficiency is served.

It is understandable that many critics find this all too pat. Even if efficiency results, equity and ecological integrity need not. With respect to equity, if we are unable to bid against other users we are compelled to give up our birthright in the amenity and health benefits of the environment whether or not we choose to do so as individuals. Such an exchange is equivalent to a forced sale except that in all likelihood we are not compensated. The welfare economist also has no convincing means for ensuring the rights of future generations. Finally, there is no reason to expect an economic optimum to coincide with long-term ecological health of the environment. It would appear that the role of economic criteria is the more limited one of allocating waste assimilative capacity within socially determined limits. Those limits may be set in the light of economic values but should reflect other values as well.

The Role of Government. The growth of capitalism saw the extension of private property, with more and more human activities falling within the ambit of the market. Since the heyday of untrammeled capitalism we have witnessed a progressive restriction of the rights of property and have sought to restore the sense of community that was dissolved by individualism. We have accepted government action to meliorate the effects of the market system through employment policy, intervention in labor markets, antitrust laws, and measures to equalize incomes, all often at the expense of property. The likelihood is that in an effort to limit adverse environmental effects we will go further down this path, while holding much property in private hands and availing ourselves of the dynamo of profit. But whether we continue to employ the market in attenuated private form or try to simulate some of its elements in public administration, we face ever more complex and novel problems in public decision making.

The institution of government itself is under attack in Western countries as being part of the system that many reject. While older liberals look to the government for solutions to environmental problems, many younger people either show a streak of anarchism or turn to smaller units as the basis of social organization. This trend seems incompatible with ultimate environmental objectives because a smaller scale is not appropriate in dealing with some (though not all) of the problems. The challenge will be to use the instruments of government to set population, income, and consumption goals consistent with ecological requirements and to manage environmental resources in a fashion to promote them. Far from having less government, we are likely to have more, and to have the government intrude into areas heretofore considered private.

A most likely candidate for governmental intervention is the size of families or, more broadly, the right to have children. A second point where government may encroach on the private sphere is in the matter of consumption. Heretofore, although squeamish at times about some forms of consumption—alcohol and drugs, for example—the government generally has been content to let the consumer decide. Faced with environmental constraints and the fact that some types of consumption are environmentally innocuous, the government will be tempted to direct consumption patterns toward those types. Presumably this can be accomplished through the market, once the terms are set. However done, it represents a departure from the assumptions of welfare economics. The government also will develop a new concern with the quality of merchandise as a means of satisfying consumer demand while minimizing environmental burden.

If government must intervene more actively in society to contain environmental threats, its very ability to function may become a problem. We live in a time when traditional social bonds seem to be weakening. The size, remoteness, and complexity of government have caused a growing number of people to question its competence and authority. Without general acceptance of government's legitimacy, its intervention by sophisticated administrative techniques may appear as simply one more evidence of an efficient tyranny.

As civilization becomes ever more dependent on an intricate technology supporting a huge mass of humanity in a world stripped of many other life forms and habitats, our survival becomes tenuous. Ever more toxic substances will be used in increasing amounts. Huge stockpiles of radioactive materials will be subject to release or misuse. Only fine control keeps the machine operating. A break in continuity and man will be hard put to regain his previous status. In this context, the prospect of social dissolution is one of the most frightening that we face. Even if we surmount our present transitional problems, can we learn enough about ourselves in time to insure against a new outbreak in the future?

The control of population and income policy which heretofore have been national concerns now may assume international importance. Environment is only one of many factors that call into question older concepts of sovereignty. However, national states are likely to be with us for some time, so long as such great cultural and income differences exist among people. Meanwhile we will need to develop an array of principles and agencies to deal with global threats. A first step will be at the scientific level to ensure worldwide monitoring of the level of insult and extent of threat. It should also be possible to establish agreement at least on the scientific level on the ecologically tolerable limits of use of certain common property resources as waste dumps. Moving from there to decisions about the level of use, amenities considered, and how to allocate use will prove far more difficult. No country will accept being "priced out" of this market. Therefore control and enforcement will be difficult to achieve except as the level of international agreement grows or there is willingness to resort to sanctions.

In the end, much depends on values. It will be possible to shape incentives and enforce rules provided a consensus exists that the expected forms of behavior are consistent with some perception of man's role and purpose. At any point in time the values of the society are given, but over a longer period they are malleable. One cannot speak confidently of how they can or should be altered. Let us assume that they will change in response to increased knowledge or awareness of the consequences of our behavior. Meanwhile, we are faced with the fact that the main tenets of Western thought are not easy to reconcile with a long-term view of the life system. The injunction to multiply, the grant of dominance, the focus on the hereafter (or its more recent opposite, a total hedonism and short-term calculus)—none provides the basis for values that preserve life. On the other hand, the habit of accumulation, the lesson of compound interest, the ideal of selflessness—all induce a sense of responsibility and forethought that can be turned to account. On the most optimistic assumptions, if this side of man should prevail, what then? If we deprive man of his ancient outlets—to make war, to compete economically, or to breed—what is left of his psychological nature? We can happily leave that problem to the future. Today, few people are aware of the full implications of our current problem or prepared to make the adjustments needed. The time in which we must make adjustment in our thinking is comparatively short and the outcome is in doubt.

Selected References

Coale, Ansley J. "Man and His Environment." *Science*, vol. 170 (October 9, 1970), pp. 132-36.

Falk, Richard A. "Proposals for International Environmental Protection." *Congressional Record* (October 9, 1970), pp. E9066-69.

Juster, F. Thomas. "On the Measurement of Economic and Social Performance." *50th Annual Report*. National Bureau of Economic Research, September 1970, pp. 8-24.

Russell, Clifford S., and Hans H. Landsberg. "International Environmental Problems: A Taxonomy." *Science*, vol. 172, no. 3990 (June 25, 1971), pp. 1307-14.

EIGHT

A SUMMARY
AND PROSPECT

A decade ago the doctrine that economic growth was the touchstone for dealing with most social problems was virtually unchallenged. Europe basked in its economic miracles, Japan loomed on the horizon as the economic success story it has since become. The United States elected a president committed to getting "the country moving again," and we stood at the beginning of a hoped-for "decade of development" for poor countries. As we surveyed the prospects for the soaring sixties, no one mentioned the environment. Yet a scant ten years later earnest orators at Earth Day observances warned that mankind had entered an environmental and demographic crisis, that if we failed to gain control of it within the next ten years we were doomed to disaster. Has the situation changed so abruptly, or are we caught up in an ephemeral obsession?

The conclusion of this study is that the situation has indeed changed, not quite so abruptly as our perception of it, but rapidly and fundamentally. If we associate the change with the quickened economic and demographic growth following World War II and project it to the end of the century, we have the makings of a crisis. It becomes a crisis because it will be difficult, in so short a period, to effect stopgap technical cures for the fast deteriorating environment and even more difficult to alter basic human attitudes toward reproduction and economic achievement or to change our perception of man's role in nature. Such attitudes are the product of many centuries of development and, at least with respect to reproduction, may be rooted in the genetic makeup of the race. Our social institutions also are resistant to abrupt change. Yet if we can turn to account the institutions and motivations that we have, make rational application of science and technology to our near-term problems, and simultaneously move toward a set of values and aspirations consistent with long-range occupancy of the earth, we can hope to surmount the crisis.

The root cause of environmental problems is economic and demographic growth. It is true that we have compounded our problems by emphasizing incentives more appropriate to achieving growth than to improving environmental quality. But even with "wrong" incentives, development at lesser rates and lower magnitudes did not impinge so strongly on natural systems and did not overwhelm them as it threatens to do now and in the future. Increasingly we exceed the capacity of natural systems to assimilate waste.

In reviewing economic and demographic growth we saw how the rates applicable to economic series often mean doubling output in the United States in less than 20 years. In the main, this has meant an equivalent increase in throughput of materials and of discharges to the environment. It is the nature of growth series that the absolute magnitudes represented build up rapidly. At the same time, this economic growth has been achieved through the more intensive application of science in processing and synthesizing materials, thereby introducing into the environment exotic materials that cannot be readily assimilated or whose effects on humans and other species are ill-understood.

There is considerable disagreement over the extent to which economic growth, as distinct from population growth, is responsible for the problem. The dispute is not very useful. We know that with present per capita income, consumption patterns, and technical levels we already sorely burden the environment. Population alone has not been the principal villain, however. In the United States, economic growth has proceeded much faster than population, as reflected in our rising per capita standard, and while we have some of the world's most severe environmental problems, we are a country of only average density. In other developed countries economic growth also is the more dynamic element. In less-developed countries where population growth is usually faster, densities greater, and income growth sometimes slow, population growth is the stronger force.

In any case, population growth cannot be exonerated as a future source of difficulty. It has a momentum that is hard to reverse. Although the transitional problems of stabilization are difficult, they must be faced at some point, and the advantages of stabilizing at a tolerable level are enormous. If we value environment, income, other forms of life, or the maintenance of options, there is everything to be said for early restriction of population growth and hardly anything to be said for its continuance. When we consider that we cannot in good conscience insist upon the stabilization of incomes elsewhere at levels below our own, the environmental implications of the increases become staggering. Whatever world problems may arise as a result of economic growth, it is a chilling thought that they will soon be doubled or quadrupled by population growth. The magnitude of the problem we must eventually deal with is closely tied to population.

Since a given output of goods can be obtained with different levels of discharge to the environment, we probably could modify our technology and produce something near our present output with considerably less environmental damage. Up to this point, both because of the reserve assimilative capacity of the natural system and because we have used it free of charge, we have had little incentive to minimize the burden imposed on the environment. Now that we recognize such a need, science plays a key role. One need is to rationalize technical processes so as to minimize harmful discharges. Another is to improve our understanding so that we can identify and forecast effects and damages from these discharges.

It is surprising to discover how little we know of the effects of man's activities on larger natural systems, on specific life communities, and on the health of man himself. This ignorance begins with a lack of information on the character and volume of many of our industrial discharges. It extends in particular to our understanding of such large systems as the dynamics of the atmosphere and the oceans. We have only a tenuous grasp of the movement of plant nutrients and their migration into water. The disposition of pesticides is poorly understood, as are some of their effects on life. The same goes for radioactivity, where the dispute rages on. We are dependent on science to describe the nature and extent of damage and to identify problems in advance, so that society can judge what risks it will take. So far we have avoided disaster, but we need a more comprehensive scientific warning system if we are to have reasonable future assurance.

So long as we choose economic and demographic growth, and so long thereafter as we aspire to improvement in environmental standards, there will be a place for technology in elaborating the techniques of abating pollution.

We have hardly begun. Processes can be designed to save materials, to recover or recycle usable materials, and to neutralize those that must be discharged. Such possibilities are strongest in industry, and with some exceptions, in agriculture. The control of materials is more difficult once they are dispersed into the hands of consumers, but we can expect improvements in methods of collection, treatment, and recovery in such areas as solid wastes, sewage, auto bodies, and the like. In some cases, the pace of technical solutions will be quickened if the manufacturer is made to assume greater responsibility for producing more durable and less noxious products, or to attend to their consequences.

Many of our more acute or immediate environmental problems appear amenable to technical solutions. Much of the BOD load of water can be traced to a few sources—inadequate sewage treatment, a few food processing industries, and pulp and paper mills. Concentrated action in these areas would make a great difference. Excessive nutrients in the water also derive from cattle feedlots, and perhaps from fertilizer use in some cases. All but the latter could be dealt with readily. We have a host of problems connected with energy use, and especially the combustion of fuels. Although they are not easily solved, we can go far toward mitigating the effects. Our failure to do so stems from inertia or unwillingness to pay the cost.

We cannot avoid the cost. We pay it in damage to health and amenity, if not in the cost of products. Wider appreciation of this fact will support the kind of measures needed to ensure that technical solutions are found. A most urgent need is to provide incentives. Technical solutions will lag as long as we allow free access to our common environmental property. If society is made aware of environmental costs and has the means for expressing its wishes, then regulation and incentives can be used to keep pollution within limits. We can establish standards of air and water quality, rationing the portion of the environment's assimilative capacity that we choose to employ and allowing product price to reflect the cost of environmental protection.

The capacity of an airshed or watershed to absorb wastes varies with a number of conditions. If we aim to maintain its quality within set limits, we have a management task to perform. It may involve the augmentation of capacity, the scheduling of use, or other matters for which systems management techniques are appropriate. When technical advances, incentives, and management are effectively coordinated, we should be able to increase the flow of useful goods we derive from the economy without equivalent increase in environmental damage. Moreover, we can aspire to do this at moderate cost.

Nevertheless, continued economic and demographic growth extended far enough into the future greatly magnifies our problem. At some stage it may overwhelm the technical and managerial measures from which we have just derived interim hope. Moreover, the availability of resources, which has not been considered a serious short-term problem, cannot be so treated if we project far enough into the future. The earth is finite and growth must stop somewhere, whether arrested first by resource limitations or environmental tolerances. Massive applications of energy permit more complete recycling of materials, and can enable us to stave off these limits, but not forever.

Rather than dream of technological utopias that promise ever more goods, perhaps we should take human needs as a starting point and consider how we can cut the cloth to fit them. Several possibilities are open. We could reduce pressure on the environment by restraining income growth, although it is hard to see how this could be attempted without major income redistribution. At the level of consumption patterns, much could be done through improved design and durability of goods to reduce the required throughput of materials. Or we could stress nonmaterial forms of consumption—education, sport, music, and theater, for example. Alas, much travel might have to be excluded from the list because of its high use of energy. Most optimistically, there is the chance that income growth—if properly channeled in terms of consumption patterns and investment in environmental technology—can be consistent both with increased consumption and improved environmental quality. The chance improves if we do not multiply the problem by population increase.

On a world scale the United States has set an example of economic performance that, even at our present level, will be hard for others to match for generations, if ever. We may progress to control of our own effluents and be able to produce and recycle the resources we need, only to find that less-developed countries aspiring to similar economic standards are willing to take environmental risks of world consequence in order to achieve them. We would have no moral basis to deny them.

During the decades ahead while we grope for possibly different values we must assume that some economic and demographic growth will occur, and we should make the best use of our scientific and institutional resources to contain its environmental impact. It will be helpful if we keep our problems in perspective, recognizing that some, while annoying and immediate, do not threaten disaster, while others, less obvious in our daily life, must be carefully watched lest they bring catastrophic damage. We have no single environmental problem but a host of them, and we have a number of means of coping with them. Without diverting our concern about the long term, we must learn to manage the present.

To illustrate the complexity of this task and some of the considerations that enter into it, we have prepared a matrix (Table 6) showing various types of environmental insult by type and by order of gravity, and tried to associate them with causative and managerial considerations. The matrix serves best if attention is centered on the captions rather than on the entries in each box. The entries are very impressionistic and are not defended too ardently. Some of the captions are troublesome also—causative factors, for example, are not entirely independent of each other. Nonetheless the matrix points up where problems fall on the scale of gravity and what kinds of things can be done about them, and it also serves as an organizational device for discussion.

As we move toward graver possible consequences we tend to find that the effects are deferred in time and enlarged in scope, that the appropriate administrative unit becomes larger, and that the remedies are more likely to be dependent on value changes. By contrast, many of the less grave threats to health or the amenities, which nonetheless are more imperative from the standpoint of public annoyance, are subject to control on a smaller scale and can be managed by extension of regulation or revision of incentive. In some cases where the problem is encountered at the consumer level and is local in effect, the leverage may have to be exerted on the manufacturer because the consumer is difficult to regulate. Sensible strategy will weight the graver threats differently, for we can take few chances with disaster. Prudence becomes more advisable with affluence because we will view increases in income as of little value. Less grave but more pervasive and immediate problems affecting amenities and health will attract concentrated attention. Generally speaking, they can be managed at tolerable cost through technological and institutional adjustments in the near term. However, this does not justify complacency, for it is uncertain that we will apply ourselves to achieve the desired result.

For some purposes, the classification of problems into short-term and long-term is useful. Short-term problems are those that already (or will within a generation or so) require remedial action to avert unacceptable congestion or to avoid permanent damage. Problems of this sort fall within a planning horizon with which we are accustomed to deal. Decisions are made by those who will bear the consequences. Long-range problems strain our conventional decision apparatus. We can ensure a future for subsequent generations only if we develop an essentially conservationist view of the earth. Linking the two periods are the actions taken today that condition the possibilities of tomorrow. These actions are not all in one direction, since today's investment in scientific capital will be useful in dealing with future problems, but at the same time we must be wary of irreversible physical consequences unless we have strong assurance of their compatibility with the life-support system.

Most health and amenity considerations are one-generation problems. We may pass on a technology that imposes burdens on our heirs, but they have the same options as we to escape their dilemma. We are left to our own standards of taste and to our willingness to pay for higher standards; we can hardly be expected to consider only the remote future. In fact, we may best serve the future by improving our science, technology, and institutions so as to allow future generations to deal with these problems in their own way.

The presence of irreversibilities changes the picture, even for health and amenity considerations, for then future generations do have a stake in our actions. We may still choose to proceed with caution. But when dealing with significant established threats to human genetics or the life-support system we cannot responsibly proceed in the face of such uncertainty. At this point we must invoke another standard—one that holds the life-support system inviolate above all else. The most difficult problem is how to evaluate the threat—its nature, extent, probability, threshold, and the like.

Over the long run, institutions are considered responsive to changes in social values. But they always lag, and early attention must be given to the technical problems of designing social means for dealing with our problems. The potentially valuable role of the market in allocating assimilative capacity has been stressed, as has the possibility of enlarged management authorities capable of dealing with a whole range of problems. Both instruments need further elaboration. Our experience with them is limited, and our hopes for their effectiveness could be disappointed.

Whatever the instruments used, the framework of social goals will be set somewhat independently. The process of arriving at the public's wishes is difficult. We all want a clean and healthy environment but disagree on who gives up what to get how much of it. The fact that the environment is held in common requires that social choices be made. Economic criteria give us important dimensions of this choice, namely the cost of the technical alternatives that scientists and engineers cast up and certain measurable costs and benefits, but in the end we fall back on political processes for arriving at policy. The level at which decisions should be made, the designing of political units of proper scope, the procedures for framing issues, the mechanics of bargaining to arrive at policy—all are part of the process.

Man's attitude toward his role in the scheme of things is fundamental to many questions. In particular the extent to which we are prepared to occupy and transform the earth hinges on this. We probably can survive (although

Table 6. An Environmental Matrix

Environmental problems by order of gravity	Causative factors 1. size of population 2. concentration of population 3. per capita income level 4. consumption pattern 5. technology	Character of insult 1. temporary insult 2. cumulative insult 3. reversible damage 4. permanent damage (human time scale) 5. synergistic potential	Problem threshold 1. continuing 2. now or soon 3. one generation 4. more than one generation	Area affected 1. local 2. regional 3. national 4. international 5. global
Amenity considerations				
Litter	4, 3	1, 2	1	1, 2
Noise	2, 5	1	1	1
Odor	5	1	1	1
Air, visibility aspects	2, 5, 4	1	1	1, 2
Water quality, recreational aspects	5, 2, 1	1, 2, 3, 5	1	1, 2, 4
City, aesthetic aspects	4, 5	N	1	1
City, convenience and efficiency aspects	2, 4	3	1, 2	1
Country, aesthetic aspects	5, 4, 1	2, 4	1, 2	1, 2, 3
Access to country and nature	4	2, 3	1, 2	1, 2
Human health effects				
Air pollution-combustion products	5, 4, 2, 3	1, 3, 5	1, 2, 3	1, 2
Water pollution:				
Pathogens	2, 5	1, 3	2, 3	1, 2, 4
Nitrates	5	2, 3	2, 3	1, 2
Industrial chemicals	5	All	2, 3	1, 2, 4
Pesticides (via food chain)	5, 1, 3	2, 3	3	2, 4, 5
Radioactivity	5, 3	2, 4	3	1, 2
Heavy metals	5	2, 4	All	1, 2, 4
Human genetic and reproductive effects				
Radioactivity	5, 3	4	3, 4	3, 5
Pesticides	5, 1, 3	4	N	3
Industrial chemicals	5	4	2, 3, 4	1, 2, 5

[a]Irrespective of source of financing.
N = none, unknown, uncertain, not applicable, negligible.

Appropriate management level[a] 1. local 2. regional authority 3. national 4. multinational agreement or authority 5. global	Possible economic approaches 1. environmental charge 2. tax on material 3. subsidy	Possible institutional approaches 1. laws and regulations 2. enlarged systems management or planning 3. court actions	Possible technological approaches 1. containment at source 2. neutralization of objectionable discharges 3. reduction in discharge volume via process and material changes 4. increased recycling	Efficacy of possible value change bringing 1. reduced population growth 2. slower income growth and more equal distribution 3. less burdensome consumption patterns 4. curtailment of property rights
1, 2	1, 3	1, 2	4, 3	3, 2
1	N	1	3, 1	N
1	N	1	2	N
1, 2	1, 3	1, 2	3, 2	2, 3
1, 2, 4	All	All	All	2, 1
1	2, 3	1, 2	N	4, 3
1, 2	All	2	N	4, 3, 2
2, 3	3	All	N	4, 2, 3, 1
1, 2, 3	2, 3	2	N	3, 1
2, 3, 4	All	1, 2	All	3, 2
1, 2, 4	3	1, 2	2	1
1, 2	2, 3	1	3, 1	3, 4
1, 2, 4	1, 2	1, 2	All	2, 1
3, 4	2	1	3, 1	3
3	N	1	3, 1	2, 1
2, 3, 4	N	1	3, 1	N
3, 5	N	1	3, 1	2, 1
3	2	1	3, 1	N
3, 4	1, 2	1, 2	All	2, 3

(Table 6 continues)

Table 6. An Environmental Matrix (Continued)

Environmental problems by order of gravity	Causative factors 1. size of population 2. concentration of population 3. per capita income level 4. consumption pattern 5. technology	Character of insult 1. temporary insult 2. cumulative insult 3. reversible damage 4. permanent damage (human time scale) 5. synergistic potential	Problem threshold 1. continuing 2. now or soon 3. one generation 4. more than one generation	Area affected 1. local 2. regional 3. national 4. international 5. global
Effects on ecological system and the earth's life supportive capacity				
Human occupancy of biospace	5, 1, 3, 4	2, 4, 5	All	3, 5
Ocean threats:				
Pesticides	5	2, 4, 5	3	5
Oil	3, 4	3, 5	3	5
Other chemicals	5	2, 4	3, 4	5
Erosion	5, 1, 3	2, 4	1, 4	1, 2, 5
Fertilizers and damage to mineral cycling	5	3	4	1, 5
CO_2, albedo, and climate	5, 1, 3	2, 5	4	5
Heat rejection:				
Local aspect	5, 2	1, 5	2, 3	2, 4
Global aspect	3, 1	3, 5	4	5

[a]Irrespective of source of financing.
N = none, unknown, uncertain, not applicable, negligible.

this is not certain) in a thoroughly synthetic environment in which most natural systems have been destroyed. If we take this path we venture into an unknown far greater than that which lay ahead of any quest of the past, for we take all of life with us and there is no return. It is hard to see that the gain compensates the risk. If we are not to go that route step by step, then we must consciously and soon restrict our range.

Our prospect viewed from the standpoint of our possibilities is reasonably optimistic. We can improve our technology and management so as to eliminate much insult and we can continue to generate a social dividend, part

Appropriate management level[a]	Possible economic approaches	Possible institutional approaches	Possible technological approaches	Efficacy of possible value change bringing
1. local 2. regional authority 3. national 4. multinational agreement or authority 5. global	1. environmental charge 2. tax on material 3. subsidy	1. laws and regulations 2. enlarged systems management or planning 3. court actions	1. containment at source 2. neutralization of objectionable discharges 3. reduction in discharge volume via process and material changes 4. increased recycling	1. reduced population growth 2. slower income growth and more equal distribution 3. less burdensome consumption patterns 4. curtailment of property rights
3, 5	All	All	1	2, 3, 1
5	2	1	3	N
5	1	1	3, 2, 1	2, 3
5	1, 2	1, 2	All	2, 3
1, 3	3	1	3	4, 2, 1
1, 3	2	1	N	2, 1
3, 5	N	1, 2	3	2, 1
2, 3, 4	1, 3	All	2	3
5	N	1	3	2, 3, 1

of which may be devoted to environmental preservation. By adjustments of consumption patterns, income, and numbers we can aspire to permanent occupancy.

The question is whether we have the will and the foresight to take all the necessary measures in time—to reform our individual thinking and to organize ourselves at appropriate levels to deal with our problems. We must truly learn to govern ourselves if we are to survive. The task calls for the most arduous personal and social discipline. While some current tendencies toward a simpler life would reduce the environmental burden, they often are accompanied by antirational attitudes and a mistrust for organization of the sort needed to manage a complex system. A new set of values is needed in which the commitment to environmental quality is wedded to personal values and life styles that do not negate our progress but seek rather to make it serve a new vision.

While a few technocrats may thrill to the vision of a far more numerous population living in a highly synthetic world, most of us cannot so readily abandon the natural system in which the race was formed. If it is our aim to come to terms with that system and occupy a role within it, then we must contemplate early limitation of our numbers and devise a technology that stringently limits environmental burden. While this may allow for some income growth as our understanding improves, it gives precedence to the preservation of major elements of the natural system. It implies a kind of responsibility which is the absolute antithesis of the query, "What did posterity ever do for me?"

As a setting for human life such a prospect promises to be far more satisfying than one in which man barely manages to survive in a mad race between technology and population. One cannot know whether we will accomplish this shift. Much depends on how we in the United States spend the scientific and social capital and momentum that we have available. The situation does not call for despair, but we urgently need sustained intelligent concern and action.

BIBLIOGRAPHY *

Barnett, Harold J., and Chandler Morse. *Scarcity and Growth: The Economics of Natural Resource Availability*. Baltimore: Johns Hopkins Press for Resources for the Future, Inc., 1963.

Borgstrom, George. *Too Many: A Study of Earth's Biological Limitations*. New York: Macmillan, 1969.

Brown, Harrison. *The Challenge of Man's Future: An Inquiry Concerning the Condition of Man During the Years That Lie Ahead*. New York: The Viking Press, 1954.

Darling, F. Fraser, and John P. Milton, eds. *Future Environments of North America: Transformation of a Continent*. Record of a Conference Convened by The Conservation Foundation in April 1965, at Airlie House, Warrenton, Virginia. Garden City: The Natural History Press, 1966.

Detwyler, Thomas R. *Man's Impact on Environment*. McGraw-Hill Series in Geography. New York: McGraw-Hill, 1971.

Dubos, René. *Man Adapting*. The Silliman Foundation Lectures. New Haven: Yale University Press, 1965.

———. *So Human an Animal*. New York: Charles Scribner's Sons, 1968.

Ehrlich, Paul R., and Anne H. Ehrlich. *Population, Resources, Environment Issues in Human Ecology*. San Francisco: W. H. Freeman, 1970.

Ewald, William R., Jr., ed. *Environment for Man: The Next Fifty Years*. Bloomington: Indiana University Press, 1967.

Great Britain. Royal Commission on Environmental Pollution. (Chairman: Sir Eric Ashby). *First Report*. Presented to Parliament by Command of Her Majesty, February, 1971. Command 4585. London: Her Majesty's Stationery Office, 1971.

Handler, Philip, ed. *Biology and the Future of Man*. London: Oxford University Press, 1970.

Helfrich, Harold W., Jr., ed. *The Environmental Crisis*. New Haven: Yale University Press, 1970.

*See also selected references at end of chapters 1, 2, 4, 5, 6, and 7.

Herfindahl, Orris C., and Allen V. Kneese. *Quality of the Environment: An Economic Approach to Some Problems in Using Land, Water, and Air.* Washington, D.C.: Resources for the Future, 1965.

Jarrett, Henry, ed. *Environmental Quality in a Growing Economy.* Essays from the Sixth RFF Forum. Baltimore: Johns Hopkins Press for Resources for the Future, 1966.

_____. *Perspectives on Conservation: Essays on America's Natural Resources.* Baltimore: Johns Hopkins Press for Resources for the Future, 1958.

Leopold, Aldo. *A Sand County Almanac and Sketches Here and There.* London: Oxford University Press, 1949.

Mishan, E. J. *Technology and Growth: The Price We Pay.* New York: Praeger Publishers, 1969.

Murdoch, William W., ed. *Environment Resources, Pollution and Society.* Stanford, Conn.: Sinauer Associates, Inc., 1971.

National Science Board of the National Science Foundation. *Environmental Science: Challenge for the Seventies.* Report of the National Science Board. Washington, D.C.: Government Printing Office, 1971.

Pitts, James N., Jr., and Robert L. Metcalf, eds. *Advances in Environmental Sciences and Technology*, vol. 1. New York: Wiley-Interscience, 1969.

Smithsonian Institution. *The Fitness of Man's Environment.* Papers Delivered at the Smithsonian Institution Annual Symposium, February 16–18, 1967. Foreword by Hubert H. Humphrey, Premise by S. Dillon Ripley, Introduction by Rt. Hon. Jennie Lee. Washington, D.C.: Smithsonian Institution Press, 1968.

U.S. Congress. *Problems and Issues of a National Materials Policy.* Papers Delivered at an Engineering Foundation Research Conference on National Materials Policy, July 1970. Committee Print prepared by the Science Policy Research Division, Legislative Reference Service, Library of Congress at the Request of Hon. J. Caleb Boggs for the Use of the Senate Committee on Public Works. 91 Cong., 2 sess. Washington, D.C.: Government Printing Office, December 1970.

_____. *Congress and the Nation's Environment—Environmental Affairs of the 91st Congress.* Committee Print Prepared by the Environmental Policy Division, Congressional Research Service, Library of Congress, at the Request of Henry M. Jackson, Chairman, Senate Committee on Interior and Insular Affairs. 92 Cong., 1 sess. Washington, D.C.: Government Printing Office, February 10, 1971.

_____. *The Environmental Decade (Action Proposals for the 1970's).* Hearings before a subcommittee of the House Government Operations Committee. 91 Cong., 2 sess., February 2–6, March 13, and April 3, 1970. Washington, D.C.: Government Printing Office, 1970.

_____. *The Environmental Decade (Action Proposals for the 1970's).* Twenty-Fourth Report by the House Committee on Government Operations. 91 Cong., 2 sess., House Report no. 91–1082, May 13, 1970. Washington, D.C.: Government Printing Office, 1970.

U.S. Council on Environmental Quality. *Environmental Quality. The First Annual Report of the Council on Environmental Quality Transmitted to the Congress August 1970*. Washington, D.C.: Government Printing Office, 1970.

U.S. Department of Health, Education, and Welfare. Environmental Health Service/Public Health Service. *Environmental Health Problems*. Washington, D.C.: Government Printing Office, 1970.

U.S. President's Science Advisory Committee. *Restoring the Quality of Our Environment*. Report of The Environmental Pollution Panel, The White House, November 1965.

Wagar, J. Alan. "Growth versus the Quality of Life." *Science*, vol. 168, no. 3936 (June 5, 1970), pp. 1179–84.

Wilson, Thomas W., Jr. *The Environment: Too Small a View*. An Occasional Paper. Aspen, Col.: The Aspen Institute for Humanistic Studies, 1970.

INDEX

Accidents, 114, 123, 134; minimizing, 150; nuclear, 71-72, 129, 140
Aerobic and anaerobic degradation, 106, 108, 109
Aerosols, 59, 60, 62, 66
Africa, 39, 41, 100
Agriculture: chemicals in, 26-27; damage control in, 26, 113-14, 182; damages to, 54, 56, 119-20; disturbance of natural systems in, 12, 25, 80; and future food demand, 145; without hazardous pesticides, 146-47; outlook for, 26, 29; persistent pollutants in, 111; pesticides in, 84-85, 146-47; problems in, 25-29; processing products of, 25, 28; residuals in, 25, 27-29, 106, 130, 144; technology in, 41. *See also* Animals; Feedlots; Fertilizers; Land use; Pesticides
Air pollution, v, 3; abatement and control, 23, 116, 119, 121, 148, 155t; as amenity loss, 51, 114; and behavior of discharges, 115; chief pollutants in, 115-21; climate effect in, 62-65, 114; cost of reducing, 121, 155t; evaluation of damage, 115; from feedlots, 94; and health, 52, 114, 115, 116-20; from incineration and open burning, 31, 34, 122; knowledge gap concerning, 116; long-term and near-term threats, 129, 142; and photosynthesis, 56, 66; property damage from, 120-21; sources, 22-23, 30, 52, 115; technology and solutions, 121; in urban

areas, 34. *See also* Combustion; Emissions; *and specific pollutant*
Air quality: nature of, 116; standards, 182
Algae growth, 109, 110
Amenities, 162; and air pollution, 51, 114; choices among, 172; damage to, 50, 51-52, 106, 109, 111, 147; and irreversibilities, 185; policy decisions concerning, 130; prospects for improving, 156, 184, 185; standards for, 131
American Chemical Society, 83n, 112n
Anderson, R. J., Jr., 121n
Animal wastes, 28, 94, 114, 131; measures to control, 147-48
Animals: and air pollution, 119; disease containment among, 53; pesticide effects on, 80-81, 83. *See also* Animal wastes; Feedlots
Antibiotics, 52, 53
Aquatic life: damage to, 78, 79, 106, 108, 109, 114; fertilizer effects on, 3, 89-90
Arsenic: as pesticide, 79
Asia, 39
Assimilative capacity: of atmosphere, 115, 116; equity of use of earth's, 170; of water, 114, 134, 148, 150
Atmosphere: air circulation pattern in, 60-61; assimilative capacity of, 115, 116; CO_2 concentration in, 62-63, 65; interaction of, with sea, land, and polar ice, 61; interference with insola-

195